Further praise for *The Age of Absurdity*

'An enjoyable and at times hilarious dissection of our instant-gratification, fast-food, celebrity-obsessed, dumbed-down society'
Choice Magazine, Book of the Month

'Intriguing . . . an investigation into 21st century satisfaction and its elusive achievement'
Good Book Guide

'Illuminated with reflections about Foley's own demons as an aging university lecturer, parent and lover, rendered in wickedly sceptical tones'
Irish Examiner

'An amusing gamble through science, religion, philosophy and literature in search for strategies for fulfilment in a contemporary culture that seems designed to resist them'
New Scientist

D0071554

The Age of Absurdity

Why Modern Life makes it Hard to be Happy

Michael Foley

**SIMON &
SCHUSTER**

London · New York · Sydney · Toronto

A CBS COMPANY

First published in Great Britain by Simon & Schuster UK Ltd, 2010
This paperback edition published in 2011 by Simon & Schuster UK Ltd
A CBS COMPANY

3 5 7 9 10 8 6 4

Simon & Schuster UK Ltd
1st Floor
222 Gray's Inn Road
London
WC1X 8HB

www.simonandschuster.co.uk

Simon & Schuster Australia
Sydney

A CIP catalogue for this book is
available from the British Library.

ISBN: 978-1-84739-627-3

Typeset by M Rules
Printed in the UK by CPI Cox & Wyman, Reading, Berkshire RG1 8EX

For Jane

Contents

PART I

The Problems

1

The Absurdity of Happiness

So I go to a wall of bookshelves, extending from floor to ceiling, with books jammed in sideways along the top of each shelf, and I think, Not a single book I want to read. Then I proceed to the ragged towers of a CD collection that, despite its size and discriminating embrace of classical, jazz, world and adult-oriented rock, does not contain one piece of music worth playing. Obviously stimulation will have to be sought elsewhere. I consult *Time Out London Eating & Drinking* – possibly the most compendious and varied collection of restaurant reviews in the world, with substantial chapters on each of twenty-two major regional and national cuisines – and flip irritably through the pages, scowling at the lack of even *one* exciting new place to eat. The answer must be to look further ahead, to the unadulterated bliss of a holiday abroad. But the websites provoke only disbelief and outrage. Why isn't there a reasonably priced apartment in the atmospheric old town, a few minutes' walk from the sea on one side and from major transport links on the other, with a barbecue-equipped roof terrace and views over the lively, bustling, colourful market? Would anyone even *consider* less?

And now I catch a glimpse of my face in the mirror – a raging gargoyle corroded by acid rain. How can this have happened to a 1960s flower child? Especially one who has yet to enjoy fully the

sexual variety promised to the flower children? Not to mention all
the new stuff. Can anyone nowadays be said to have lived life to
the full without experiencing group sex, bondage and a pre-op
transsexual?

This is crazy, of course. But who, in the Western world, has not
been deranged by a toxic cocktail of dissatisfaction, restlessness,
desire and resentment? Who has not yearned to be younger,
richer, more talented, more respected, more celebrated and,
above all, more sexually attractive? Who has not felt entitled to
more, and aggrieved when more was not forthcoming? It is possible that a starving African farmer has less sense of injustice than
a middle-aged Western male who has never been fellated.

Of course many also become aware that demanding everything
is absurd. Then the questions arise. How did such inordinate
expectation come about? What is the alternative? If there is an
alternative how can it be achieved? Do the best minds of past and
present offer any useful advice? Is there a consensus in what
they say? If so, what is it and how does it apply to living in the
twenty-first century? These are the questions addressed by this
book – but there are no simple answers.

Even defining the goal is difficult. The alternative to discontented craziness is contented sanity – happiness. But this word
presents all kinds of problems. Many, including myself, can hardly
bear to utter a word so contaminated by the excesses of happy-
clappiness and self-help. It immediately brings to mind beatific
grins, tambourines, orange robes and T-shirts saying, 'Today is the
first day of the rest of your life' (the poet Derek Mahon made this
a couplet with the line, 'Tell that to your liver; tell that to your ex-
wife'[1]). We are too knowing, too sophisticated, too ironical, too
wised up, too post-everything for a corny old term like happiness.
The word 'happiness' would draw an equally derisive snort from
a philosopher, a novelist, a poet and a cab driver, though all of
these would no doubt secretly want the experience. Many may
claim that life stinks – but no one wants to *feel* like shit.

Alternative terms are even less satisfactory. The academic

community has proposed 'Subjective Well-Being', which reduces to an impressive acronym, SWB, but is lifeless jargon. More recently populists have suggested 'Wellness', which sounds like an obscure English coastal town (stony beach, but charming despite that).

It will have to be embarrassing old 'happiness'. And, not only is the word agony to use, it is impossible to define. The Oxford English Dictionary shockingly offers a misapprehension corrected over two thousand years ago by Socrates: 'good fortune or luck; success; prosperity'. More scrupulous attempts to define the concept get lost in infinite ramification. The Buddhist kingdom of Bhutan in the Himalayas set up a Gross National Happiness Commission and one of the Commission's first tasks was to define what it was created to promote. So far it has identified four pillars, nine domains and seventy-two indicators. But the country is still no better than others at resisting lamentable trends. As a spokesperson glumly conceded, 'In the last century a young person asked to identify a hero would have invariably chosen the king – but now it is the rap artist 50 Cent.'[2]

And useful testimony on happiness in practice is as difficult to find as convincing theory. Unlike its opposite, depression, happiness is averse to self-definition. The misery memoir is a well-established genre – but there is no equivalent for happiness (in fact a happy childhood is a crippling handicap for a writer). It seems that only the painful experiences are a source of inspiration.

Perhaps a condition of being happy is an unwillingness to analyse the state, because any attempt at definition will kill it. Perhaps it is not even possible to be *consciously* happy. Perhaps it may be recognized only retrospectively, after it is lost. Jean-Jacques Rousseau first elaborated this view: 'The happy life of the golden age was always a state foreign to the human race, either because it went unrecognised when humans could have enjoyed it or because it had been lost when humans could have known it.'[3] In other words, if you have it, you can't be aware of it and, if you're aware of it, you can't have it.

And happiness tends to be thought of as a permanent state, when it may be only occasionally achievable. The philosopher Hannah Arendt has argued that the human condition is a cycle of exhaustion and renewal, so that going up is possible only after going down and attempts to remain permanently up will fail: 'There is no lasting happiness outside the prescribed cycle of painful exhaustion and pleasurable regeneration, and whatever throws this cycle out of balance – poverty and misery where exhaustion is followed by wretchedness instead of regeneration, or great riches and an entirely effortless life where boredom takes the place of exhaustion . . . ruins the elemental happiness that comes from being alive.'[4]

And the happiness state, when examined more closely, turns out to be not a point but a range, with contentment at the bottom and exaltation at the top.

Alternatively, happiness is not a state but a process, a continuous striving. Aristotle defined it as an activity. Marcus Aurelius, an earthier Roman, likened it to wrestling. Or maybe it is both a state *and* a process. The ancient Greek term, *eudaimonia*, captures something of both interpretations and translates roughly as *flourishing*. This is an appealing idea: to be happy is to *flourish*. (And Eudaimonics would be an impressive title for Happiness Studies – there's nothing like a Greek word for intellectual heft.)

Then again, there is the assumption that only one version of happiness is achieved by the fortunate few. But, given our bizarre uniqueness, it is unlikely that even any two happy people are experiencing exactly the same phenomenon. There are probably as many forms of happiness as there are of depression.

As for how to attain this indefinable thing . . . The United States Declaration of Independence has that famous phrase, 'the pursuit of happiness'. But many believe that happiness may not be pursued, that it is an accidental consequence of doing something else – an insight possibly first expressed by John Stuart Mill in the nineteenth century: 'Those only are happy . . . who have their minds fixed on some object other than their own happiness . . .

Aiming thus at something else, they find happiness by the way . . . The only chance is to treat, not happiness, but some end external to it, as the purpose of life.'[5]

Hence another question – what is the 'something else', the 'end external'? Living well? Virtue? Wisdom? These are as difficult to define as happiness itself. One of the problems in thinking about happiness is that every line of thought leads off into some vast area of contention with a contradictory literature going back centuries. Arendt said that virtuous acts are, by definition, not meant to be seen. So, a double whammy: goodness is invisible and happiness is mute.

And goodness has the same access problem. It is not possible to be good by trying to be good. This is also true of many other desiderata – originality for instance. It is not possible to be original by trying to be original – those who attempt this in the arts will be merely avant-garde. Originality is the product of an impulse so intense and overwhelming that it bursts the conventions and produces something new – again more by accident than design. Also attainable only indirectly are wisdom and authority, perhaps even humour and love. Is there a General Theory of Desiderata in this?

Only the surrogates of happiness yield to pursuit – success, fame, status, affluence, fun, cheerfulness – though it is possible that the lowest level of the happiness range, contentment, is directly achievable. Gustave Flaubert thought so: 'Happiness is not attainable though tranquillity is'[6], which sounds more like an admission of defeat and surrender. But, as a literary man rather than a philosopher, Flaubert was a bit inconsistent and did leave open a narrow window of opportunity: 'Stupidity, selfishness and good health are the three prerequisites of happiness, though if stupidity is lacking the others are useless.'[7]

In fact, these quotes are from Flaubert's good days. Essentially he subscribed, like many others before and since, to a form of Manicheism, the belief that man is a fallen creature who can *never* find happiness.

Then there is the view that the pursuit of happiness is itself the main cause of unhappiness, that the pursuit is intrinsically self-defeating. Immanuel Kant put it like this: 'We find that the more a cultivated reason devotes itself to the aim of enjoying life and happiness, the further does man get away from true contentment.'[8]

So the absurdity of happiness is that it is embarrassing to discuss or even mention, impossible to define or measure, may not be achievable at all – or, at best, only intermittently and unconsciously – and may even turn into its opposite if directly pursued, but that it frequently turns up unexpectedly in the course of pursuing something else. There is no tease more infuriating.

Besides, hasn't every thinker since Socrates pondered all this and left the world not much wiser? Questions seem to breed only more questions. Agonizing leads only to bewilderment and frustration. Or to banalities – watch less television and smile more at strangers. It is tempting to forget the whole thing and simply fall back on the couch with a remote control in one hand and a beer in the other.

But there is a compelling reason to develop a personal strategy for living. Rejecting issues, which often feels liberating, is actually enslavement. Those who do not produce their own solution must be using someone else's. As Nietzsche warned: 'he who cannot obey himself will be commanded'.[9] Worse, the someone else who commands is likely to be the average contemporary, and the solution a weak mixture of contemporary recommendations and anathemas. This has a parallel in writing. Many would-be novelists and poets read only their contemporaries and often not even these, justifying this laziness as a bold bid for freedom from influence. But this attempt to escape specific influence results in unconscious surrender to the worst kind of general influence – current popular taste.

Of course there is the phenomenon of the happy brute, whose instincts and talents perfectly match the demands of the age but are not inhibited by sensitivity or scruple, and who is therefore hugely successful and happy to enjoy the approbation and spoils – the palaces, courtiers, servants and seraglio. In earlier eras this would have been a warrior. Now it is more likely to be an entrepreneur. One of capitalism's most successful confidence tricks is its promotion of the illusion that anyone can make millions. But there is room at the top for only a few and few have the aptitude to claim a place.

There is also the happy fantasist who lives blissfully on illusions. And is this not a convenient and harmless way of feeling good? The problem is that life takes a malicious pleasure in shattering illusions and this experience is more painful and costly than dispelling illusions or preventing them from developing in the first place. Illusions can become immune to reality only by turning into full-blown delusions. You really have to believe you *are* Napoleon. So, once again, it comes back to understanding the world and the self and how these interact.

Nature abhors a vacuum – and nowhere more than in the human mind. For our understanding of how the mind can be colonized we should thank Karl Marx and Sigmund Freud, thinkers revered in the twentieth century and often reviled in the twenty-first. But their great central insights remain valid and relevant: Marx showed how much of what we assume to be independent thought is actually imposed by society; Freud how much actually arises from the unconscious. So there is intense and relentless pressure from both directions – without and within – and the result may well be no independent thought at all.

However, there is no hope of escaping entirely – or even largely – from either pressure. To live in the world but outside of its prejudices is an impossible ideal. As we live in the age so the age lives in us. And ages are as narcissistic as the people who belong to them: each believes itself to be unassailably superior and demands to be loved more than the others. These demands are usually met. We tend to prize our own age as we prize our native country – it has to be good if it produced *us*.

The current age has been hugely successful at inspiring fealty – and a key factor may be its ability to promote the illusion that fulfilment is not only possible but *easy*, even *inevitable*. Regular economic crises expose this illusion – but usually only to some people, for a short period, and in a limited way. There is a questioning of the mechanics of the system but not its underlying assumption that, if there is unlimited personal freedom and infinite choice, then anyone can *be* anything and *have* anything. No thought or effort is necessary. Only want and ye shall become and possess – this is the message propagated covertly by advertising and overtly by the self-help industry. And the age's ideal is the 'bubbly personality', its symbol the smiley face and its mantra 'Have a nice day'. But there is a fundamental axiom: you do not have to pretend to be what you are. So it should come as no surprise that the bubbly, smiley age of nice days is increasingly dosing itself with antidepressants. The brightly smiling depressive seems to be a phenomenon of the times. Depression memoirist, Sally Brampton, says of herself and a fellow sufferer, 'We both know that each of us is capable of smiling and talking cheerfully while at the same time planning our own deaths.'[10] Now those too far out are both waving *and* drowning. And, if everyone is presenting a bubbly personality, it appears as though there must indeed be automatic, universal fulfilment. So the depressive cannot understand what has gone wrong and feels atrociously isolated among the smiley faces, perhaps not even aware of also presenting a bright smile.

This is an example of what Erich Fromm identified as a new phenomenon in modern society – 'anonymous authority'[11] – a cultural pressure all the more effective for being invisible and sourceless and therefore difficult to detect and resist. Like Satan, authority has realized that the smart move is to convince everyone you no longer exist.

And anonymous authority is becoming even more anonymous and therefore even more insidious and difficult to counteract. In Western society there is no longer any overt repression. Most of the old taboos have faded away. On prime-time television a serious, distinguished-looking older woman, a doctor, sits at the

centre of a semicircle of earnest, attentive young women, holding
in her lap what appears to be some sort of anatomical model. Is
this an Advanced Midwifery seminar? No – a masterclass in delivering a blowjob, described with breezy familiarity as a 'BJ'. 'But it
always gives me jaw ache,' complains one of the young women.
The doctor explains soothingly that the secret is taking the strain
with the right hand, which she demonstrates on the model.
Meanwhile the left hand should be expertly engaged with the
often-forgotten testicles: 'I call them the stepchildren because
they're always neglected.'

As for overt authority, the last vestiges have disappeared, with
presidents and prime ministers discussing their family pets and
favourite football teams on the sofas of chat shows, religious
leaders playing the bongo drums and doing parachute jumps for
charity ('Archbishop in 12,000 feet leap of faith') and managers
publishing in the company newsletter photographs of themselves
passed out at the Christmas party with trousers down and anal
cleavage packed with cream cheese. So where is the problem?
Where is the coercion? Everyone is cool now. Even God has
been obliged to attend anger management classes for wrath.
Anything goes, provided of course that it does not denigrate
women or those of a different race, religion or sexual orientation
and causes no damage to the environment or suffering to animals.

Anonymous authority's most effective trick is making its recommendations self-evident. It is impossible to argue against the
self-evident. Only a crank would attempt to do so. This too is self-
evident. The way we live now is the natural law.

So resistance will incur charges of crankiness. Worse, it may be
that a resister must not just *appear* but also actually *be* a crank.
This alarming insight came to me many years ago while watching
a film based on the autobiography of Frank Serpico, an ambitious
young New York cop who eventually made it to detective, only to
discover that his new colleagues were all corrupt. They pooled
and shared out bribes as calmly and coolly as if they were running a coffee cooperative. And these weren't repulsive characters

but ordinary, friendly guys prepared to accept and like Frank. So, when he refused to join the club, he was obviously a crank. But here is the twist that made the movie so fascinating. The scenes from Frank's personal life revealed that *he really was a crank*: attractive and engaging girlfriends left him; his friends found him impossible.

This suggests that to behave with principle it is necessary to be a crank. Think of any principled objector. Even Christ was a crank.

So who wants to be a crank in this cool, relaxed, open-necked age, when everyone, and especially the boss, is one of the guys?

Then there are the pressures from within, from the under-self with its toxic pit of desire and aggression and its dangerous ability to persuade the upper self to do its bidding, to put a plausible and even sophisticated veneer on its demands. So, even as I deride television, I am fantasizing about propagating this view on talk shows. And even as I give the impression of being coolly indifferent to the opinion of others, I am coolly calculating the best way to impress. What I want is to be loved for never wanting to be loved.

There are resourceful enemies without and within – the ad and the id – and each is cunning and relentless, constantly adopting new guises to appear acceptable. Neither may be defeated and merely to keep both at bay requires unremitting vigilance. But, since thinkers of various kinds have been exercising vigilance for thousands of years, there are rich sources to be tapped. In the last century philosophers mostly abandoned happiness as an unserious and, worse still, unfashionable subject (black became as sexy for intellectual thought as for cocktail dresses) but, more recently, other specialists, in particular psychologists and neuroscientists, have provided fascinating discoveries and insights.

So the approach in this book is to trawl philosophy, religious teaching, literature, psychology and neuroscience for common ideas on fulfilment, then to investigate how easy or difficult it might be to apply such strategies in contemporary life and finally to apply them to areas of near-universal concern. Most of us have to work for a living, many of us would like to enjoy a lasting relationship with a partner and, in spite of tremendous advances in cosmetic surgery, all of us are still obliged to endure growing old. 'One can live magnificently in this world,' said Tolstoy, 'if one knows how to work and how to love, to work for the person one loves and to love one's work.'[12] And, he might have added, one can even grow old, if not quite magnificently, then at least without feeling entirely worthless.

However, investigating the sources is unlikely to produce a set of instructions. An axiom for literature also applies more generally: the only prescription is that there can be no prescriptions. The complexities of individuals and their circumstances make universal prescriptions impossible. In fact, the demand for prescriptions is another sign of the times. It is only our own impatient, greedy age that demands to be told how to live in a set of short bullet points.

But another useful axiom is that defining a problem is the beginning of a solution. Developing a richer awareness of problems may be one way of indirectly generating the miraculous by-product, happiness. Which may in turn generate its own miraculous by-products. Which may then enhance the original. For happiness, like depression, is a self-reinforcing cycle. Depression is a descending spiral where being depressed reduces volition, which in turn increases depression . . . and so on down. Happiness is an ascending spiral where being happy enhances volition, which in turn increases . . . and so on up. The greatest gift of happiness may not be the feeling itself as much as the accompanying thrill of possibility. Suddenly the world is re-enchanted and the self born anew. Everything is richer, stranger and more interesting. The eye sees more clearly, the mind thinks more keenly, the heart feels more strongly – and all three unite in enthusiasm, delight and zest.

PART II

The Sources

2

The Ad and the Id

There is a faery land, never buffeted by wind or lashed by rain, without clocks, closed doors, beggars, litter, graffiti, garbage, vermin or dark alleys, where the temperature is always pleasantly constant and the light evenly bright and the Pipes of Pan vie in sweetness with the tinkling of euphonious fountains at the intersections of the broad esplanades. On all sides shining emporia display garments, shoes, lingerie, creams, lotions, fragrances, chocolates, toys, mobile phones, games, televisions, flowers, music players, jewellery, sports gear and digital picture frames restlessly changing content every few seconds. In WH Smith, on parallel racks that extend into the distance, hobby magazines gleam, sleek and fat, bulging with complimentary booklets, vouchers, sunglasses, CDs, DVDs, and samples of personal fragrances. In Cards Galore there are facetious congratulations for every occasion from birth to retirement ('Our workmate who art retiring, pensioner be thy name . . .'). In the Disney Store a multitude of creatures, in a variety of sizes, colours and materials, offer identical wide eyes and innocent smiles. In Build-A-Bear Workshop there is an invitation to 'Make Your Own Furry Friend (the pawfect furreal gift)'. In the open area Le Munch Bunch Sandwicherie announces a special offer for any roll, cake and cold beverage. For dessert Joe Delucci's proposes a Cow Fodder

Sundae of chocolate and baked cream ice cream, soft marshmallow and chunky caramel. Outside the SingStar™ booth a youth in
a World War II flyer's helmet, several layers of fleece and outsize
jeans with the fork at his knees, holding three carrier bags in his
left hand and a microphone in his right, nevertheless manages to
boogie energetically while singing along to the video of 'Get This
Party Started'. Behind him a queue of restless hoodies is further
unsettled by the gaze, from the doorway of Essensuals, of an
eight-foot young woman in bra, pants, suspenders, black stock-
ings and stiletto heels, pouting mischievously. A real pouting
princess, a senior nail technician (from California Nails), golden
haired from organic colouring (in Hairport) and golden skinned
from vertical turbo tanning (in Stand By Your Tan), strides past
Sunglass Hut and a great wooden horse that has overweight children swarming all over it but no foes concealed within.
Approach, knock for resonance. Wooden all through.

Everything about a shopping mall is designed to encourage the
feeling that not to want anything would be atrociously churlish.
Firstly, a mall eliminates distractions such as depressing weather
and accusing clocks. Then, if it is a multi-storey building, a soaring
atrium or central well makes an immediate, profound impression.
Planners, from the architects of Gothic cathedrals to those of contemporary corporate headquarters, have understood that the key
to inspiring awe is redundant space, especially overhead. Any
structure with its own firmament must have been created by God.
To enhance the religious atmosphere there may be background
piped music as soothing as organ chords. And there will certainly
be many fellow worshippers to provide reassurance. The most
persuasive argument for any activity is that everyone is doing it –
and here everyone is shopping. The company of the faithful is
immensely comforting but, as in church, there is no need to
engage. The real engagement is with the icons in the window displays, promising to confer distinction, enhanced status and sexual
attractiveness. These material goods even enhance the religious
feeling. Brain scans have shown that high-end brands evoke the

same neural response as religious images; that, shocking and lamentable though it may be, an iPod has the same effect as Mother Teresa.[13] Also, the windows displaying these material icons extend from floor to ceiling, completely exposing the bright interiors, and the entrances are wide and doorless, so the instinctive fear of entering an unfamiliar enclosed space is overcome. Inside, young, attractive sales staff approach, seeking eye contact with friendly encouraging smiles, creating the illusion of youth and attractiveness in the shopper. The loud soul music suggests a bar or club where mutual attraction can blossom but, unlike the brutally competitive bars and clubs, here there is no possibility of rejection. Spending money is the easiest orgasm. Open the wallet and flash the bright card.

So the ad woos the id in the traditional way – by impressing, flattering and stimulating.

THE AD: Regard the mighty vault soaring to Heaven.
THE ID: SHEEZ!
THE AD: Now regard the many shining prizes.
THE ID: WANT!
THE AD: All of this is for you.
THE ID: ME!
THE AD: You are indeed uniquely wonderful.
THE ID: Lights! Cameras! Put me on prime-time!
THE AD: Nor need you concern yourself with others, but
be an infant till you die.
THE ID (scowling): Don't you mean, be an infant *forever*?
THE AD: I said, be an infant for *eternity*.
THE ID: WHOOP-DE-DOO!
THE AD: Never shall your desires diminish or your
appetites abate.
THE ID: MORE!

The ad smiles in satisfaction, as well it might. Never have ads been more numerous. The average American is now subjected to

over 3,000 adverts per day.[14] Never have ads been more inclusive.
Having learned the lesson of the Jesuits – get them early and you
have them for life – the ad has already colonized childhood and
will soon be seeking techniques for establishing brand loyalty in
the womb. And never have ads been more cunning. Is this a documentary? No, an ad. A news feature? No, an ad. A famous
London stadium? No, an ad for an oil-rich Middle Eastern country
keen to develop its brand.

Is this a cinema urinal? Yes, but, as your head tilts back to enjoy
relief, there comes into view on the ceiling a red plastic urinal
bearing the legend, *Spider-Man 3 . . . Coming Soon.* So, to gaze at
the ceiling is no longer safe – but at least the sky is still free. Ah,
a little aeroplane! Someone has escaped into the infinite. No, it is
merely a tow truck for an advertising banner. At least there is
nature. No, an enterprising Dutch hotel chain has begun placing
ads on live sheep. So the ad, which has become increasingly
good at pulling the wool over our eyes, now also pulls our eyes
over the wool.

Never has the ad been more sneakily aggressive. There is 'tar-
geted marketing', 'ambush marketing', 'guerrilla marketing', 'viral
marketing'. The ad has no scruples about using biological war-
fare. Most sneaky of all is neuromarketing, which uses
neuroscience to infiltrate the brain, study its defences and find
ways around them.

Never has the ad been more entertaining. One of the most ran-
corous disputes I have had with my daughter was over my habit
of muting the television during ads. When she objected I gave her
the standard lecture about ads making us want things we don't
need. She snapped back angrily that, of course, she understood
this and was entirely impervious to such persuasion, but had to
see the ads because they were discussed by her friends as entertainment just like the programmes. Only a crank would wish to
deprive her of this.

And, no longer content merely to match entertainment, the ad
has begun to infiltrate films and television programmes through

'product placement'; increasingly the product determines the story rather than the other way round. Surveys have shown that making the product seem an integral part of the story is more effective than any direct advertising because it cunningly evades the brain's resistance.[15] 'Content marketing' takes this approach to its logical conclusion by creating so-called entertainment solely for the purpose of advertising.

And the ad is no longer content to be passively observed. You no longer decode the ad, it decodes you. The latest digital billboards have concealed cameras and software that establish who is looking and display the appropriate ad – so a young man will see a bimbo advertising beer and a middle-aged woman will get details of a pampering-day offer at a health spa. Eventually these billboards will be able to recognize individuals and personalize the offering – seducing me with great 2-for-1 deals on Chinese poetry and hard-bop jazz. Then it may be necessary to go about in disguise, perhaps even to cross-dress, to bamboozle the ad.

Such bamboozlement would be an example of 'culture jamming', the new resistance movement dedicated to sabotaging consumer culture. This resistance is coordinated by websites such as the BADvertising Institute and the Canadian magazine *Adbusters*, which publishes anti-consumerist articles and spoof ads (for example, for a vodka called Absolut Nonsense) and sponsors initiatives such as Buy Nothing Day and Watch No Television Week. In the UK an organization known as Modern Toss arranges subversive events and produces T-shirts, carrier bags, posters and coffee mugs with salutary injunctions such as BUY MORE SHIT OR WE'RE ALL FUCKED.

These ventures are excellent fun but unlikely to start a revolution. Rather than attempting to defeat the ad, it would be wiser to work from the other end and attempt to control the id.

This is not easy either. The contemporary id is rampant and in no mood to be tamed. Never have so many wanted so much so badly. Never has the id been so flattered and indulged. This is the golden age of the id.

Once upon a time the id was despised and feared. For Plato it was the bad horse in the team, a 'companion to wild boasts and indecency, he is shaggy round the ears – deaf as a post – and just barely yields to horsewhip and goad combined'.[16] For Marcus Aurelius it was 'the secret force hidden deep within us that manipulates our strings'.[17] For Buddhists it was projected outwards as Mara, for Christians as Satan. For the Sufis it was the 'al-nafs al-amara', the bitter lower soul that 'knows only how to sleep, eat and gratify itself'.[18] In medieval Europe it was the violent, greedy ogre of 'Jack and the Beanstalk' and other tales. For Arthur Schopenhauer it was the will-to-live and for Nietzsche the self. Kafka personified it as the dark figure that suddenly appears on deck and wrests the helm from its legitimate guardian. And for our own age there is a materialistic explanation – it is the old reptile brain lurking at the base of the new brain. The names of the id vary – but everyone agrees on its nature. It is greedy, impulsive, angry, cunning and insatiable. No amount of gratification is ever sufficient.

Two and a half millennia before Freud, Buddha recognized that the core problem for the self is unconscious desiring. There is a striking myth of the confrontation between Buddha and Mara, the personification of the id, who appears mounted on an elephant brandishing a weapon in each of his thousand arms and, when this fails to intimidate, calls down nine frightful storms that make even the gods flee in terror. Buddha is left alone – but sitting in the 'unconquerable position' so Mara is obliged to enter into dialogue: 'Arise from this seat which belongs not to you but to me.[19] Buddha stays put, delivers an analysis of Mara's ugly character and concludes that he is more entitled to the seat than Mara.

This is like a dramatisation of Freud's project: 'Where there was Id there shall be Ego.'[20] The ego ejects the id and takes its seat. Mastery of the unconscious is the crucial victory.

According to Buddha, the root problem is ignorance, which encourages attachments that lead to desires and cravings, which bring dissatisfaction and discontent. And, if ignorance is the problem, the solution must be knowledge. So insight is redemption. Understanding is salvation.

The first requirement is the difficult work of self-knowledge. Long before Christ, Buddha realized that we see the faults of others clearly, but are conveniently blind to our own. And Buddha's version of the insight is better because it recognizes the endless ingenuity of self-justification: 'One shows the faults of others like chaff winnowed in the wind, but one conceals one's own faults as a cunning gambler conceals his dice.'[21]

The problem of ignorance can be appreciated rationally, but Buddha's solution requires a deeper, total understanding achievable only through meditation – which is not the heavy-lidded, somnolent trance suggested by Buddhist icons, but an intense mental activity described as 'mindfulness', 'wakefulness' and 'watchfulness'. *The Dhammapada*, the collection of aphorisms attributed to Buddha, has several chapters devoted exclusively to these concepts: 'Those who are watchful never die: those who do not watch are already as dead.' So the goal of meditation is not quietude and indifference but awareness, alertness, keen purposeful clarity – Buddha's metaphor for the liberated mind was a sword drawn from its scabbard.

From the practice of meditation Buddha developed a theory of consciousness like that of contemporary neuroscience. Consciousness has no substance or direction but is an endlessly flickering, fluctuating shadow play of perceptions, fantasies, delusions, associations and memories. 'The mind is wavering and restless, fickle and flighty' – the mind has the caprice of a monkey that 'grabs one branch, and then, letting that go, seizes another'. And so the idea of a unified self is an illusion: 'There is no one invariable self. What is subject to change is not mine, it is not I, it is not my self.' This recognition of ceaseless change was another central insight. All is flux. Everything is transient – 'All things are on fire.'[22]

As a consequence there is no permanent self to attack or

repress. The greed, the cravings and lusts, are as fleeting as every-thing else and will simply wither away in the bright light of intense and prolonged scrutiny. To recognize them for what they are makes them impossible to indulge. So Buddha did not denounce vice but dismissed it as 'unskilful' behaviour. Buddhism has none of the self-loathing so common in Christianity, the hatred and fear of the body and frenzied mortification of the flesh.

Hence a radical extension of an already radical idea – knowl-edge is not just the beginning of a solution but *the entire solution.* Understanding is itself transformation. But the transformation is neither immediate nor easy – nor even perceptible: 'Just as the ocean slopes gradually, with no sudden incline, so in this method training, discipline and practice take effect by slow degrees, with no sudden perception of the ultimate truth.'[23] The secret is to per-sist in the method until 'reasoned, accurate, clear and beneficial' behaviour becomes habitual. To be is to become – so the seeker of enlightenment must be 'energetic, resolute and persevering'. Buddha's last words were: 'All accomplishment is transient. Strive unremittingly.'[24]

Another key word is 'method'. Buddhism is not a creed but a method, a set of procedures for dealing with the chain of con-sequences following from ignorance. But Buddha refused to speculate on the cause of ignorance itself. So there is no theory of the fall of man, no original sin. In fact he refused to answer any metaphysical questions, not because he himself did not speculate but because such speculation was unhelpful: 'It is as if a man had been wounded by an arrow thickly smeared with poison, and his friends were to procure for him a physician, and the sick man were to say, "I will not have this arrow taken out until I have learnt the name of the man who wounded me".'[25]

This refusal to construct a Great Unified Theory of Everything was profoundly wise. For, if there is no dogma, there can be no doctrinal disputes, no heresies, no schisms – and so no inquisitions, no torturing, no burning at the stake. The two main Buddhist sects, the Theravada and Mahayana, have always coexisted in harmony – compare and contrast with the history of Catholicism and Protestantism. And in Buddhism there are no supernatural interventions, no gods, no miracles, no divine revelation, no divine grace or divine incarnation. So there is no need for faith. In fact, Buddha expressly rejected the idea of faith as an abdication of personal responsibility – no one should believe anything just because someone else says so. Each individual must work out a personal solution.

It is ironic that Christianity, the religion of the rational West, is, in fact, completely *irr*ational, inconsistent and even absurd, whereas Buddhism, the religion of the mystical East, is completely rational, consistent and even practical – not a creed requiring a leap of faith into absurdity, but a method that can be shown to work. And it is even more ironic that the attractive features of Buddhism make it unattractive to the modern age; while the other major religions are all gaining believers, Buddhism is losing ground.[26]

Christian doctrine blamed the flaw in man on original sin, which could be redeemed only by the mysterious workings of divine grace. For over a thousand years this ruled out any investigation of the self or belief in terrestrial fulfilment. It was not until the Enlightenment that thinkers gave the individual hope and scope.

The ideas of the seventeenth-century Dutch philosopher Baruch de Spinoza were startlingly similar to those of Buddha. The Enlightenment thinkers worshipped reason, but Spinoza realized that reason was riding a tiger, that human nature is driven by largely unconscious 'appetites' which enter consciousness as 'desires'. His expression of this insight could have come from *The Dhammapada* or the writings of Freud: 'Desire is man's very essence.'[27] And his views on consciousness could have come from a contemporary neurobiologist: 'The human mind is the very idea or knowledge of the human body.'[28] However, like Buddha, he believed that drives may be controlled by being understood: 'An emotion ceases to be a passion as soon as we form a clear idea of it.'[29]

And, like Buddha, Spinoza is often dismissed as a mere seeker of tranquillity – but what he valued most was joy, which he defined as a sense of empowerment created by the understanding mind. But, again as in the teachings of Buddha, understanding is not a passive, final state, but a process requiring ceaseless effort. In another insight prefiguring neurobiology, which defines living organisms as systems for optimizing life conditions, Spinoza suggested that our very nature is to strive. His Latin word for human nature, *conatus*, means 'striving' or 'endeavour': 'The striving by which each thing attempts to persevere in its being is nothing other than the actual essence of the thing.'[30] And the striving has to be difficult to be valuable: 'If salvation were readily available and could be attained without great effort, how could it be neglected by almost everyone? All that is excellent is as difficult to attain as it is rare.'[31]

But seventeenth-century Europe was not ready for this. Where Buddha was revered as a master, Spinoza was reviled as a heretic. His Jewish community in Holland first tried to bribe him (an annuity of a thousand florins) to shut up, then they tried to murder him (the attempted stabbing was foiled by the voluminousness of Spinoza's cloak) and finally they declared him anathema in fine Old Testament style: 'With the judgement of the angels and of the saints we excommunicate, cut off, curse and anathematize Baruch de Espinoza . . . with the anathema wherewith Joshua cursed Jericho, with the curse Elisha laid upon the children, and with all the curses which are written in the law. Cursed be he by day and cursed be he by night; cursed be he when he lieth down, and cursed be he when he riseth up; cursed be he when he goeth out and cursed be he when he cometh in . . .' So it thunders and thunders before commanding that no one may read Spinoza's writing, communicate with him or even venture within four cubits of him. Spinoza's response: 'This compels me to nothing that I should not otherwise have done.'[32]

After Spinoza's death his writings and ideas were ruthlessly suppressed and it was not until the nineteenth century that Schopenhauer expressed a similar set of insights. His term for the id was the 'will', which he defined as 'a blind driving force' that causes 'man' to be ruled by urges 'which are unknown to him and of which he is scarcely aware'.[33] And Schopenhauer expressed, with matchless eloquence, the insatiability of appetite: 'the desires of the will are boundless, its claims inexhaustible, and every satisfied desire gives rise to a new one. No possible satisfaction in the world could be enough to subdue its longings, set a limit to its infinite cravings and fill the bottomless abyss of its heart.'[34] Foremost among these appetites is the sex urge: 'Man is deluded if he thinks he can deny the sex instinct. He may *think* that he can, but in reality the intellect is suborned by sexual urges and it is in this sense that the will is "the secret antagonist of the intellect".' Sex is 'the ultimate goal of nearly all human effort' – and sexual repression will cause neurosis. Schopenhauer was a remarkably insightful psychologist, but he did not believe in social progress or personal fulfilment: 'In a world where no stability ... is possible, where everything is restless change and confusion and keeps itself on the tightrope only by constantly striding forward – in such a world, happiness is not so much as to be thought of.'[35]

Nietzsche too came up with similar ideas, which he imagined were thrillingly new when, in fact, many were several thousand years old. He too acknowledged an unconscious driving force, which he called the 'Self': 'Your Self laughs at your Ego and its proud efforts. "What are these mental gymnastics to me?" it says to itself. "Only a roundabout way to my goal. I am the Ego's lead violin and I prompt all its ideas".'[36] And this lurking 'Self' is the most persistent and dangerous adversary: 'But you yourself will always be the most dangerous enemy you can meet; you yourself lie in ambush for yourself in forests and caves.'[37] Nietzsche also had the intuition that the drive to optimize is the essence of all living things: 'Wherever I came upon a living creature, there I found will to power.'[38] The ceaseless striving of the human organism he defined as 'Self-Overcoming': 'Life revealed to me this secret: "Behold, it said, 'I am that *which must overcome itself again and again*'."'[39] And the friction of self overcoming self would generate enough heat and light to make life fulfilling. Nietzsche welcomed difficulty with typical grandiloquence: 'Whatever does not kill me makes me stronger.'[40]

In the twentieth century Freud proposed a similar ego-and-id model of the self that he claimed was not only new but rigorously scientific. And to establish mastery of the id by the ego there was the 'scientific' method of psychoanalytic therapy, which sought to match the cunning of the id by catching it in unguarded moments, exposed in neurosis, free association or dreams (after a hard day's manipulation of the ego, the id likes to party all night). But the therapist would have to be a special person: 'The analyst must be in a superior position in some sense, if he is to serve as a *model* for the patient in certain analytical situations, and in others to act as his *teacher*.'[41] In other words, the analyst would have to be as inspiring as a Buddhist Master. But there is an ongoing and acute worldwide shortage of Masters. Few analysts were willing or able to be models or teachers and many settled for being well paid to listen to wealthy neurotics for an hour a week – or, worse, became psychological cosmetic surgeons. I can remember being appalled when the theatre critic Kenneth Tynan revealed in an interview, with no sense of embarrassment or irony, that he had paid an analyst to remove his guilt at leaving his wife.

And recent neuroscience research confirms the model of the self proposed by thinkers – except that the division between reason and emotion, the ego and the id, is not as clear as Freud and his predecessors believed. According to neuroscientists such as Joseph LeDoux, the brain's emotional response is largely activated by the amygdala (in the limbic system, the old reptilian brain) and the rational response by the prefrontal cortex (directly behind the eyes).[42] So, to put it very, very crudely, the ego is the prefrontal cortex and id is the amygdala. But the emotional brain is capable of thought and the rational brain, with an autoroute directly to the amygdala, is hugely influenced by emotion. And many of the impulsive responses of the emotional brain (for example, intuition) are good, while many of the considered responses of the rational brain (for example, self-delusion) are bad. So it is not exactly true that the ego is the hero and the id is the villain. But, in general, the rational brain makes wiser decisions than the emotional brain. Take the case of Mary Jackson, an intelligent, highly motivated 19-year-old student who planned to go through medical school, marry her boyfriend and establish a paediatric clinic in her deprived inner-city area. Suddenly she stopped attending classes and began drinking, taking crack cocaine, sleeping around and flying into violent rages if criticized. When she was eventually referred to a neurologist, Kenneth Heilman, he discovered from a brain scan that a huge tumour had damaged the prefrontal cortex, making it unable to resist impulses and maintain long-term goals.[43] And, in the mid-twentieth century, many surgeons actually *caused* similar effects by carrying out frontal-lobe lobotomy, a procedure supposed to cure many conditions from epilepsy to schizophrenia. This crude technique, used on thousands of people in prisons and mental homes, involved inserting a scalpel under the eyelid and hammering it through the bone to sever the connections between the prefrontal cortex and the rest of the brain. (Anyone in awe of the Nobel Prize should bear in mind that the 1949 prize for medicine was awarded to the two surgeons who pioneered this lobotomy procedure.)

The neuroscientist Jonathan Cohen has actually observed the conflict between the emotional and rational brains by putting subjects into a scanner and giving them the option of receiving a gift certificate immediately or a certificate for a larger amount in a few weeks' time. The prospect of receiving a certificate right away activated the emotional brain, while the prospect of a larger certificate in the future activated the rational brain, the prefrontal cortex – and the area with the strongest activation decided the choice. So Cohen may be the first person to witness the oldest struggle in human history – the ego arm-wrestling the id. And it grieves my prefrontal cortex to reveal that the id mostly won.[44]

3

The Righteousness of Entitlement and the Glamour of Potential

The limitation of much thinking about the self is that it considers the self as an isolated and immutable entity, independent of personal history and social circumstances. But, of course, there is no such self. Everyone is influenced by temperament and history and the prevailing social climate.

Marx was the first to recognize the importance of cultural conditioning: 'It is not the consciousness of men that determines their social being, but, on the contrary, their social being that determines their consciousness.'[45] And Freud added to the id and the ego the concept of the superego, the internalized repository of society's precepts that, like the id, operates below consciousness. But both these models were too simplistic. Conditioning is not a simple one-way transfer but a complex circular process fed by constant feedback loops. What often happens is that changing social attitudes cause a few people to develop a new need or a more urgent version of an old need and an astute entrepreneur notices the development and provides an appropriate product or service. This legitimizes, reinforces and spreads the new attitude, so more people express the need more openly and more entrepreneurs service it. Soon the phenomenon has become a new norm; everyone is doing it. Eventually it becomes the natural law and influences even those who do not have the need and wish never to have it.

Marx was also too simplistic in assuming that conditioning always comes from the right. In recent times it has just as often come from the left. The 1970s was the decade of liberation, of anger at injustice and demands for recognition and rights. But, over time, the demand for specific rights degraded into a generalized sense of entitlement, the demand for specific recognitions into a generalized demand for attention and the anger at specific injustice into a generalized feeling of grievance and resentment. The result is a culture of entitlement, attention-seeking and complaint.

The demand for attention is increasingly strong and various, a consequence of inner emptiness requiring identity conferred from without: I am seen, therefore I am. At the lowest level this is expressed as a need to be physically seen. So, in a typical example of feedback, social space is increasingly organized to provide visibility: open-plan design is now the norm in homes, offices, restaurants and bars; there is more and more year-round alfresco eating and drinking; and more and more public areas designed to facilitate 'people watching', where the pleasure is as much in being watched. If separation is unavoidable, the walls are transparent, as in the transparent manager's office and the transparent elevator. The transparent home was an inevitable development – so, in Manhattan, the glass curtain wall is now as characteristic of the architecture as red brick and limestone in the 1920s. And, if all this visibility does not provide enough attention, those with sufficient disposable income can pay to be put under surveillance and/or stalked. This may seem an unlikely way to spend money but apparently such services are increasingly popular because they give their customers a unique sense of significance. As the founder of one such service puts it, 'We've had clients who say that they wear nicer underwear or start taking better care of themselves simply knowing they're being observed. Just knowing there's attention on them can be enough.'[46]

At the next level of attention-seeking, there is the need to be acknowledged as an individual. In its extreme form this becomes a craving for celebrity, the desire to be noticed not just now and then by a few, but to be bathed always in a universal warm glow of recognition, admiration, envy and desire. The contemporary prayer is: Let perpetual light shine upon us – spotlight. And this demand for celebrity is now so overwhelming (31 per cent of American teenagers sincerely believe they will be famous[47]) that the traditional means of supply – talent fêted by the media – has become completely inadequate. It was inevitable that celebrity should become available to the talentless (by becoming stars of reality television, for example) and that it should have developed new channels open to everyone (such as self-promotion on the internet).

And at the level above the individual is the demand for recognition of group identity. Here, attention-seeking, entitlement and complaint combine in the increasingly common phenomenon of taking offence, where some powerful group decides that its right to appropriately reverent recognition has been violated and that it is due retribution. The beauty of taking offence is that the threats of the bully can be presented as the protests of the victim so that the ego can bask in virtue while the id exults in aggression. The arbitrariness is also appealing. Anyone can decide to take offence at anything and this ever-present potential creates a climate of fear satisfying to bullies.

Of course no one foresaw any of these developments back in the 1970s during the heady liberation of women, gays, black people, youth and sex. Liberation was exhilarating, an unqualified good. As soon as the yoke of oppression was lifted everyone would inevitably flourish.

Many on the political right were appalled; others saw an opportunity. Money, too, demanded to be liberated – and had its wish in major financial deregulation. Free at last to express the gypsy in its soul, money became restless, promiscuous and irresponsible. It would lie with anyone attractive but rarely stay a full night. Investors were no longer prepared to wait for the long-term return of dividends; they demanded a quick return by reselling shares at a profit – so share price rather than performance became the measure of company success. And share price tended to rise when companies seemed to be doing something new and exciting. So financial sexiness came to depend on appearing dynamic, flexible and innovative. Stability, on the other hand, became a dowdy frump – *ugh*.

The smart move was to attack one's own organization with a chainsaw. So began the mania for restructuring, even in institutions without shareholders, such as government departments, universities and the BBC. But there are a limited number of structures, so anyone who remained in an organization long enough found that their first structure, long since discarded as hopelessly out of date, eventually came round again as the newest thing. It was only after many years of employment that I began to see something in Nietzsche's concept of eternal recurrence.

Newly liberated money was even sexier than liberated women, so the most significant change was a worship of change itself, which gradually spread into the wider culture as a superstitious belief in the magic of potential. One consequence is that, because change is now believed to be intrinsically good, politicians can mount successful campaigns based entirely on the promise of 'change'.

As Schopenhauer pointed out, human nature has always tended to live in anticipation, another id attribute – but entitlement and worship of change have combined to put the contemporary age completely under the spell of potential, the enchantment of imminence. The result is that means become ends in themselves.

So money, the universal means, becomes the universal end. But the effect has many manifestations. In relationships, for instance, sexual attractiveness tends to become detached from the sex it is supposed to facilitate. Increasingly, attractiveness wants to be admired rather than touched. Certainly it does not expect, God forbid, to have to *work*. I offer to psychology the theory that the greater the sexual attractiveness the lazier the sexual performance. This hypothesis may turn out to be invalid – but it would certainly be fun to test.

In the workplace, restructuring, innovation, flexibility, talent, training and mobility are all revered as good in themselves. This explains the obsession with training programmes (often employees are required to fill training quotas regardless of need) and the rise in status of 'talented' professionals such as designers, museum curators, graphic artists and chefs.

Reverence for potential is a form of greed that believes there is always something better just ahead. But the spell of potential enchants the future at the expense of disenchanting the present. Whatever is actually happening today is already so yesterday, and the only true excitement is the Next Big Thing – the next lover, job, project, holiday, destination or meal. As a consequence, the most attractive solution to problems is flight. If there are difficulties in a relationship or at work, the temptation is to move on. This, in turn, rules out the satisfactions of confronting and surmounting problems and destroys the crucial ability to make use of tribulations, to turn to advantage whatever happens.

And, of course, for the problem-averse, whatever happens must be agreeable. The only fortune is good fortune – random bad luck is just not acceptable. The philosopher Julian Baggini conducted a survey on the nature of contemporary complaint and discovered that what people most complain about is bad luck, fate, all that is outside their control.[48] Few are willing to accept that, as neo-stoics tersely put it, shit happens. Tragedy has to mean something – and something good must come of it. So bereaved relatives appear on television to ensure that such a terrible thing can never happen again: 'We don't want anyone else to have to suffer like us.'

In the leisure world, shopping and travel have become ends in themselves because they are activities of pure potential – all possibility and promise. Shopping combines many forms of potential – the intoxication of adventure, the mystery of the quest, the danger of gambling, the serendipity of creative work, the transcendence of religious faith and the sensuousness of foreplay. No wonder everyone loves it. And the excitement of potential can be prolonged even after the purchase. A few years ago a 17-year-old named Nick Bailey was so enamoured with his newly purchased Nintendo Wii gaming system that he filmed himself taking it out of the packaging and, as one does with such life-changing experiences, posted the film on YouTube. But who would want to watch a teenage geek unpacking his latest gadget? In fact, 71,000 people in the first week alone. Soon there were websites devoted exclusively to the thrill of unpacking and unwrapping.[49] And so was born a new vicarious shopping experience, at two removes from the actual merchandise.

This is an extreme case of the tendency for shopping pleasure to become detached from the reality and utility of the goods. Shopping is no longer so much about the gratification of desire as the thrill of desire itself, which must be constantly renewed. The actual purchases become less and less satisfying. Potential is always infinite but whatever is chosen is always finite. For the addict of potential every climax is an anticlimax. The magical talisman is revealed as mundane and the transcendent shopper returns to the familiar, disappointing self. Frequently the gorgeous clothes are never worn, the amazing gadget never used, the fascinating book never read and the thrilling CD never played.

My own compulsion is buying books and CDs in the hope of acquiring secret esoteric knowledge and enjoying secret ecstatic transports. But my shelves have CDs that have never been played (although none is still in cellophane because ripping off cellophane is part of the potential, the foreplay), and there are many more CDs that I have played only once. As soon as music issues from speakers a CD loses its magical aura and becomes just another CD. And because books are cheaper but take longer to read I have increasing numbers of unread purchases. A new book retains its lustre of potential for about six weeks and then changes from being a possible bearer of secret lore into a liability, a reproach, a source of embarrassment and shame.

One solution to the problem of unnecessary purchasing is to justify it as collecting so, not surprisingly, collecting of every kind is on the increase. How much more satisfactory for the ordinary shopper to be reclassified as a collector, with the term's suggestion of professorial expertise and connoisseur's discrimination, and for the useless junk to become collectibles, a word suggesting not unjustifiable extravagance but canny investment. And the compulsive purchaser of books and CDs can do even better. Buying these is not shopping but 'building a library'.

Travel is also based on expectation. The new place will be different in so many unexpected ways, inspirationally exotic, and a new transfigured self will be born. But the new place, though probably warmer, is still just another *place*, with sky, buildings, people and trees – and the dreary old fretting self has insisted on coming along for the trip. In *The Art of Travel* Alain de Botton tells a story about a Caribbean holiday with a girlfriend. Before setting off, they dream of a new harmony inspired by beaches, blue seas, palm trees and magnificent sunsets, but, as soon as they arrive, they end up arguing about the size and appearance of their restaurant desserts. They both get the same dessert but his portion is better presented whereas hers is bigger. She swaps them over and justifies pleasing herself by claiming she is pleasing him. They quarrel and return to the hotel in a resentful sulk, oblivious to the glorious scenery that was supposed to inspire them.[50] We have all had experiences like this – and conveniently forgotten them. For the next holiday is already lined up and will surely bring true bliss.

So compatible are travel and shopping that they increasingly get together. There are shopping opportunities at the airport, on the plane, in the train station, in the hotel lobby and even in the hotel room via the internet, though, of course, these only serve to keep things ticking over until the main experience – entirely new shopping opportunities in the new place.

The perfect combination of travel and shopping, however, is the luxury cruise. In fact, since the cruise experience also involves constant entertainment and pampering, the cruise ship is the perfect symbol of the contemporary age – an enormous, mobile pleasure palace conveying outsize infants in pastel leisurewear round a series of shopping venues.

David Foster Wallace's hilarious and terrifying account of a Caribbean cruise, *A Supposedly Fun Thing I'll Never Do Again*, is scrupulous documentary realism, but also a fable for our times – for the cruise displays, in exaggerated form, all the new cultural trends. There is the inability to experience directly and the need to film everything to believe it has happened – all the passengers are heavily laden with sophisticated camera equipment. There is the universal sense of entitlement – everyone believes that they thoroughly deserve this holiday. There is the infantile need for pampering – the cruise ship offers constant servicing by an army of assiduous servants. There is the relentless, even fanatical, cheerfulness of the staff. There is the refusal of thought among the infantile passengers. Wallace notes: 'I have heard upscale adult U.S. citizens ask the Guest Relations Desk whether snorkeling necessitates getting wet, whether the skeetshooting will be held outside, whether the crew sleeps on board, and what time the Midnight Buffet is.'[51] There are the endless shopping opportunities on board and at the ports, and endless distractions and entertainments – pools, gyms, multiple sports facilities (including even a driving range), casinos, piano bars, discos, cinemas and a Celebrity Show Lounge with nightly Celebrity Showtime featuring an impressionist, a juggler of chainsaws, a husband and wife duo singing Broadway show-tune medleys and a hypnotist claiming to have entranced both Queen Elizabeth II and the Dalai Lama.

Many of these contemporary trends are interrelated. The infantile tendency is surely a reaction to the age of liberation. It is a common mistake to assume that liberation is in itself enough for fulfilment, that everything will be fine if one can just escape the soul-destroying job, oppressive relationship, dreary town. But it turns out that freedom does not lead automatically to fulfilment. Instead, freedom leads to unremitting hard work. The old traditions may have been oppressive but living without them is uncertain, complicated, confusing and stressful. Having to think every decision through from first principles is exhausting. The potential of infinite opportunity becomes the perplexity of infinite choice. And so to the backlash – a deep yearning to act from impulse rather than deliberation, to follow emotion rather than reason, to prefer anything certain, simple, easy and passive. The arduous responsibility of being an adult induces a deep nostalgia for the luxury of basking in unconditional love, eating, drinking, filling a nappy and dozing off to a lullaby.

The ad is of course only too happy to pander to emotion and impulse, and the entertainment industry to sing Big Baby to sleep. The only good thing about the new infantilism is that the need to protect baby often cancels out the need to indulge. A London hotel, known for innovative services such as dog weddings and a mustard sommelier, came up with an idea worthy of a luxury cruise ship: for a fee, two members of staff would come to a guest's room and one would recreate the magic of childhood by starting a pillow fight with the guest while the other acted as referee. This new service was enormously popular but, of course, had to be discontinued 'on health and safety grounds'. However, if the demands for pampering and attention are not met, Big Baby will become very cross indeed. The new infantilism has contributed to the growing sense of self-importance and entitlement, the diminishing sense of self-awareness and obligation and the increasing recourse to resentment and outrage. Big Baby is frequently red in the face.

And the new infantilism is one reason for the rise of PC – not Political Correctness but Professional Cheeriness. A cheerful expression, drained of subtlety and nuance and infused with exaggerated brightness, is the demeanour an adult presents to a child. Another possible source of PC is the shift from manufacturing to service economies, which has made the user interface increasingly significant. Not only is the customer always right, the service always has to be bright. This obligation spread through the American service industries and then around the world. Even the sublimely disdainful waiters of Paris have had to adapt. No one did contempt like the French – as with their great wines and cheeses, it was based on centuries of tradition – but they too have had to learn to wish their despised clientele a nice day. Jean-Paul Sartre, so proud at how Paris opposed 'Nazi venom', would have been horrified to see it succumb to American sugar.

And a further factor is the modern tendency to become a commodity in a world of commodities, to develop not as a person but as a brand – and in the contemporary marketplace this means being bubbly and smiley.[52]

This marketing orientation has been further encouraged by the rise of the team. The new 'flexible' organizations often replaced established departments and long-term staff with teams working on specific projects under short-term contracts. So, for the individual, institutional loyalty has become meaningless and the crucial skill is the ability to perform anywhere as a 'team player'. Collaboration is as important as individual effort, and ability to fit in as important as performance.

In the 1970s two Americans combined a smiley face with the fateful slogan 'Have a Nice Day' and copyrighted a symbol whose worldwide popularity rivalled that of the Cross. In fact, the original smiley face was created by an earlier American adman, Harvey R. Ball. But that was back in innocent 1964, before money became sexier than sex, so Ball never bothered to trademark the symbol and was paid only $45 for his work. An old-school guy despite being an adman, Ball, when asked how he felt about missing out on a stupendous revenue stream, responded with a remark worthy of a Stoic philosopher: 'Hey, I can only eat one steak at a time.'

All these developments have combined to produce a shift in values – favouring change over stability, potential over achievement, anticipation over appreciation, collaboration over individuality, opportunism over loyalty, transaction over relationship, infantilism over maturity, passivity over engagement, eloping over coping, entitlement over obligation, outwardness over inwardness and cheerfulness over concern.

Seduced from the left by the righteousness of entitlement and from the right by the glamour of potential, it is easy to believe that fulfilment is not only a basic right but thoroughly deserved, and that attaining it requires no more thought, effort or patience than an escalator ride to the next level of the shopping centre.

The problem is that the major developments all seem benign. Isn't 'freedom' the most inspirational of words and the unassailable concept at the heart of modern society? Isn't a sense of potential the essence of happiness? Aren't we obliged to change ourselves? And obliged to behave unto others as we would like them to behave unto us? But freedom, which originally meant the freedom to participate in government, has come to mean the freedom to resist intervention by government. A sense of personal potential is indeed necessary to make life worth living – but the need is for a sense of potential within – whereas contemporary potential is entirely external, dependent on activities such as sexual adventure, promotion, shopping and travel. 'You must change yourself' is a fundamental commandment, but it does not imply worship of change for its own sake – change must always be balanced against the need for responsibility and commitment. Cheeriness is desirable – no one prefers surly bad manners – but it is often the appearance of goodwill without the substance and discourages deeper reactions such as irony, scepticism and dissent. It even discourages passionate enthusiasm by making it appear alarmingly excessive. Worst of all, it discredits the smile itself by making it seem insincere and manipulative so that the only sincere expression is the furious grimace of a gargoyle.

What can be done? There is little prospect of changing the culture. One of capitalism's greatest strengths has been its ability to co-opt everyone into its project by encouraging them to become property owners, shareholders and entrepreneurs. And to its promise that anyone can be a millionaire has recently been added the promise that anyone can be a celebrity. Its other great strength is the ability to neutralize dissent by absorbing it. So capitalism effortlessly assimilated the working class, as it later swallowed the 1950s beats, the 1960s counterculture, the 1970s punks and, more recently, the culture-jamming movement. The Adbusters company now manufactures a running shoe and of course advertises it in *Adbusters*. Will you be punished for transgression if you publish a novel on the pleasures of hanging young boys, exhibit a partly decomposed skull supporting a bluebottle colony or pelt a concert audience with pig intestines and then bite the head off a live bat?[53] No, instead you will be rewarded with wealth and fame. Capitalism actually seeks counterculture to consume as the roughage in a healthy diet.

Similarly, television and advertising have learned to defuse opposition by ironic self-mockery. One of the most successful recent TV sitcoms featured a stupid, passive family who do nothing but slump in their living room watching television. But, of course, the families in their living rooms watching on television the family in its living room watching television did not feel stupid and passive but knowing and superior – they had been let in on the joke. And advertising offers parodies of ads and even mocks the very idea of advertising. This is the trick of the sophisticated conman who ensures complicity by winking at you throughout the con.

Do thinkers offer any advice on resisting the conditioning pressures of the world? Rarely. Thinkers tend to withdraw in contempt and horror – Buddha's solution to the world was to abandon it.

But the Greek and Roman Stoics – Epictetus, Seneca and Marcus Aurelius – were very much in the world. Aurelius was an emperor, Seneca was a wealthy banker, possibly the only banker to write philosophy, and Epictetus was an ex-slave. And the world they moved in was a late, affluent civilization with many similarities to our own. Their writings are also surprisingly lively, not at all 'stoic' in the word's contemporary meaning of grim resignation to adversity. These three were neither grim (Seneca: 'It is more civilized to make fun of life than to bewail it'[54]), nor resigned (Marcus Aurelius: 'The art of living is more like wrestling than dancing'[55]) and as much concerned with surviving prosperity as enduring adversity (Seneca: 'While all excesses are in a way hurtful, the most dangerous is unlimited good fortune'[56]). The problem, they argued, is not that affluence is bad in itself but that it encourages character defects such as self-importance, contempt, resentment, impatience, restlessness, and, worst of all, desire for yet more wealth. They understood all too well the madness that makes too much never enough. Epictetus compared this to a fever that creates a thirst no amount of water can slake. Seneca cites Alexander the Great's insatiable need for new lands to conquer: 'He still desired to pass beyond the Ocean and the Sun.'[57] The problem, then as now, is the spell of potential in an affluent society. As Seneca put it: 'The greatest hindrance to living is expectancy, which depends upon tomorrow and wastes today.'[58] So, as though written expressly for the twenty-first century, the Stoic works abound in reminders of the futility of attention-seeking, shopping, anger, taking offence and travel for its own sake ('Nothing here is any different from what it would be up in the hills or down by the sea'[59]).

The key Stoic virtue is detachment – if it is not possible to influence the world, it is at least possible to moderate the world's influence on the self – but the purpose of this detachment is understanding rather than contempt. And it does not imply withdrawal or fatalistic indifference. The Stoic strategy is not to avoid experience or to accept it passively, but *to make something of it*: 'If our inner power is true to Nature, it will always adjust to the possibilities offered by circumstance. It requires nothing predetermined and is willing to compromise; obstacles are merely converted into material for use. It is like a bonfire mastering a heap of rubbish.'[60] Complaining is, of course, entirely out of the question – Epictetus: 'The proper goal of our activity is to practise how to remove from one's life sorrows and laments and cries of "alas" and "poor me".'[61] But Aurelius has the maxim for the coffee mug: 'To refrain from imitating is the best revenge.'[62]

Unfortunately, this fruitful speculation on how to live in the world was obliterated for over a thousand years by Christianity's rejection of the possibility of terrestrial happiness. Yet Christ, often regarded as the most unworldly of men, was in fact much concerned with the world and offered useful advice on how to deal with it. Firstly, he rejected, with startlingly consistent vehemence, loyalty to family and tribe: 'a man's foes shall be they of his own household'.[63] Then he considered the phenomenon of the Pharisees, the Scribes. These were men with power but no authority – a crucial distinction. Authority earns respect, power demands it; authority requires no trappings, power needs imposing robes; authority is forthright, power is secretive; authority is the open heart, power is the closed fist. So Matthew says of Christ: 'For he taught them as one having authority and not as the Scribes.'[64] The Scribes believed in rules rather than principles, status rather than achievement, hypocrisy rather than virtue. So they were always trying to drag Christ into case law and make him contravene prohibitions – and Christ always refused rules and insisted that every case be decided from first principles. If a sheep falls into a pit on the Sabbath do you obey the prohibition on work or pull the sheep out?[65] And he consistently denounced hypocrisy, a key theme in the New Testament, but rarely mentioned by Christians.

Christ's conflict with the Pharisees is permanently relevant because there are Pharisees in every period and culture. Like the poor, the Pharisees are always with us. They rarely seize power or define its supporting ideology, but they will serve any regime and implement any plan. They are the French civil servants who delivered their Jewish fellow citizens to the Nazis, the communist apparatchiks who betrayed their neighbours to the secret police, the righteous zealots who imposed political correctness at the end of the twentieth century – and the colleagues who speak at length in every meeting, in loud confident tones that suggest critical independence, but never deviate from the official line. Pharisees are among the most important transmitters of cultural norms and they will switch effortlessly to new values without even being conscious of the move. So they have learned to be PC in both senses. Where for centuries they were solemn, they are now Professionally Cheerful, although they still have no sense of humour. And, as Christ understood, they can never be defeated because they always hold the power, propagate official ideas and follow official procedure. Christ's advice was 'Render therefore unto Caesar the things which are Caesar's'[66] – give to power only the necessary minimum and no more.

The Pharisee is the type defined by Fromm as the 'authoritarian character'[67], who worships power for its own sake, reveres the powerful and despises the powerless. In other words, the orientation is sadomasochistic – kiss up and piss down. This type will also fear, loathe and seek to suppress those like Christ who have authority and do not need or seek power.

These ideas – the Stoic belief in making use of inevitable adversity, Christ's insistence on a morality based on principle rather than prescription, and the Freudian understanding of the sadomasochistic nature of power – came together in the mid-twentieth century in existentialism, one of the few philosophical movements fully to consider the relationship of the self to the world. The key concept is personal responsibility. As Sartre expressed it: 'Man is fully responsible for his nature and his choices.'[68] But this is not an excuse for withdrawal and isolation. On the contrary, it makes engagement necessary at all levels, from personal relationships to group membership. For responsibility requires the unremitting exercise of choice, which, though frequently painful, is the only way of transcending circumstance and self. But every choice ends in finitude so there can be no question of living in perpetual anticipation. Søren Kierkegaard, the proto-existentialist, wrote, 'This is the despair of possibility. Possibility then appears to the self ever greater and greater, more and more things become possible, because nothing becomes actual. At last it is as if everything were possible.'[69] Kierkegaard argued that the self needs a balance of necessity and possibility –

it will suffocate in too much necessity but vaporize in too much possibility. Throughout history, crushing necessity has been the usual problem, but the contemporary self is being driven mad by infinite possibility. Rejection of necessity is the contemporary sickness.

And Sartre defined not potential but finitude as the essence of freedom: 'To be finite . . . is to choose oneself . . . to make known to oneself what one is by projecting oneself toward one possible to the exclusion of others. The very act of freedom is therefore the assumption and creation of finitude.'[70] But the chosen finitude must be fully accepted – it is always necessary to *follow through*. And this exercise of responsibility rules out grievance: 'It therefore makes no sense to complain since nothing foreign has decided what we feel, what we live, or what we are.'[71]

So the Stoic insistence on making use of what happens is raised to the level of a core belief – whatever you have been made into you can make something out of. Indeed this making is an obligation. Sartre denounced the passive acceptance of social roles and cultural conditioning as 'bad faith', lack of 'authenticity', the lazy excuse of 'this is the way I am'. The self must be constantly made and this making becomes a way of transcending the self. Living is perpetual self-transcendence.

As for relations with others, the freedom of the individual is the crucial factor. So in love there is no question of either surrendering or demanding surrender – masochism or sadism. It is difficult to have a relationship without some element of power struggle but the ideal is that the autonomy of the partner should always be respected; the consequence of following this ideal, though, is not eternal bliss but eternal conflict. Danger and risk are unavoidable but give the relationship intensity – and intensity rather than serenity is the existentialist goal.

Similarly, in group relations there should be no submission to the group ethos, what Sartre defined as 'us-consciousness', nor any use of power to subjugate the freedom of others. As in love, the exercise of power in the group is often sadomasochistic.

What the authoritarian personality, the Pharisee, usually demands is compliance with hierarchy, regulations and procedure but what it really craves is surrender of internal freedom. So it may always be frustrated by being given *only* external compliance. This is the existentialist triumph, the preservation of a secret self and personal freedom by rendering to Caesar only the things that are Caesar's.

So existentialism rejects team-player malleability, emphasizes finitude rather than potential, advises making use of whatever happens and embraces the difficult because it confers intensity. No wonder this philosophy has gone out of fashion.

Another key concept is absurdity, again an extension of Stoic thought. If life is insignificant and meaningless, it must be absurd. So this is also the age of absurdity in the philosophical sense.

For Sartre, always solemn and portentous, absurdity was tragic, even justifying suicide and certainly ruling out happiness. But Albert Camus saw that not only is happiness possible, it is symbiotically linked to absurdity – each can reinforce the other: 'Happiness and the absurd are two sons of the same earth. They are inseparable. It would be a mistake to say that happiness necessarily springs from the absurd discovery. It happens as well that the feeling of the absurd springs from happiness.'[72] Camus applied this to the situation of Sisyphus, eternally condemned to push a rock up a hill, a myth with profound resonance for all those obliged to work for a living: 'Sisyphus teaches the higher fidelity that negates the gods and raises rocks. He, too, concludes that all is well. This universe henceforth without a master seems to him neither sterile nor futile. Each atom of that stone, each mineral flake of that night-filled mountain, in itself forms a world. The struggle itself towards the heights is enough to fill a man's heart. One must imagine Sisyphus happy.'[73]

Unfortunately the existentialists were entirely humourless. *The Myth of Sisyphus* is Camus' classic work on the absurd but it too has portentous moments, especially on the subject of suicide. In fact Camus' actual death was appropriately absurd. Though intending to return to Paris from Marseilles by rail, he was persuaded to accept a lift from his publisher – who drove off the road and into a tree. So Camus died in a car with a train ticket in his pocket – an absurdist parable on the consequences of accepting someone else's route.

It was left to other writers to draw the opposite conclusion to Sartre's – that absurdity is not tragic but comic, a reason not to reject life but to draw from it a strange new sustenance and relish. As a character in one of Samuel Beckett's plays remarks: 'How can one better magnify the Almighty than by sniggering with him at his little jokes, particularly the poorer ones?' The character is Winnie, who is first buried up to the waist and then up to the neck in the play called – what else? – *Happy Days*. 'Oh this *is* a happy day!' she cries, 'This will have been another happy day!'[74]

4

The Old Self and the New Science

You can have anything you desire and become anyone you wish to be. There are no limits to potential, achievement and reward. The universe is an endless conveyor belt of prizes. Such are the seductive claims of the self-help industry in its annual outpouring of books with titles such as: *The Joys of Much Too Much: Go For The Big Life – The Great Career, The Perfect Guy, And Everything Else You've Ever Wanted.*

The covers are brightly coloured, the titles are long and greedy, the tone is frenziedly cheerful and the argument has three basic assumptions: that fulfilment is a consequence of worldly success (*God Wants You To Be Rich*); that there are a number of simple steps for achieving fulfilment (*Life Is Short – Wear Your Party Pants: 10 Simple Truths That Lead To An Amazing Life*); and that anyone who follows the prescribed steps will discover vast, untapped potential (*Awaken the Giant Within*). Self-help must take some of the blame for fostering the illusion that fulfilment is easy.

Distaste for the fatuous breeziness of self-help has also possibly encouraged a rejection of all psychology as lightweight and worthless. But the message of serious psychology is the opposite of that of self-help – fulfilment is not easy, but exhaustingly difficult. Theorists of the self insist on understanding and transformation but psychology has shown how difficult these can be. Attempts at self-understanding will be strenuously opposed by the id's cunning use of self-deception, self-justification and self-righteousness. There seems to be no delusion too absurd, no justification too irrational and no righteousness too extreme for the human mind to accept.

The delusions begin with the very idea of happiness. Everyone everywhere, regardless of age, gender, social status or wealth, reports a happiness level over 5 on a scale of 1 to 10 – and, stranger still, is certain of even greater happiness in the future. The American psychologist Jonathan Haidt claims that there are similar delusions for all the desiderata, that most Europeans and Americans rate themselves above average on a wide range of talents including virtuousness, intelligence and of course sexual performance. This made me think of my self-important teaching colleagues – and, sure enough, Haidt says of college professors, '94 per cent of us think we do above-average work.'[75] Needless to say, I am among this 94 per cent. And it turns out that teachers are even more deluded than students – a mere 70 per cent of students believe they are above average. The temptation to laugh is checked by another troubling thought: most of my colleagues believe themselves to be terrifically amusing; everyone also has an above-average sense of humour.

But, as so often, there is an intriguing exception. Haidt observes that the desiderata delusion is weaker in east Asian countries, and possibly non-existent in Japan. Is this evidence of the beneficial influence of Buddhist culture, which attempts to dispel illusion and reduce attachment to the self?

But we exaggerate only our own virtues. On those of others we are realistic. Two psychologists, Nicholas Epley and David Dunning, asked people to predict whether they would behave selfishly or cooperatively in a game played for money. The result: 84 per cent claimed that they themselves would play cooperatively – but the estimate of cooperative behaviour in others was only 64 per cent. And, in fact, 61 per cent did play cooperatively.[76] In other words, as Buddha and Christ said repeatedly, we are hypocrites.

There is at least the consolation that many of the psychologists' findings support the insights of religious and philosophical thinkers, in particular the conclusion reached at the very beginning by the Greeks and repeated by everyone since, but still not generally accepted – that success and prosperity alone will not make anyone happy. A certain level of affluence is of course required to provide the basics, as Aristotle acknowledged, but more will do little to increase satisfaction. Many of the experts produce a graph of happiness level against income. This rises steeply at first and then levels off. After a certain point, having more has no effect. There is even an equivalent graph for countries, which shows happiness levels rising at first with stages of economic development but then tailing off – so increasing wealth is as ineffective for nations as for individuals. And the same phenomenon may be observed over time – the increasing affluence of the West over the last few generations has brought no corresponding increase in happiness.[77]

There is also evidence that, as Buddha and Spinoza claimed, resisting the desire for immediate gratification can bring long-term fulfilment. In 1970 Walter Mischel sat a succession of four-year-old children in front of a marshmallow on a plate and explained that he had to leave the room for a moment but that, if the marshmallow was still uneaten when he returned, the reward would be two marshmallows instead of one. Around a third of the children scoffed the treat straight away, another third tried to hold out but succumbed at various stages, and the final third succeeded in waiting for the double pay-off. When Mischel surveyed the children fifteen years later he discovered that those with self-control had turned out more successful in every way, both educationally and personally, whereas those unable to delay gratification were more likely to be low achievers, to have drug and alcohol problems, and, interestingly, to become bullies, a confirmation that desire for power is a kind of greed indulged by the unfulfilled. Further investigation revealed that the key talent of the self-controllers was not so much willpower as detachment, an ability to think of something other than the treat on the plate.[78] It is encouraging to know that a third of four year olds are little Buddhas – but this classic experiment was conducted in 1970, just before the era of rabid consumption. Today's four year olds would probably wolf down the marshmallow and then complain that marshmallows are rubbish.

Other experiments have confirmed the age-old insight that the more we have, the more we want; that life is a progression, not from satisfaction to satisfaction, but from desire to desire. The economist Richard Easterlin asked young people to identify the consumer items they thought essential for the good life; sixteen years later he asked the same people the same question. What happened was that they had moved up the scale of desirables – television, car, house, overseas holidays, swimming pool, second home, etc. – and wherever they had arrived it was always the next item that would finally make them happy. No sooner was one thing acquired than they got used to it, took it for granted and wanted the next.[79] This study investigated only attitudes to consumer goods, but the effect applies to everything desirable – welfare benefits, pay rises, promotions, holidays, gourmet food and gourmet sex. As Schopenhauer remarked: 'With possession, or the certain expectation of it, our demands immediately increase and this increases our capacity for further possessions and greater expectation . . . to attain something desired is to discover how vain it is.'[80] The psychologists' terms for this are 'adaptation', 'habituation' and 'the hedonic treadmill'.

And it occurs to me that there is also negative adaptation – we think we will be less unhappy if we do less of an unpleasant chore, but the less we do the less we want to do. This happens when you feel atrociously overworked, manage to get the workload reduced but soon once again feel atrociously overworked. In fact the expectation of relief may mean that having to do less is even more vexing.

And from my own experience I can add that habituation applies not just to money, goods and pleasures, but also to fame. Artistes usually claim to want only a modest level of recognition – publication, exhibition, opportunities to perform – but as soon as this level is achieved they crave more. And there is no upper limit. Even the hugely famous are irritated by a single dissenter. This is a vulnerability worth remembering – by refusing to join in the adulation, even the most insignificant of us can infuriate a celebrity.

So the human capacity for self-deception is extraordinary – but there is another capacity that is even more impressive. The talent for self-justification is surely the finest flower of human evolution, the greatest achievement of the human brain. When it comes to justifying actions, every human being acquires the intelligence of an Einstein, the imagination of a Shakespeare and the subtlety of a Jesuit. One example that especially impressed me was the argument of a wife-beating husband who explained patiently that the punches and kicks requiring hospital treatment were a proof not of his own, but of his wife's, atrocious behaviour – if a gentle soul such as he was driven to violence then the provocation must have been intolerable. And this was an intelligent, sensitive man, a well-known poet famed for his honesty, tolerance and love of women.

The classic experiment on self-justification was carried out over fifty years ago when a psychologist called Leon Festinger infiltrated a cult that was based on the belief that a flying saucer would arrive at midnight on 20 December 1954 to save true believers from the end of the world on 21 December. Many cult members left their jobs and gave away their savings and, on the evening of 20 December, gathered with their leader to await deliverance. When midnight came and went without a spaceship there was naturally a certain amount of apprehension. But at 4.45 a.m. the leader finally realized what had happened – the unshakeable faith of the true believers had caused the world to be spared: 'Not since the beginning of time upon this Earth has there been such a force of Good and Light as now floods this room.'[81] Hallelujah! The ecstatic group contacted the press to report a miracle and then rushed out into the streets to convert the unbelieving world.

So not only does irrefutable evidence fail to destroy a delusion; it can actually reinforce and intensify the false belief. For this astounding feat of mental trick cycling Festinger coined the drab term 'cognitive dissonance'. Unable to tolerate two dissonant beliefs, the mind simply eliminates the more inconvenient of the two. And, whereas contradictory evidence is uncritically rejected, confirming evidence is uncritically accepted. If there happens to be no evidence either way, this too is taken as confirmation. I discovered this myself during the Troubles in Northern Ireland when an exultant group of nationalists informed me that, as result of a successful IRA action, the local hospital morgue was overflowing with the bullet-riddled bodies of British soldiers. 'But there's been nothing in the papers or on TV,' I objected. They laughed in contempt at this naive response: '*Exactly.*'

No mental feat is too difficult for self-justification – and memory distortion is one of the easier tricks. As all dictators understand, those who wish to alter the future must first alter the past. So, ability to cope with the future is encouraged by exaggerating problems overcome in the past – hence the popularity of accusing parents of bullying or neglect; not only does this make the child seem more resourceful, it is a convenient way of attributing blame for any lingering imperfections. Our own past bad behaviour is, of course, conveniently suppressed. Nietzsche understood this: '"I have done that," says my memory. "I cannot have done that," says my pride, and remains inexorable. Eventually memory yields.'[82]

And creating memories, even the most bizarrely implausible, is only a little more difficult than distortion. There are several million Americans who sincerely believe that they have been abducted by aliens.[83] The clinical psychologist Susan Clancy interviewed several hundred of these 'experiencers', as they describe themselves, and found the same pattern. All of them had suffered from mental distress and dysfunction and then had had an alarming sleep experience – actually a phenomenon known as 'sleep paralysis' – which they subsequently explained by an abduction story. The aliens were then blamed for the original problems. As a

woman suffering from sexual dysfunction explained, 'I understand that it's related to what the beings did to me. I was a sexual
experiment to them from an early age.'[84] This is an extreme way
of evading responsibility – but it might cause less damage than
blaming parents . . . unless the aliens get hold of Clancy's inter-
views, realize that they have been made scapegoats and decide
that, as innocent victims, they are entirely justified in mounting an
alien invasion of the USA.

Of course, the experiencers are familiar with the scientific
explanation and vigorously reject it ('I swear to God, if someone
brings up sleep paralysis one more time I'm going to puke'),
greatly supported in this by mixing with fellow experiencers and
sharing stories, for justification also operates at the group level.
The 'us-consciousness' described by Sartre creates an overwhelming urge to justify anything done by Us and to condemn
anything done by Them. Such Us/Them distinctions can be based
on the most minor differences – and have been created artificially
by researchers – but are strongest when the distinction is long-
standing. Religion, of course, provides the ultimate differentiation,
with a divinely anointed Us and a divinely damned Them. And
anyone who has lived in a long-term conflict area will be familiar with the line, 'Their atrocities are always so much more vile
than ours', or, from the more passionate group advocates, 'Our
atrocities were actually committed by *Them* to discredit *Us*'.

The perpetrators of violence often follow a cycle where the
innocence of a victim requires a drastically contemptuous justification that actually intensifies the hatred and rage. So the more
helpless the victim the more violent the attack, and the more desperate the need to re-establish moral superiority. Dictators
invariably see themselves as self-sacrificing patriots working only
for the good of their countries. The writer Louis Menand spotted
a wonderful poster in the Haiti of the infamous Jean-Claude 'Baby
Doc' Duvalier: 'I should like to stand before the tribunal of history
as the person who irreversibly founded democracy in Haiti –
signed, Jean-Claude Duvalier, President-for-Life.'[85]

Of course novelists have always understood the subtleties of
self-justification. There is a minor episode in *War and Peace*
that is so convincingly horrifying it has stayed with me long after
I have forgotten all the war scenes. After the battle of Borodino the
Russian army, reneging on a solemn pledge, abandons Moscow to
Napoleon – and anyone who can afford transport flees the city. A
mob, angry at being duped and deserted, gathers outside the residence of the governor, Count Rostopchin. This shrewd official
realizes that a scapegoat is needed and orders his soldiers to fetch
a youth imprisoned for distributing leaflets criticizing the authori-
ties. 'This man,' Rostopchin cries to the mob, 'is the scoundrel who
has lost us Moscow.' But, when the youth is brought out, he is pitiful – shabby, emaciated, shuffling in leg irons. Worse still, he
seems to expect justice and compassion: 'Count,' he pleads timidly,
'there is one God who judges us.' But Rostopchin, rather than
being moved to mercy, is driven into a frenzy. 'Cut him down,' he
screams at his men and, at a muttered command from an officer, a
dragoon hits the youth on the head with the flat of his sword. The
resulting cry of shock and pain incites the mob to finish the job.
And, while they are distracted with beating and kicking the youth
to death, Rostopchin makes his way through to the back of the residence and is borne away in a carriage with 'swift horses'.

Then begins the work of self-justification. At first Rostopchin is
sickened by his own cowardice and cruelty and chilled by the
youth's mention of God. But, little by little, he convinces himself
that his behaviour was not only irreproachable, but necessary 'for
the public good'. As an individual he would have acted differently, but as governor it was essential to safeguard both the
dignity of the office and the life of its current holder. Soon he is
congratulating himself on so astutely killing two birds with one
stone – appeasing the mob and punishing a criminal – and, by
the time he reaches his country estates, he has 'completely
regained his composure'.[86]

But, if anything can be justified, what hope is there for self-
knowledge and self-transformation? The psychologists point out

that delusion, justification and righteousness are successful because they operate below consciousness. Once exposed to awareness they lose most of their power. This is, of course, the understanding advocated by Buddha, Spinoza and Freud.

But psychology has identified another obstacle to change in the 'set point'[87], a kind of default setting or equilibrium state of the self. Schopenhauer defined this as 'our primary and inborn character'.[88] So even the effects of something as positive as winning a lottery or as negative as paralysis will eventually wear off. The time limit for extreme effects is a year or so; after lesser disturbances we revert much more quickly. This explains why we always overestimate the impact of future events – we are never as happy or as miserable as we expect to be. In other words, our natural temperament is always reasserting itself; people can get used to almost anything. In Kafka's *Metamorphosis* Gregor Samsa experiences only 'slight annoyance' about turning into an insect and is soon scampering happily across the ceiling of his bedroom.

But there are interesting exceptions that resist the gravitational pull of the set point. On the positive side, cosmetic surgery is reported to have a long-term beneficial effect that refuses to fade.[89] So perhaps I should pay more attention to those emails promising a penis capable of extra duty as a backscratcher. And on the negative side, no one ever learns to tolerate excessive noise. This was surprising at first but soon made sense. I like to think of myself as a strong-minded individual who can withstand heavy psychological pressure – but any malign regime wishing to break me would have only to lock me in a room and play loud rap music. After a few hours I would betray my wife, daughter, friends and every ideal I have ever held dear.

This apparent fixity of the set point has led to claims that it is genetically determined. David Lykken and Auke Tellegen analysed the long-term moods and traits of several thousand sets of twins, and concluded that the subjective well-being of identical twins was similar whether they had been reared together or separated, whereas this was not true for non-identical twins.

Lykken's conclusion was unequivocal: 'Nearly 100 percent of the variation across people in the happiness set point seems to be due to individual differences in genetic makeup.'[90] So there was a further conclusion: 'trying to be happier is like trying to be taller' – hence *The New Yorker* cartoon showing two middle-aged men in leisurewear sipping cocktails in front of a fake chateau, with one saying to the other, 'I could cry when I think of the years I wasted accumulating money, only to learn that my cheerful disposition is genetic.'[91]

There are several possible objections to Lykken's conclusions. Firstly, there is the difficulty of measuring accurately something as abstract as a psychological set point. Then the study does not seem to have considered, much less investigated, deliberate attempts to *move* the set point. Those in the study may have been as fatalistic as most people in accepting their temperament, but what would be the effect of a conscious, informed, determined and prolonged attempt to alter the default state? In fact, there is a physical equivalent to the psychological set point – the biochemical equilibrium state that our bodies maintain in a regulatory system known as homeostasis, a sort of thermostat effect. But as the neurobiologist Steven Rose has explained, these default values are not permanent: 'The set points around which the moment-by-moment fluctuations in an individual's biochemistry oscillate on the microscale themselves change during the trajectory of a lifetime.'[92]

So, if physical set points can change, why not the mental equivalents? The evidence on cosmetic surgery and noise already shows that this is possible. And a recent survey suggests that the set point follows a U curve over a lifetime, starting high, then dropping to a minimum in the middle years but climbing back, amazingly, to the high level of youth.[93]

And factors other than age make a difference. Those with religion are happier than unbelievers. Married people are happier than singletons.[94] But is this a confusion of cause and effect? Those happy to begin with may make better spouses. And countries report different levels of happiness, with the former communist states at the bottom of the table, confirming that the project of mass happiness led to mass misery.

Also, some forms of status do confer meaningful benefits. Those in professional jobs are happier, not because they earn more or have greater prestige, but because they have more control over what they do. They have the priceless gift of autonomy and so are free to exercise personal responsibility.

But the importance of most forms of status is relative. We will be happy with very little if everyone else has a little less – and miserable if this distinction is eliminated or reduced. So workers' unions have been justified in protesting at 'eroded differentials' – indeed a genuine and painful affliction. And this explains why a pay rise may make an employee howl with rage. If someone else at an equivalent level got more, then the smaller rise is not merely worthless, but *an insult*. The issue is not the money but the ranking it signifies. Money used to buy status; now it *is* status.

But little in human psychology is simple. A survey of Olympic medallists showed that bronze medal winners tended to be happier than those taking silver.[95] How is this possible? Consider the differentials. Bronze is aware only of the vast gap between itself and the unmedalled many *not even close to the podium* – whereas silver sees only gold one hateful step up.

And, if there are no genuine distinctions, artificial differentials must be created. Every community is minutely calibrated in terms of social superiority – not just district by district or even street by street but frequently house by house. I have no doubt that, even in shanty towns, there is virulent snobbery – the early settlers regard themselves as aristocrats and the new arrivals as scum.

In the age of entitlement everyone wants to appear superior to everyone else, but traditional marks of superiority, such as birth, wealth, professional status and exclusive district, are by definition difficult or impossible to acquire. The solution is to establish new forms of superiority, for instance by becoming cool and thus infinitely superior to the multitude of the uncool. Coolness is a cheap form of exclusivity available to everyone – like culture snobbery, my own differential. Becoming superior to philistines is not only cheap but relatively unassailable. There is little chance of a stampede to read and rave about Proust (and I would be profoundly annoyed if too many followed my recommendation and made Marcel popular). But staying cool is hard work because the cool is constantly destroyed by mass adoption. It was cool to get a tattoo when tattoos were the insignia of the dangerous outlaw – but soon even suburban housewives had tattoos on their bums.

Needless to say, consumer culture is aware of the universal hunger for differentials and has provided an artificial form of exclusivity in the brand. The genius of branding has been to disguise the undesirable conformity of consumption as its highly desirable opposite, distinction. So conformity is the result of everyone striving for distinction in the same way.

Occasionally brands get caught in their own contradiction of attempting to make everyone want to have what not everyone can have. Burberry, a clothing brand based on a landed-gentry image, launched a marketing campaign to increase sales but was adopted by soccer hooligans, which destroyed the image. But, in general, branding continues to flourish, with consumers paying exorbitant prices for what is supposed to distinguish them from the crowd, but only reveals them to be part of it. Much consumption is driven by a futile attempt to get ahead of the pack – or a defensive need to avoid falling too far behind.

And another discovery of psychology is that the emotions are asymmetric, with the negative more powerful and long lasting than the positive. Schopenhauer also understood this: 'the weakness of wellbeing and happiness, in contrast to the strength of pain'.[96] The positive emotions are capricious day-trippers, but the negative emotions are imperialists – determined to invade, overwhelm, occupy and subjugate. And the key to imperialism is to get the natives to do your dirty work. Think of how anger possesses the entire being, feeding itself in every possible way, forcing the intelligence to create justifications and the memory to resurrect ancient grievances. Whereas the positive emotions are butterflies that flit through, alight briefly and fly off. And there is an equivalent imbalance in the eye of the beholder. We tend to forget favours quickly, but remember dirty tricks forever. This is one of the problems of marriage – it takes a huge amount of good behaviour to make up for one slip. It is easy to sin but a bitch to atone. Jonathan Haidt extends this principle to finance and gambling by explaining that the pleasure of gaining a sum of money is less intense than the pain of losing the same amount. Bad is always stronger than good. But Shakespeare was on to this long ago: 'Men's evil manners live in brass; their virtues we write in water.'[97]

This explains why anxiety and depression can so easily become chronic. They occupy the mind and convince it to support the feelings with negative thoughts. The psychologist Aaron Beck identified an unholy trinity of views common to many depressives: 'I'm no good'; 'The world is bleak'; 'My future is hopeless'.[98] And supporting this trinity of general views is a quartet of negative reactions to specific situations: personalization (blaming yourself for accidents or bad luck); overgeneralization (believing yourself to be always the victim of terrible events); magnification (exaggerating adverse effects); and arbitrary inference (drawing negative conclusions without evidence). Beck then developed Cognitive Therapy, which trains sufferers to identify such thoughts, write them down and classify them as bullying by one of the Gang of Four – psychology's version of the Buddhist and Freudian techniques for achieving transformation by understanding.

Independently of Beck, psychologist Albert Ellis also developed a version of Cognitive Therapy known as Rational Emotive Behaviour Therapy. This was intended not so much for the multitude suffering from depression as for the even greater multitude suffering from unrealistic expectations. Ellis's unholy trinity was the three crippling 'musts': 'I must succeed'; 'Everyone must treat me well'; 'The world must be easy'.[99] He defined belief in these three as 'musturbation', a form of self-abuse possibly even more widespread than masturbation. Such a familiar litany of demand! The first 'must' is the curse of perfectionism, the second is the curse of neediness and the third is the curse of stupidity. So much anguish and outrage could be prevented if towns and cities floated over their streets every day three giant balloons, showing the messages: 'Failure Is More Common Than Success'; 'Many Will Dislike You Whatever You Do'; and, on a balloon even larger than the other two, 'The World Does Not Oblige'. The essence of the Ellis approach is that the problem is not with events themselves but with our illusions concerning them and our reactions to them – both of which can be controlled.

This strategy is of course classic Stoicism, and Ellis's views and style are remarkably similar to those of Epictetus. Both understood the deviousness of the human brute but believed in rationality and detested whining. And both refused to be respectful towards their illustrious predecessors: Epictetus called Epicurus 'that foul-mouthed bastard' while Ellis accused Freud of being 'full of horseshit'.[100] Perhaps their robust pragmatism was a consequence of difficult early lives. Epictetus began as a slave; Ellis was neglected by his parents and, in the Depression era, made a living by buying up second-hand jackets and trousers and reselling them as suits. He came late to the academy and was never affected by intellectual snobbery, publishing books with titles such as *How to make Yourself Happy and Remarkably Less Disturbable* and *How to Stubbornly Refuse to Make Yourself Miserable About Anything – Yes, Anything!*

Cognitive Behavioural Therapy is not universally accepted. The clinical psychologist Oliver James argues that its effects are merely cosmetic and temporary. In particular, it will not solve deep-seated problems caused by childhood maltreatment.[101] This is probably true. Buddha, Spinoza and Freud all agree that the process of self-understanding and transformation is lengthy, so a few sessions of CBT are unlikely to be life-changing. But anything that dispels illusion must be worthwhile – and there is evidence that those who have undergone CBT are less vulnerable to the many biases of self-deception and self-justification.[102]

Echoing many earlier thinkers, psychologist Daniel Nettle posits the theory that the struggle *is* the meaning: 'The purpose of the happiness programme in the human mind is not to increase human happiness; it is to keep us striving.'[103] The human creature is designed for striving. Buddha, Spinoza and Schopenhauer, among many others, agreed. Schopenhauer put it with typical clarity: 'We take no pleasure in existence except when we are striving after something.'[104] The neuroscientist Antonio Damasio claims that this striving is based in our neurobiology: 'The innate equipment of life regulation does not aim for a neither-here-nor-there neutral state . . . Rather, the goal of the homeostasis endeavour is to provide a better than neutral life state, what we as thinking and affluent creatures identify as wellbeing'.[105]

So we are not only born to strive, but to strive for *well-being*.

And striving implies effort applied over time, with obstacles, difficulty and the possibility, even likelihood, of failure. If we could feel good without effort we would no longer feel good. Back in the 1970s, before virtual reality had been invented, the philosopher Robert Nozick postulated a machine offering life that felt real in every way but provided only pleasant experiences. And he suggested that no one would want such a life because it would lack authenticity.[106] But perhaps the true lack would be effort. The difficulty is crucial. Everything worthwhile has to be *earned*.

5

The Quest and the Grail

AT LAST SCIENCE DISCOVERS WHY BLUE IS FOR BOYS BUT GIRLS REALLY DO PREFER PINK announced the headline in *The Times*[107]. The story beneath reported a survey that demonstrated that this gender difference does indeed exist. But why? Cue the theory of the moment – evolutionary psychology – which explains human behaviour as survival mechanisms evolved in the Pleistocene era: 'girls preferred pink because they needed to be better at identifying berries'. The possibility of cultural conditioning was not even considered, either by the authors of the report or the journalist, though it has to be acknowledged that the evidence for cultural influence is in obscure sources. For instance, the *Ladies' Home Journal* of 1918: 'The generally accepted rule is pink for the boy and blue for the girl. The reason is that pink being a more decided and stronger colour is more suitable for the boy, while blue, which is more delicate and dainty, is prettier for the girl.' The cultural explanation is that tastes changed during the twentieth century when blue became associated with men's uniforms and workwear and pink with homosexuality. But theories of cultural conditioning are out of fashion.

Instead, evolutionary psychology is the universal explicator. This is the problem with theories. Every Big Idea is a megalomaniac bent on world domination: Marxists interpreted everything in terms of class; Freudians in terms of childhood; and feminists in terms of gender. In the end, the new way of seeing becomes a new set of blinkers. All three of these big ideas have gone out of fashion – but there are always new contenders for intellectual imperialism.

Many old contenders are also still striving for dominance. Religions are the most ferocious intellectual imperialists. A religion is by definition a Grand Unified Theory of Everything, providing, for those prepared to offer absolute brand loyalty, a one-stop shop for all intellectual and spiritual requirements (Buddhism is an honourable exception). And what a luxury to have every problem explained and provided with a ready-made solution.

The temptation to surrender to a system is strong and the prospect of independence can be terrifying. And there is evidence that believers are happier. So why not believe? It is even possible to believe while knowing that the belief is absurd. Kierkegaard's famous leap of faith was a conscious leap into absurdity.

But for those incapable of such a leap there is a responsibility to pick and mix ideas. According to Freud: 'Every man must find out for himself in what particular fashion he can be saved.'[108] The English philosopher John Armstrong has defined this approach as 'pandoxy'[109] – once again Greek provides an impressive term. So, when asked about belief, it is satisfying to be able to shrug and say, 'Oh, I'm a pandoxist, of course'. But this does not help with the fundamental problem of what to pick, how to mix and, even more perplexing, in what way to apply the mix to everyday life?

Buddha's ideas are attractive – but can enlightenment be attained by anyone in a Western country permeated by the Four Ignoble Truths?

1. We can't sit still.
2. We can't shut up.
3. We can't escape self-obsession.
4. We can't stop wanting things.

Nietzsche is invigorating – but who would attempt to put his ideas into practice? To live as an Übermensch would be as impossible as to live as a Christian.

One of the many absurdities of trying to work out how to live is that the best guides to life have themselves fastidiously refrained from what most people regard as living. Few of them have had wives or children or suffered the indignity of earning bread by the sweat of their brows. Spinoza, for instance, is invariably described as a lens grinder but even he had only a few years of daily grind. As for the family men, Buddha not only abandoned his wife and child but sneaked away during the night – so much for honesty. Socrates did not walk out, but he was notoriously dismissive of his family. And, as German philosopher Karl Jaspers remarked drily of Confucius, 'His relations with his wife and children were less than cordial.'[110] The story of Sartre and his women is even less edifying: Sartre's existentialist lover, Simone de Beauvoir, seduced young, attractive and impressionable female students and then passed them on to Sartre, who dumped them when he had had his fun. Several of these girls were blighted for life by the experience. There is even a strain of misogyny in thinkers from the axial age on, and it is particularly virulent in Schopenhauer and Nietzsche. What have these men to say to those who work for a living, remain with a partner and rear a family?

And then speculative thought is so elusive, so hard to grasp and retain, never mind apply. It seems to pass through the mind like a breeze through a tree – there is a brief excited stirring and then the leaves return to their dream.

But re-reading Erich Fromm for the first time in thirty years was a revealing experience for me. I was sure I had retained nothing of his books, but kept coming across sentences that I had been repeating myself almost word for word without being aware they were not my own. So ideas do remain in the mind – but imperceptibly, below consciousness – and must influence behaviour in the same way. It is not a matter of receiving and applying prescriptions, as the self-help books suggest, but of absorbing ideas and permitting them to fertilise fruitful behaviour unconsciously. The old tree may be stirred in its roots after all. This, too, is an old idea. Socrates believed that merely pondering and discussing concepts like honesty and justice made people more honest and just, an example of Buddha's insight that any understanding is already a transformation, though the change is likely to be gradual and imperceptible. So it is useful to investigate ideas even if they provide no specific instructions and appear to have no discernible effect. And when the same ideas turn up in widely different periods they are massively reinforced.

The American psychologists Christopher Peterson and Martin Seligman examined many cultures and traditions to find the virtues believed to be essential for living well. Their aim was to find a consensus; the virtues had to be universally accepted. This proved impossible – but the following six kept turning up: justice, humaneness, temperance, wisdom, courage and transcendence. The list is short but so predictable that many readers will have gone to sleep before reaching the only mild surprise – transcendence. The researchers acknowledge this as the odd one out, 'the most implicit'[111], a sense of meaning or purpose, not necessarily religious, which infuses a tradition. So it is not strictly a virtue in the sense of requiring specific behaviour.

The problem with the other five is over-familiarity. Everyone accepts these as undeniably good. And the word 'virtue' is irremediably associated with humourless piety and righteousness. At the mere mention of this word many will first faint with boredom, then get up and run a mile. Even though virtue is undoubtedly a major factor in finding fulfilment, as much research has demonstrated,[112] exhorting people to be virtuous is probably a waste of time.

The Peterson and Seligman approach is too broad and diffuse, both in searching for something as general as virtues and in looking across entire traditions (including even Boy Scout manuals). If every source is consulted and common denominators sought, the results are likely to be platitudinous. An alternative is to read only original thinkers and writers and to seek only exciting insights. This is the luxury of being an independent seeker. There is no requirement to be comprehensive or to persist with anything boring. And an element of surprise is needed to render an insight memorable and useful, to make it penetrate and lodge.

There is no guarantee of finding common ground but it is exciting when original thinkers in widely different times, cultures and specialisms come up with the same strategies. When several guidebooks recommend the same restaurant, that's where you go to lunch.

The good news is that there are indeed such strategies. The bad news is that all of them are discouraged by contemporary Western culture. The great achievement of the age has been to make fulfilment seem never easier, while actually making it never more difficult.

Here are the concepts that keep turning up in philosophy, religious teaching, literature, psychology and neuroscience: personal responsibility, autonomy, detachment, understanding, mindfulness, transcendence, acceptance of difficulty, ceaseless striving and constant awareness of mortality.

Most of these concepts are mentioned repeatedly by thinkers and a few are universally acknowledged. Awareness of mortality, for instance, is urged by everyone from Buddha to Sartre, who believed that only intense and constant consciousness of death exposes the emptiness of convention and breaks the crust of routine; only death is the guarantor of intense life. But even this universal recommendation is being increasingly rejected. Woody Allen was in tune with the times when he explained that he had no wish to achieve immortality through his work; instead he wanted to achieve it by the more direct strategy of never dying. And where there is a will there is a way. We will live forever if we consume enough organic blueberries and pomegranate juice.

But, for the age that expects everything to be easy, the most crucial revelation is that everything worthwhile is difficult. In fact, attempts to find easy solutions will cause the very problems these attempts were meant to evade. The poet Rainer Maria Rilke understood that the modern age increasingly demands effortlessness: 'People have sought easy solutions to every problem – and the easiest of the easy. Yet it is clear that we must hold to what is difficult; every living creature holds fast to it.'[113]

This echoes Spinoza and uncannily prefigures the discoveries of neuroscience. As Rilke explained, he advocated difficulty not because it was noble but because it was *necessary*: 'You are mistaken in calling it your *duty* to take on difficulties. It is your survival instinct that pushes you to do it.'[114]

To survive is to strive. The problem is the tendency to strive for the wrong things, especially to emulate those who have found worldly success. The human creature is a search engine of great power and sophistication, but with little idea of how to choose search parameters or evaluate results. So, when misguided striving fails to provide satisfaction, there is a tendency to believe that the alternative must be a rejection of all striving, that the answer is to lie on a Caribbean beach lathered in coconut oil.

The striving is not only difficult but its goal is obscure – a theme repeated endlessly since the axial age, around the middle of the first millennium BCE, when the human ape accidentally acquired consciousness and began asking the questions which will still be the FAQs on God's website when He gets around to setting it up. In this period – named the 'axial age' by Karl Jaspers because it brought such a profound change in human awareness – there was Socrates in Greece, the Hebrew prophets in the Middle East, in India Buddha and in China Lao Tzu and Confucius. The poet of Ecclesiastes expressed most beautifully the necessity and difficulty of seeking after truth: 'And I gave my heart to seek and search out by wisdom concerning all things that are done under heaven: this sore travail hath God given to the sons of man to be exercised therewith.' The result is usually frustration: 'I perceived that this also is vexation of spirit.' But the poet is unable to abandon the search for understanding: 'Who is as the

wise man? And who knoweth the interpretation of a thing? A
man's wisdom maketh his face to shine, and the boldness of his
face shall be changed.'

These early thinkers expressed the need for striving in abstract
form – but it had already found expression in narrative. There is
a rich and unbroken tradition of quest literature running from *The
Epic of Gilgamesh* in 1000 BCE to *The Wizard of Oz* in the twentieth century. The scholar of myth, Joseph Campbell, has shown
how the quest saga has been important in every period and culture and always has the same basic structure, though local details
may vary. Each saga begins with a hero receiving a call to adventure which makes him abandon his familiar, safe environment to
venture into the dangerous unknown. There, he undergoes a
series of tests and trials, negotiates many difficulties and slays
many monsters. As a reward he wins a magical prize – a Golden
Fleece, a princess, holy water, a sacred flame or an elixir of eternal life. Finally he brings the prize back from the kingdom of
dread to redeem his community.[115]

This is the plot of *The Wizard of Oz* and also of *Gilgamesh* three
thousand years earlier. The hero, Gilgamesh, a Mesopotamian king,
becomes disenchanted with his kingdom and life and departs on
a quest, which involves dealing with ferocious lions, scorpion men
and a beautiful goddess who attempts to detain him with surprisingly modern temptations: 'Day and night be frolicsome and
gay; let thy clothes be handsome, thy head shampooed, thy body
bathed.'[116] Nevertheless, the hero persists in his quest and, diving
to the bottom of a deep sea, plucks the plant of immortality. But
the ending has a nasty twist that would have to be changed in any
movie version: when Gilgamesh lies down to rest a serpent steals
the plant, eats it and attains eternal youth. In mythology the snake
is always the villain.

Campbell argues that these narratives symbolize an essentially
inward journey – the hero breaks free from the conventional
thinking of his time, ventures out into the dark of speculative
thought, finds the creative power to change himself and wishes to

share this with others. The prize won after much uncertainty and danger is knowledge: 'The hero is the one who comes to know.'[117] So the narrative has four stages: departure, trial, prize, return; these are the same as the goals of the abstract seeker: detachment, difficulty, understanding, transformation.

A similar four stages are common in the initiation rites of 'primitive' cultures: separation, ritual wounding, initiation and return. The young person is taken away from the village, symbolically wounded in some way, instructed in the rites and returned to the community. So becoming an adult requires the same four stages – detachment, difficulty, understanding and transformation. It is only our own culture that believes in prolonging adolescence for life. In the contemporary version of the story the hero remains at home with his parents and ventures out into danger by playing EverQuest online in the basement.

As Campbell points out, the stories of Buddha and Christ also follow the quest saga structure. Both men reject their families, go forth, endure many trials, experience doubt and despair, but finally win through to transfiguration and return to share their knowledge with the world.

Only institutionalized religion demands passive conformity. In the iconography Christ is always sorrowfully submissive and Buddha smugly quietist. But neither man was remotely passive. They constantly questioned, prodded, goaded, unsettled and disturbed. Far from advocating passivity, they would let no one rest: Christ: 'I came not to send peace, but a sword'[118]; Buddha's last words: 'Strive unremittingly'.[119]

The problem with religions is that the inspirational founders become an embarrassment to the small-minded followers who turn ideas into dogma, principles into regulations and initiatives into ritual. The founders reject kin worship; the followers revere family. The founders go forth; the followers remain at home. The founders are tormented by doubt; the followers bask in certainty. The founders seek authority; the followers seek power. The founders attract and convince; the followers confront and coerce.

Frequently the followers are so successful at distortion that their message becomes exactly the opposite of the original. In the Irish Catholic culture I knew as a boy, the faithful – both clerical and lay – violated the principles of the New Testament so comprehensively and precisely that it almost seemed as though they had read it.

A perfect example was my mother's repeated and vehement command always to go up to the front at Mass. Respectable people sat at the front, the lower orders in the rows behind – and only the worst kind of corner boy stood at the back. What would she have said if I had showed her Matthew 23:6 with Christ's denunciation of the Pharisees for loving 'the chief seats in the synagogues'? She would have become even more angry at this further example of smart-alec cheek. Slave all your life to give your children a higher station in life and what thanks do you get for it? Nothing but smart remarks.

The concept of the quest permeates all culture, religious and secular, early and late, low and high. Many of the greatest literary works of the twentieth century were quest stories. James Joyce's *Ulysses* is the story of one ordinary hero's going forth, trials and tribulations and return home to rebirth. Proust's huge novel *À La Recherche du Temps Perdu* is the story of a lifelong quest for meaning, in which the meaning is eventually revealed to be the writing of the story. And Kafka gave the quest saga a modern twist by making the quest always futile and the prize always out of reach: 'There is a destination but no way there.'[120] So K, despite all his efforts, never manages to get into the Castle. Yet he never gives up – and neither do any of Kafka's other frustrated seekers. In 'Before the Law' – a mere page and a half – a man comes from the country seeking admittance to the Law but is barred by a boorish Doorkeeper. The man tries various stratagems – wheedling, bribing, seeking intimacy – but none succeeds. The Doorkeeper remains adamant. Years pass and eventually the seeker, realizing that he is dying, puts one final question: '"Everyone strives to reach the Law," says the man, "so how does it happen that for all these many years no one but myself has ever begged for admittance?" The Doorkeeper recognizes that the man has reached his end, and, to let his failing senses catch the words, roars in his ear: "No one else could ever be admitted here, since this gate was made only for you. I am now going to shut it."[121]

In fact, many versions of the quest acknowledge that the striving is endless – though not futile. The twelfth-century Sufi poem, *The Conference of the Birds* by Farid Ud-Din Attar, is like a parable by Kafka. The birds of the world meet for a conference, which turns fractious. A hoopoe rises and, quelling the multitude with natural authority, suggests that what the birds lack is a spiritual leader, a Simorgh, to show them an alternative to aggressive craving. They must all fly off in search of this Simorgh. But many birds are deterred by the prospect of a long and arduous quest. The hawks prefer the power of worldly princes, the herons their desolate shoreline, the ducks their cosy pond. The finches fear for their frailty, the nightingales for their song. But eventually a group sets off, traversing seven valleys – the Valley of the Quest, the Valley of Love, the Valley of Insight into Mystery, the Valley of Detachment, the Valley of Unity, the Valley of Bewilderment and the Valley of Poverty and Nothingness. In each valley they endure dangers, vicissitudes and temptations, and are told stories of exemplary characters. These include Jesus who says, 'The man who lives and does not strive is lost,' and Socrates who replies, to the disciples enquiring about where to bury him, 'If you can find me you are certainly clever for I never found myself.'[122]

When the birds finally arrive at the court of the Simorgh only thirty remain and they are ageing, exhausted, bedraggled and soiled. A haughty palace herald flies out and, contemptuous of their shabby appearance, tells them they are unworthy and must return whence they came. But the birds demand entry, and are finally admitted. The palace is indeed glorious – but empty, save for mirrors. Around and around they fly, frustrated and heartsick – to have come so far and endured so much for no reward. But, bit by bit, a strange feeling of joy steals over the birds. Suddenly they realize the significance of the mirrors. They have found the Simorgh after all. They are looking at the Simorgh in the mirrors. Because *they* are the Simorgh (which in Persian also means thirty birds). The Simorgh is *them*.

This expresses a profound truth – that the search for meaning is itself the meaning, the Way is the destination, the quest is the grail.

Many others have discovered this over the centuries and expressed it in a variety of ways.[123] One of the most memorable formulations was by C.P. Cavafy in his poem 'Ithaca'.

> Always keep Ithaca fixed in your mind.
> To arrive there is what you are destined for.
> But don't hurry the journey at all.
> Better if it lasts for many years,
> So you're old by the time you reach the isle,
> Wealthy with all you have gained on the way
> And not expecting Ithaca to make you rich.
>
> Ithaca gave you the beautiful journey.
> Without her you'd never have set out.
> But she has nothing more to give you now.
> And if you find her poor, Ithaca won't have deceived you.
> Wise as you have become, after so much experience,
> You'll have understood by then what these Ithacas mean.[124]

PART III
The Strategies

6

The Undermining of Responsibility

A student fails to submit a project on time and then misses an appointment with his supervisor to discuss the problem. The university sends the student a letter informing him that he has been given a mark of zero for the project. Now the student not only comes to the supervisor but barges into his office without an appointment.

'This project must be accepted late,' he demands.

'Why is that?'

'Because I'm suffering from TCD.'

'Which is?'

'Time-Constraint Disorder – a chemical imbalance in the brain that means I can't meet deadlines or turn up in time for appointments.'

I invented TCD as a joke, forgetting that it is impossible to satirize the contemporary world, and then discovered that a Professor Joseph Ferrari of DePaul University genuinely wants procrastination recognized as a clinical disorder[125] and included in the standard reference work for mental-health professionals, the *Diagnostic and Statistical Manual of Mental Disorders* (DSM). This tome has already been through four editions, accumulating new disorders in each, with 297 defined in DSM-IV – and many more due in DSM-V. Consider, for example, Antisocial Personality Disorder (APD),

which is defined as a 'pervasive pattern of disregard for and violation of the rights of others that begins in childhood or early
adolescence and continues into adulthood' – in other words the
vice formerly known as selfishness. So, the key to indulging a vice
is to redefine it as a Disorder and give it a resonant acronym. 'It's
a *condition,*' you then announce with aggressive outrage if your
behaviour is challenged, 'a *Disorder.*' Those who spend too much
time online will be glad to know that surfing the web has just been
identified as a clinical disorder by Dr Jerald Block of the Oregon
Health and Science University: 'Internet addiction appears to be a
common disorder that merits inclusion in DSM-V.'[126]

My own candidate for inclusion in DSM-V is Disorder
Addiction Disorder (DAD), an uncontrollable compulsion to classify all undesirable human behaviour as Disorders.

These new 'Disorders' are of course welcomed by Big Pharma
because sufferers can be encouraged to buy drugs. But, in a classic
example of cultural-conditioning feedback, the pharmaceutical
companies also create their own Disorders by redefining previously
normal states (a practice known as 'condition branding'). So Social
Anxiety Disorder, the attribute previously known as shyness, is
now a 'condition' requiring GlaxoSmithKline's drug Paxil or Pfizer's
Zoloft. Paxil and Zoloft were just two more anti-depressants until
their manufacturers launched major campaigns to promote them
as cures for Social Anxiety Disorder. Sales immediately soared. A
major company may well seize on Time-Constraint Disorder (TCD)
and promote one of its poor-selling products as a miracle drug
that activates the urgency centres of the brain.

But the Disorder phenomenon is only one consequence of
a contemporary desire to evade personal responsibility. No one
is prepared to accept blame any more. Instead, everyone wants
to be a victim – and frequently succeeds, even in the most
unpromising circumstances. When Newham Council in East
London pursued Z-Un Noon for non-payment of a series of parking fines, Noon was so outraged that he took the council to
court for causing him 'emotional distress'.[127] Better still, he won

his case and was awarded £5,000 for the distress caused by each of the four tickets, making a total of £20,000. And when the incredulous council ignored this ruling, bailiffs turned up at the council offices with a 'notice of seizure' and began to disconnect and take away computers. Faced with the prospect of total paralysis, the council paid up.

When was the last time anyone said, 'It's my fault'? Already it seems like centuries since Sartre declared, 'Man is fully responsible for his nature and his choices.'[128] Now the opposite is true. Man is responsible neither for nature nor choices.

How has this come about? The concept of personal responsibility – that we can and should decide our own destinies – is at the heart of modern society and considered axiomatic by most of its citizens. Yet this concept is now being steadily undermined, from both above and below, from both high and low culture – from scientists, philosophers and writers denying free will and from the age of entitlement denying obligation. In science there is the Holy Trinity of Determinism – genetics (behaviour is determined by genes); evolutionary psychology (behaviour is determined by evolved survival mechanisms); and neuroscience (behaviour is determined by the modules of a hard-wired brain). Of course, many scientists have expressed reservations and qualifications, but the subtleties tend to be in the small print – it is easier to remember headlines announcing the discovery of genes for depression, obesity, criminality, homosexuality and, the latest, anxiety[129] and male infidelity.[130]

And here is a contemporary philosopher with no reservations – John Gray, until recently Professor of European Thought at the London School of Economics: 'There are many reasons for rejecting the idea of free will, some of them decisive. If our actions are caused then we cannot act otherwise than we do. In that case we cannot be responsible for them. We can be free agents only if we are authors of our acts; but we are ourselves products of chance and necessity. We cannot choose to be what we are born. In that case, we cannot be responsible for what we do.'[131]

Gray also attacks the idea of progress, rejects as illusory the concepts of morality, justice and truth, dismisses any possibility of dealing with the world's problems and asserts that the world is inexorably bound for tyranny, anarchy, famine, pestilence and the eventual extinction of the human race. This is a contemporary version of the old 'original sin' concept in its extreme Manichean form. The human creature is fatally flawed and the world is rushing to inevitable ruin. All that has changed is the nature of the flaw: once it was implanted by God as a punishment; now it is the animal nature inherited from our ancestors. The program in the genes is the new original sin.

This determinism is attractive to many at each end of the social scale. For an authoritarian elite it justifies firm control of the essentially evil human brute and for the individual it justifies self-indulgence because this is inevitable in a fallen creature. Both are absolved of obligation. Attempts to improve either social conditions or personal behaviour would be equally futile.

But has anyone ever argued that behaving *well* is determined? Has anyone ever protested: 'Hey, it's my nature, I just can't help being good'? Determinism is invoked only to excuse behaving badly. No, on second thoughts, I recall reading somewhere about a criminal using genetic determinism as a legal defence. The wise old judge nodded affably: 'I can quite accept that you are genetically determined to break the law. The problem is that *I* am genetically determined to uphold it.' And he smiled apologetically. 'So I have no choice but to impose on you the maximum sentence.'

John Gray bases his rejection of personal responsibility on the theory that action is unconscious, citing the work of neuroscientist Benjamin Libet, who claimed to have discovered that action takes place half a second before the brain makes a conscious decision to act. It is certainly true that much, perhaps even most, of what we do involves no conscious thought. This may even be true of decision-making, where conscious control is assumed to be essential. For several years I taught a course called Decision

Theory, which explained various mathematical techniques for weighing the effects of a complex set of factors on an outcome. But gradually there grew the suspicion, which I did not reveal to students or colleagues, that this was merely superstitious mumbo-jumbo, another example of physics envy. And, finally, I slipped into the heresy that, not only did no manager ever use these techniques, but that the business of decision-making was barely rational at all. This was confirmed by a rare experience of decision-making in practice. As a teacher of database theory I was co-opted on to a team with the responsibility of choosing a new Database Management System, which would be used on all database teaching and for the university's own information systems. There were three major database contenders and the team went to each corporation, sat through lengthy demonstrations and asked probing questions. But, in the end, without anyone publicly admitting it, we were exhausted by technical detail and opted for the presenters we liked best. In fact, their database became the market leader whereas the other two died. Hence, a useful technique – assess the vendor not the product.

This emotional basis for decision-making has also been demonstrated by Antonio Damasio, who discovered in the 1990s that some brain-damaged patients could no longer feel emotion, though their intelligence and ability to apply reason and logic were unimpaired.[132] Delivered from the maelstrom of emotion, these people should have been able to make lucid, rational decisions based on a logical analysis of choices. In fact, it was just the opposite. They were unable to make *any* decisions, even the most simple. They could analyse the pros and cons of each possibility but, without feeling, they were unable to choose one over the others. So intuition or 'gut feeling' is not merely a part of the process but an essential feature of it.

Building on Damasio's discovery, Joseph LeDoux proposed that the brain has two routes to decision, the 'low road' and the 'high road'.[133] The low road involves no conscious reasoning or awareness and processes sensory data in the amygdala, the brain's emotion centre. This route to action is instantaneous, over-whelmingly powerful and immensely difficult to control – and it is the route supporting the Gray/Libet theory. But there is also a high road to action via the prefrontal cortex, the centre for analysing, planning and conscious decision-making. This centre is connected directly to the amygdala so there is always an emo-tional input to the reasoning, as Damasio realized. But, according to LeDoux, the prefrontal cortex can – and frequently does – override the amygdala's primitive desires and drives. And aware-ness of the emotional brain increases the power of the prefrontal cortex.

Damasio makes the same point: 'We can be wise to the fact that our brain still carries the machinery to react in the way it did in a very different context ages ago. And we can learn to disre-gard such reactions and persuade others to do the same.'[134] Unusually for a scientist, Damasio has a thrillingly specific sug-gestion for the exercise of free will: 'We humans . . . can *wilfully* strive to control our emotions. We can decide which objects and situations we allow in our environment and on which objects and situations we lavish time and attention. We can, for example, decide not to watch commercial television, and advocate its eter-nal banishment from the households of intelligent citizens.'[135]

So the neuroscientific view of human behaviour is entirely consistent with the Buddha/Spinoza/Freud model of the self and Sartre's insistence on personal responsibility and choice.

Neuroscience even rescues us from the tyranny of the genes. Matt Ridley, the genetics writer and author, states: 'By far the most important discovery of recent years in brain science is that genes are at the mercy of actions as well as vice versa . . . They are cogs responding to experience as mediated through the senses. Their promoters are designed to be switched off and on by events.'[136]

Ridley's conclusion is magnificently unequivocal: 'Free will is entirely compatible with a brain exquisitely prespecified by, and run by, genes.' And, en route, he dispels the idea of genetics as an evil science endorsing selfishness, ruthlessness and brute strength. For instance, there is a question that may have vexed visitors to the zoo: if chimpanzees are only a fraction of the size of gorillas, how come their testicles are sixteen times as large? Since male gorillas have harems, which they need to protect, they have developed impressive size and fearsome appearance – but they do not need prodigious equipment to fertilize since they have no competition. In other words, they need only appear to have balls. Chimp females, however, are promiscuous, so the males who ejaculate frequently and copiously are more likely to have offspring. Male chimps really do need big balls. Which is better – to look big and ferocious but have modest testicles and limited orgasms, or to be small and unintimidating but have huge balls and come like an exploding supernova? Nature seems to be teaching the same lesson as Stoic philosophers – that the little guy unconcerned with appearances has lots more fun.

As for evolutionary psychology (EP), the theory is that behaviour is determined by the human brain evolving in certain ways as a result of natural selection during the Pleistocene period, with no development since because there has not been enough time. EP explanations of behaviour can seem dauntingly scientific but often the reasoning is dubious and the evidence thin or non-existent. This is a self-validating theory like that of divine will. If everything that happens is planned by God, then the task of establishing meaning is to provide plausible divine intentions – and these, in turn, validate the original theory. Similarly, if everything we think, feel and do is the result of a survival adaptation, then the task is to suggest plausible adaptation stories – and this requires only imagination since there is little evidence of what went on in the Pleistocene period. For instance, I could argue that imagination itself evolved because ability to con the gullible greatly improved survival prospects.

There is a Steve on each side of the determinism debate – so both sides can say, 'Our Steve is smarter than your Steve'. The psychologist and determinist Steven Pinker has argued that, as a consequence of evolution in the African savannah, humans have a universal preference for art depicting green landscapes and water.[137] But I can supply evidence disproving the 'universal preference' – Duke Ellington hated grass because it reminded him of graves.

The biologist Steven Rose suggests that the preference for greenery, if indeed it exists, is as likely to be due to the pastoral nostalgia of urban societies. I can also propose evidence for this theory – the hunger for landscape art is overwhelmingly strong in southern England, which also happens to be nearly all motorways and concrete.

Rose argues that living organisms are not mere passive vehicles separating genes and environment. 'Rather, organisms actively engage in constructing their environments, constantly choosing, absorbing and transforming the world around them. Every living creature is in constant flux, always at the same time both *being* and *becoming*.'[138]

Neuroscientists have also challenged the 'hard-wired brain' theory, suggesting instead that the human brain is extraordinarily plastic. Far from being fixed millions of years ago, the individual brain constantly rewires itself throughout a lifetime in response to experience. It is true that, broadly speaking, specific functions are carried out by specific parts of the brain, but the detailed processing is likely to be different in each brain. And, if a functional area is damaged, the brain may be able to rewire itself to process the function in a different way. More importantly for everyday life, almost any form of persistent, attentive activity produces new brain configurations. The neurons that fire together wire together. Musicians who play stringed instruments have larger brain maps for the left hand, taxi drivers have larger hippocampi (the area that stores spatial information), experienced meditators have bigger and thicker prefrontal cortices (the area responsible for attention and concentration). The bad news is that less desirable activities – anxieties, obsessions, compulsions, addictions, bad habits – also develop their own dedicated brain networks, which become efficient and self-sustaining and difficult to change.[139]

So, the 'chemical imbalance in the brain' form of determinism, the supposed cause of 'disorders', may be a confusion of cause and effect. If certain chemical brain states correlate with behaviour, it may be the behaviour that has produced the states rather than the other way round. For instance, there is a high correlation between attention disorders and television viewing in early childhood.[140]

There is no justification for the old excuse, 'This is just how I am.' Individual temperament (formed by a combination of genetic inheritance, family influences and cultural factors) certainly encourages attitudes, behaviours and moods and is extremely hard to override, never mind permanently change. This is what psychology defines as the 'set point'. But, as well as temperament, there is character. Temperament is what you are – but character is what you do. Temperament is a given; character may be forged. We can choose to oppose the dictates of temperament and, if we act differently in a certain way for long enough, the new behaviour will establish its own brain connections. As Hamlet says to his weak mother: 'Use, almost, can change the stamp of nature.'[141] That 'almost' is the touch of genius. Shakespeare seems to have understood even the nature versus nurture debate – and, as always, avoided taking sides.

The word 'character', however, has a fatally old-fashioned ring. The age of entitlement does not seek character, which demands obligation, but identity, which demands rights. Identity can be sought in money, status or celebrity but is most easily conferred by belonging to a group – usually based on ethnicity, race, religion or sexual orientation. The group will be especially attractive if it can claim to have suffered injustice. Then its members can be victims and enjoy the luxury of having someone else to blame.

And blame is the new solution to the contemporary inability to accept random bad luck. Once misfortune was explained as the mysterious ways of God – the suffering had a purpose, which would be revealed in the fullness of time. Now, what makes misfortune meaningful is culpability. Someone must be to blame and it is never the victim. Shit happens – but it is always some other shit's fault. Just as the pharmaceutical industry is happy to cash in on blaming disorders, the legal profession is more than willing to be paid for blaming the other shit. The medical profession is also willing to oblige. The *British Medical Journal* recently initiated an extraordinary project aimed at removing the word 'accident' from the English language. 'Purging a common term from our lexicon will not be easy', conceded the august journal. Nevertheless, 'The *BMJ* has decided to ban the word accident.'[142]

This inability to accept randomness is what makes conspiracy theories so attractive. Such theories invest the banal and random with glamour and significance, and put the blame for personal irresponsibility on secret, sinister forces. It is so much more satisfactory to believe that Diana, Princess of Wales, was murdered in a car crash engineered by the Duke of Edinburgh and that Marilyn Monroe was killed by a poisoned suppository inserted on the orders of Robert Kennedy. The pitiful truth would expose too much personal irresponsibility – that one was killed by a drunk driver and the other by alcohol and drug abuse.

The problem with shifting blame is that now no one is prepared to accept blame. Here is a twenty-first century story. A 37-year-old man, Gary Hart, divorced from his first wife and separated from his second, meets a woman called Kristeen Panter in an internet chat room and stays up until 5 a.m. talking to her online. Then he sets off on a 145-mile journey driving a Land Rover with a trailer. But he falls asleep at the wheel and runs off the road down an embankment into the path of a train, causing a crash that kills ten people and injures seventy-six more. Hart ('My life is 1,000 miles per hour – it's just the way I live'[143]) is charged with dangerous driving but, at the trial, denies falling asleep and claims that the problem was mechanical failure, though a meticulous reconstruction of the Land Rover has revealed no problems. Hart is convicted and given a five-year prison sentence. When he gets out of prison he appears on a television documentary about the incident, denies any responsibility and claims that he, too, is a victim. Invited to consider photographs of the carnage, Hart does express sadness – but for the mangled wreckage of his Land Rover: 'I loved that old truck.'[144]

Of course, this story is only one extreme example – but it would be difficult to imagine an attitude like Hart's in an earlier era.

Parallel to the refusals of responsibility are the claims to *deserve*. Everyone now *deserves* a holiday (meaning not just a break but a trip abroad to a desirable location); students invariably *deserve* higher grades (regardless of assessment criteria, the argument is always, 'but I spent x hours on this'); employees *deserve* promotion (even when they meet none of the requirements for the new level); artistes *deserve* more recognition (everything written *deserves* to be published, everything painted *deserves* to be exhibited, every performer *deserves* a stage); lovers *deserve* a dream partner next time (not despite but *because of* all the past failures they themselves probably caused but for which they accept no responsibility). Failure is an obsolete concept. No one is willing to accept that few are worthy of high grades or artistic recognition and that there is no such thing as a dream partner. So failure is the new taboo F-word. In an initiative comparable to that of the *British Medical Journal*, my own university has come up with an imaginative solution. Students achieving less than 40 per cent in a module are recorded as having not taken it – which not only avoids the F-word but suggests that the embarrassing lapse never happened at all.

This sense of deserving has surely been a factor in the growth of debt. The development of entitlement since the 1970s coincides exactly with a steady rise in personal debt. If you are entitled to a certain lifestyle then borrowing the money to fund it is simply claiming what is rightfully yours – and there is no obligation to pay it back. So the lender attempting to recover money is an ugly bully harassing an innocent victim. Attitudes to debt are a great example of how cultural conditioning can change: not so long ago debt was a sin, then an unpleasant necessity for buying a home, then the way to fund a deserved lifestyle and finally something so obviously good that only a fool would refuse it. At this stage the debt house of cards became so ridiculously huge that the removal of one card was almost enough to destroy the world's financial systems. And, of course, everyone blamed the bankers for the disastrous consequences. Drag out the bankers and hang them!

The problem with an overwhelming sense of entitlement is that it promises satisfaction but usually delivers its opposite. Entitlement encourages all three of Albert Ellis's disastrous 'musts' – 'I must succeed', 'Everyone must treat me well', 'The world must be easy'. And when none of these happens, the conclusion is not that the demands were unjustified but that malign, powerful, hidden forces are denying them. So the sense of entitlement becomes a sense of bitter grievance.

Another consequence of entitlement is the contemporary worship of 'diversity' and the, often concomitant, belief that the demands of all groups are equally valid. The problem is that there are two types of diversity – diversity of opportunity, which is a question of rights, and diversity of ethics, which is a question of values – and the necessity of recognizing the first has led to unthinking acceptance of the second. Demanding justice for minorities who have suffered discrimination on the basis of race, ethnicity, gender or sexual orientation is entirely valid. But ethical diversity is a contradiction in terms. If the values of others are valid, then one's own must be equally arbitrary and therefore without value. The inevitable consequence of this relativism is a fatal loss of nerve – it becomes impossible to uphold values and make value judgements. On contentious issues we murmur that there is much to be said on both sides. About political conflicts we say, 'One side is as bad as the other', and about politicians, 'One is as bad as the other'. We see people making foolish decisions that will inevitably lead to disaster but we say nothing to them; to ourselves we say, 'I have no right to intervene', 'The advice would be rejected', 'It would only cause divisiveness', and 'What do I know about anything anyway?'

This leads to abdication of authority and the bizarre but common reversals of children bullying their parents, students assessing their teachers and employees exploiting their bosses.

And, in the absence of values and principles, ethics becomes merely legalism, restricted to situations and transactions, a matter of resolving dilemmas and drawing up contracts – I agree to do this if you agree to do that.

Another problem with 'celebrating diversity' is that it aims to promote inclusiveness but often promotes its opposite, separatism. The groups who feel deprived of rights blame other groups and demand to be separated from them. If the group is ethnically or religiously based it will demand its own country. And, if not its very own country, then at least a substantial chunk of some other group's country. But separatism, rather than easing divisions, reinforces and exacerbates them. Sartre described the ugly consequences of Us-and-Them consciousness, and psychology experiments have demonstrated that even artificial and arbitrary separation can cause conflict. In fact, the resulting conflicts were so serious that this type of experiment is now considered too dangerous. One of the last was undertaken in 1966 by Muzafer Sherif on a group of eleven and twelve year olds living harmoniously in a large cabin on a holiday camp. Sherif divided this group into two, with pairs of friends deliberately split up, and put each of the new groups in a separate cabin. Soon there was tension between the cabins, with taunting and insults becoming common, and even former friends coming to hate each other. Over time aggressive leaders emerged in each cabin.[145] So an entirely arbitrary separation produced a division, which became increasingly bitter. The lesson is that separatism causes the very problems it is supposed to prevent, which is then used as evidence for the bigotry that motivated the separation in the first place, so making the separatism even more strident.

But perhaps the worst consequence of entitlement is a sense of grievance – which encourages the human tendency to whinge. To my knowledge no major thinker has ever recommended or endorsed whingeing. Philosophy from the Stoics to the existentialists rings with denunciations of complaint. Has anyone ever become happier by whingeing?

There is often a temptation to think that one could be happier if only responsibility could be evaded or transferred to someone else, which explains the growing numbers of consultants, advisors, instructors, gurus, therapists, counsellors, personal trainers and, the inevitable development, life coaches. In Don DeLillo's satirical novel *White Noise*, the narrator's wife teaches an adult course on 'Standing, Sitting and Walking', which is such a success that she is asked to develop another course on 'Eating and Drinking'. When the narrator suggests that this might involve labouring the obvious, she explains that people need to be reassured by someone in a position of authority.[146]

Being instructed may seem a luxury, but philosophers and psychologists agree that only personal responsibility brings fulfilment. This was demonstrated by a famous study in which elderly residents on two floors of a care home were given plants for their rooms. On one floor residents were permitted to choose and water plants; on the other floor the plants were distributed and maintained by staff. On the floor with control the residents became happier, more active and alert and required less medication. And similar results were observed in other studies involving choice of films and timing of visits from volunteers. Conversely, loss of control caused unhappiness and depression. (But would it have been different if they had been card-carrying stoics? Is awareness and acceptance of lack of control itself a form of control?) Even more surprisingly, it was discovered in the six-month follow-up to the plant study that twice as many no-control as control residents had died (30 per cent compared to 15 per cent). So personal responsibility may be a matter of life and death.[147]

The less personal responsibility is exercised, the greater the

likelihood of conformity. A series of classic experiments on conforming was conducted in 1955 by the psychologist Solomon
Asch. Volunteers were required to perform a simple matching test.
When left alone, they got it right 99 per cent of the time. But
when assigned to a group (all the experimenter's accomplices
except for the single volunteer) that every so often gave a unanimous wrong answer, volunteers agreed with the incorrect group
answer 70 per cent of the time. And, when informed of the
deception afterwards and invited to estimate the extent of their
conformity, all the volunteers underestimated it.[148]

The interesting question, of course, is the mental process of
conforming – how do people convince themselves to accept
things they would otherwise reject as wrong? When the Asch
experiments were repeated recently using brain imaging on the
volunteers, the incorrect group-influenced judgements caused
changes in the brain areas dedicated to vision and spatial awareness but no changes in the areas for monitoring and resolving
conflict. So the alarming conclusion was that no self-convincing
seemed to be needed – the volunteers *actually saw* what the
group *only claimed to see*. As Gregory Berns, the neuroscientist
who conducted the new research, concluded, 'We like to think
that seeing is believing, but the study's findings show that seeing
is believing what the group tells you to believe.'[149] As for independent judgements consciously disagreeing with those of the
group, these caused activity in the brain area associated with
emotion, suggesting that autonomy and opposition are stressful.
This stress was shown to be justified in other experiments simu-
lating jury discussions where a minority opposed a majority
verdict, the scenario in the film *12 Angry Men*. The minority view
prevailed if it was expressed consistently, confidently and undog-
matically – but no one liked the minority people. This is evidence
of the crank effect: promoting principle and truth may eventually
be effective, but the promoters will be dismissed as cranks.

Even more shocking were the Milgram experiments on obedience where, at the behest of a grave authoritarian figure in a

laboratory coat, volunteers administered what they believed to be electric shocks of increasing intensity to people (middle-aged and mild-mannered) who answered questions incorrectly. Before the experiment Stanley Milgram invited forty psychiatrists to estimate the level of volunteer compliance. Their view was that only 1 per cent of sadists would continue to the maximum shock level. In fact 65 per cent went all the way to 450 volts, despite hearing what they believed were appeals to desist and even screams of pain. And, if the volunteers were permitted to delegate the actual operation of the shock lever to someone else, the compliance level rose to 90 per cent. The only good news was that the level could be reduced to 10 per cent if volunteers saw someone else refusing to administer shocks.[150] These variations demonstrate once again the power of example, good and bad.

The psychologist Philip Zimbardo has spent a lifetime studying conformity and obedience in a variety of situations ranging from the corporate world to Nazi Germany and the Abu Ghraib prison in Iraq. He has conducted many experiments, including the notorious Stanford University prison experiment in 1971, when volunteers were asked to role-play as prisoners or guards and many of the guards became increasingly sadistic. Zimbardo's conclusion is that group influence may be resisted by a combination of detachment (the exercise of scepticism and critical thinking), humility (willingness to admit personal limitations and mistakes), mindfulness (transforming habitual inattention into habitual awareness), autonomy (preserving independence within groups) and, above all, responsibility: 'We become more resistant to undesirable social influence by always maintaining a sense of personal responsibility and by being willing to be held accountable for our actions.'[151]

Considering the possible consequences of evasion should be enough to establish that personal responsibility is essential and that determinism must be rejected, both in theory and practice. An autonomous, attentive, sceptical and critically minded individual, aware of undesirable personal and group inclinations, can resist these and persuade others to do the same. The human creature is the only animal that knows it is only an animal . . . and therefore the only animal with the option of not behaving like an animal. We can be entirely determined not to be entirely determined. As Katharine Hepburn said to Humphrey Bogart in *The African Queen*, 'Nature, Mr Allnut, is what we are put into this world to rise above.'

Accepting personal responsibility may also be extended into the development of a personal code. This was the essence of the existentialist philosophy. Of course, it will be hard to justify such a code absolutely. And frequently its demands will appear ridiculous and arbitrary. So why bother? Just for the satisfying difficulty of it. Just for the sheer hell of the thing. As Flaubert exhorted: 'Since all the alternatives are absurd, let us choose the most noble.'[152]

7

The Assault on Detachment

Some hard thinking is needed and a proper Italian double espresso would kick-start the sluggish brain – but the Italian café has a giant screen showing models endlessly flouncing along catwalks, while its sound system is playing loud soul music and the two girls behind the counter are discussing photographs of themselves on a night out in high, excited tones punctuated by shrieks of laughter. Then your smartphone announces a text message from one of your several thousand network friends, and investigation, briefly distracted by a pop-up offering a choice of three exclusive picture galleries (rebellious rock vixens, the world's 100 sexiest women and movie stars embarrassed by wardrobe malfunction), reveals an email from your manager scheduling an emergency meeting in the morning and five other emails from fellow team members wondering what the hell is going on.

What you need is detachment, concentration, autonomy and privacy, but what the world insists upon is immersion, distraction, collaboration and company.

A few images of the times:

A flushed, sweating figure in a tracksuit running furiously to stay in place on a gym machine while watching the French Open tennis championships on a gigantic television and listening to Primal Scream on headphones.

A woman at the hairdresser's flicking through the celebrity wedding pictures in *HELLO!* while having a combined wash and head massage, listening with one ear to the cheery babbling of a radio DJ and with the other to the sad story of the hairdresser whose boyfriend can get an erection only by throttling her to the brink of unconsciousness ('he's an ex-soldier and blames it on Afghanistan').

A young man lying back on a sofa sipping vodka and Red Bull while watching a double-penetration porn scene and being vigorously fellated by a kneeling blonde.

Anyone doing fewer than three things at once is not living to the full, failing to take advantage of the age of simultaneous multiple distractions and permanent multiple connexity – the multitasking, hyperlinked, immersive network world.

Not only are more and more gadgets demanding attention, their solicitations are ever more cunning. My television and laptop both behave as though they are on first-name terms with their owner and have intimate knowledge of his personality and tastes. So the television service is constantly suggesting programmes to watch, all insanely inappropriate, while the website I use for book ordering has the impertinence to say, to a man of my fastidiousness and discrimination, 'Michael, we have recommendations for you.' The obvious next stage is for these gadgets to conspire. Then the smartphone will contact the sat nav: 'Listen, this asshole is a wine snob who loves Sancerre and raves on about grapefruit notes and vibrant astringency. But he's also a cheapskate who joins wine clubs for the special offer introductory case and then cancels his membership. It's just *so embarrassing* to deliver these cancellations. Anyway, tell him that, on the next left, there's a shopping centre with a supermarket offering a case of a dozen Sancerre for the price of ten. And when he gets there, mention that Waterstone's has a three for two promotion on Penguin Classics. The guy is a culture snob as well. He just *adores* the gravitas of those black Penguin Classics.'

And the shops will have a multitude of further distractions. Both the real and virtual worlds are becoming jungles of hyperlinks where every distraction is surrounded by multiple enticements to other distractions. So a smartphone with text messaging and email is the essential accessory, because it is a repository of hyperlinks, providing the facility to distract and be distracted anywhere and at any time. The content of the communications is unimportant – the connexity itself is the reassuring message. As the pleasure of shopping has become detached from the purchases, and the pleasure of travel from the places visited, so the pleasure of distraction has become an end in itself, independent of the actual distractions.

Being constantly the hub of a network of potential interruptions provides the excitement and importance of crisis management. As well as the false sense of efficiency in multitasking, there is the false sense of urgency in multi-interrupt processing.

In a study of information workers – analysts, programmers and managers – psychologists discovered that all three types of professional were interrupted on average once every three minutes. But the most interesting finding was that they interrupted themselves as often as they were interrupted by others.[153] Being constantly interrupted first became normal and then necessary so that the workers ended up doing it to themselves.

What effect does continuous divided attention have on the brain? The first point is that, as with most forms of greed, multitasking is self-defeating. Psychologists who have studied the phenomenon in detail concluded: 'Multitasking may seem more efficient on the surface but may actually take more time in the end.'[154] And neuroscientists using brain scans of multitasking came to an even more definite conclusion. Performing two tasks one after the other was faster than performing the same two tasks almost simultaneously. It was the prefrontal cortex that processed the multitasking and it turned out to be unable to concentrate on more than one task at a time.[155]

Of course these discoveries will deter no one, least of all me.

I used to read a book to the end before beginning another but, increasingly, I start new books without finishing the old ones – so I have more and more books with strips of newspaper sticking out of them.

And constantly switching attention may have long-term effects on the brain. Neuroscientists have discovered that, for people in the age range between thirty-five and thirty-nine, electronic interruptions have little effect on concentration on cognitive tasks, whereas for those between eighteen and twenty-one, interruptions cause a marked deterioration in performance.[156] The suspicion is that, for the distracted generation, the constant need to process interruptions prevents the prefrontal cortex from developing fully. This is possible because the prefrontal cortex, which can be thought of as the brain's manager, the ego, is the last part of the brain to mature and is fully formed only after adolescence – one reason why adolescents are often id-controlled, demanding, impulsive, ungrateful and angry. So the crucial executive controller is not only distracted by interruptions and hyperlinks but may be prevented from developing properly. Chronic distraction weakens the prefrontal cortex – and, with the opposite effect, long-term meditation strengthens it.[157]

However, it is becoming impossible to avoid distraction. The new built environment is a text sprinkled with physical hyperlinks. The very concepts of separation and boundaries are becoming obsolete. Airports, railway stations, office blocks, hotels and hospitals have become mini-cities with large, bright, high-ceilinged, open-plan areas offering a distracting range of products and services. And the cities themselves have become increasingly porous, with living, working, shopping, eating and drinking areas leaking into each other. New city developments such as London Docklands are designed according to this principle, known to architects as 'caves and commons', which blurs the distinctions between inside and outside, work and leisure, public and private.

No one wants to be separate. Even the open-plan office cubicle provides too much separation. The new workplaces have no partitions of any kind. Mother, an ultra-hip advertising agency in London's ultra-hip Shoreditch, has a single giant 250-foot work-table, possibly the largest worktop in the world. And it has removed the old-fashioned separation of a building into storeys by using open ramps like those in a multi-level car park.

On the other side of London, the Natural History Museum proudly announces a new exhibit in the multimillion-pound extension – its own working scientists exposed to the public like the stuffed animals in glass cases. And visibility is not confined to the professional classes. Rolls-Royce has introduced a glass-walled production line exposed to the world. Many chefs now work in kitchens exposed to the diners. In the most fashionable restaurants diners can pay extra for the privilege of eating in the kitchen with the chef. In the cheaper hip restaurants there are no separate tables and chairs but only communal benches as in school canteens.

And at these benches the diners of course enjoy fusion cooking, to a background of fusion music, wearing fusion design – and can pay for all this thanks to a fusion education. The new city academies scornfully dismiss as hopelessly old-fashioned the idea of students studying French or History – instead they simply study Napoleon. Museums dismiss as equally dated the idea of displaying art according to period or movement – instead Cézanne is supposed to be involved in an intriguing 'dialogue' with conceptual art. (The dialogue actually goes like this – Conceptual Work: 'You're so *over*'; Cézanne: 'You're such *shite*.'). And why should art be confined to museums? So there are artistic 'interventions' in buildings everywhere and anywhere. And string quartets play in railway stations, ballerinas dance in department stores, theatre groups perform in shopping centres, writers take up residence not just in universities but in prisons, museums, hospitals, football clubs, corporations, hotels and zoos.

Everything mixes with everything else – which is why 'synergy' is the word of the moment, an impressively pseudo-scientific term for mixing.

Imagine someone sitting alone in a room without television, radio, computer or phone and with the door closed and the blinds down. This person must be a dangerous lunatic or a prisoner sentenced to solitary confinement. If a free agent, then a panty-sniffing loser shunned by society, or a psycho planning to return to college with an automatic weapon and a backpack full of ammo.

No wonder the current *Diagnostic and Statistical Manual of Mental Disorders* (DSM) defines detachment as a condition known as 'depersonalization disorder', a sense of being 'detached from, and as if one is an outside observer of, one's mental processes or body'. So anyone capable of detachment is *mentally ill*, indeed scarcely even a person at all.

Yet, achieving personal detachment was considered to be a key factor in mental health by every thinker from Buddha to Sartre. Even Christian thinkers have valued detachment, and one of the most passionate endorsements comes from the thirteenth-century Dominican Meister Eckhart: 'I have read many works by the pagan teachers and the prophets, in both the Old and the New Law, and I have inquired, carefully and assiduously, to find which is the greatest virtue . . . and as I study all these writings, as far as my reason can lead and teach, I find no virtue better than a pure detachment from all things.'[158] Eckhart goes on to place detachment above humility, mercy and even love, adding in a curious but striking phrase, 'detachment compels God to come to me'. A secular version of this is that detachment from the world compels the world to approach. The paradox is that informed detachment can actually inspire a more intense engagement. It is like standing back from a painting in order to see it more clearly.

As difficult as detachment from the world is detachment from the self, a form of humility opposed by a culture that instead worships self-esteem. It is a contemporary axiom that lack of self-esteem is the root of all evil, especially social evils such as violence, delinquency and academic underachievement, and that strong self-esteem is the solution to all problems both personal and social. In the USA there is even a National Association for Self-Esteem, NASE, whose mission is 'improving the human condition through the enhancement of self-esteem', further evidence that it is impossible to satirize the contemporary world. And, at the personal level, there is a burgeoning sub-genre of self-help devoted to boosting self-esteem (*Self-Esteem: Your Fundamental Power; Ten Days To Self-Esteem; The Self-Esteem Bible*). There was a time when, in fables, people asked questions of mirrors and waited fearfully for the response. But this is no longer a questioning age. Instead we are encouraged to begin each day by shouting into a mirror the relevant delusion – for sales staff, 'I *am* uniquely persuasive. I will meet all my sales targets'; for managers, 'I *am* uniquely masterful. I will command universal obedience'; and, for lovers, 'I *am* uniquely beautiful. I will inspire eternal love in the object of my desire.'

The problem with self-esteem is that it has no values or principles and does not even require effort. Self-respect, which is subtly though crucially different, implies achievement worthy of respect, but self-esteem, in its contemporary usage, makes no demands on the self – only on others. Self-respect comes from within and self-esteem from without. Spinoza understood this distinction: 'Self-respect does not extend to anything outside us and is attributed only to one who knows the real worth of his perfection, dispassionately and without seeking esteem for himself.'[159] Self-esteem is narcissistic, demanding that the world reflect back whatever image is presented, and so it can never have any lasting benefit, although few have acknowledged this. Exceptions include Albert Ellis with his book *The Myth of Self-Esteem*[160], and a study by a group of American psychologists who conclude drily: 'We have found little to indicate that indiscriminately promoting self-esteem in today's children or adults, just for being themselves, offers society any compensatory benefits beyond the seductive pleasure it brings to those engaged in the exercise.'[161] In fact, these psychologists suggest that pumping up self-esteem may well exacerbate the very problems it is meant to solve. If the world does not comply with the demands of a high self-estimate, and the world is frequently slow to oblige, the outraged self-believer may resort to violence to make the world fall into line. One obvious example is the 'respect' obsession in youth culture, where failure to show sufficient respect, such as by bumping into someone in a hamburger queue, can get the disrespectful shot dead. Another example is the total confidence that many parents instill in their children. The problem with this kind of high self-esteem is that it is accompanied by low self-awareness. Such children grow up with no understanding of their own faults – or even go so far as to believe that their own faults are *endearing*. As the hunchback said happily, 'On *me* it looks good.'

The psychologist Oliver James, in an investigation of depression, was intrigued by a World Health Organization table showing prevalence of emotional distress in different countries during a twelve-month period. At the top was the USA with 26.4 per cent and at the bottom was China (Shanghai) with just 4.3 per cent. The trend in the table was for more developed countries to have higher rates of depression – but Shanghai is a fully developed city. James went to Shanghai to investigate and concluded that a crucial difference was in attitudes to self-esteem. In America government task forces, schools, parents and self-help books promote the boosting of self-esteem but in China the Confucian insistence on modesty produces a focus on personal shortcomings. Furthermore, whereas in America worldly success is the only ratification of self-esteem, the Chinese are satisfied with striving itself. And James also cites studies showing that the most aggressive Americans are those with 'grandiose self-esteem', who are likely to become violent if their self-estimate is not acknowledged.[162]

Hence a profound irony – the boosting of self-esteem, which is intended to promote a sense of well-being and to discourage aggression, may instead be a cause of depression and violence. And attempts to realize children's potential by praising them for their talents may instead inhibit or destroy potential. Parents would be wiser to take the Chinese approach and praise their children for effort rather than innate ability.

The psychologist Carol Dweck actually tested this hypothesis by giving several hundred New York schoolchildren a test and afterwards praising half for effort ('You must have worked really hard') and the other half for intelligence ('You must be smart at this'). Then the pupils were offered a choice of two further tests – one at the same level as the first or another more difficult. Of those praised for effort, 90 per cent chose the harder test and of those praised for intelligence a similar majority took the easier option. So the form of the single short sentence of praise had an enormous effect – showing once again that it is better to concentrate on the striving than the outcome. Dweck's conclusion was that the intelligence group became scared of failure, while the effort group was encouraged to learn from mistakes. When the two groups were invited to look at the test papers of those who had done better than themselves or those who had done worse, the intelligence pupils almost all chose to boost their self-esteem by comparison with those below, while most of the effort pupils wanted to understand their errors by examining better test papers. And, in subsequent tests, the effort pupils raised their average scores by 30 per cent, while the intelligence average dropped by 20 per cent.[163]

So the way to success is to focus on failure. And in general it would be wiser to concentrate on our shortcomings. But it is supremely difficult to see ourselves as we really are. The mind shies away from its own insignificance as strenuously as from the prospect of its own extinction. It takes a kind of wilful, unnatural act, a leap of anti-faith, to understand that one's own self is a raw, quivering, insecure, fearful and puny thing. The inner giant is really a trembling dwarf – and a half-crazed, neurotic, greedy, enraged, deformed dwarf at that. All that distinguishes one dwarf from another is the nature and strength of its disguises and self-deception (whose final task is to erase all the ingenious processes of self-deception).

The good news is that we can summon help in the heroic task of exposing our unheroic natures. Literature abounds in reminders of our laughable paltriness – Shakespeare, for instance: 'The fool doth think he is wise but the wise man knows himself to be a fool.'[164] The further good news is that this exposure is liberating, even exhilarating. Hence another exquisite paradox – the inner giant may be awakened only by recognizing it as a dwarf.

However, the serious seeker of detachment will have to embrace the Holy Trinity of Ss – Solitude, Stillness and Silence – and reject the new religion of Commotionism, which believes that the meaning of life is constant company, movement and noise. Commotion is life, repeat these new faithful; solitude, stillness and silence are death.

Already the word 'solitude' has an archaic ring to it, as though it were some weird ascetic practice of the Desert Fathers, like taking a vow of chastity or wearing a hair shirt. When a team of psychologists asked people to rank common activities in order of preference, spending time alone came out second last, just ahead of being interrogated by the boss.[165] There are many possible reasons for this. Like detachment, solitude can be frightening. It may expose the insignificance, ugliness and emptiness we are trying so hard to conceal. And, within relationships, a desire for solitude may be interpreted by a needy partner as rejection or a failure to provide the constant company craved, or both, and this partner will scheme, bully and intrude to prevent the other being alone. Then there are the demands of relatives, colleagues and friends, the last two categories being increasingly significant. In the survey cited above, spending time with friends was by far the most popular activity.

Has anyone researched the phenomenon of contemporary friendship? My feeling is that young people have increasingly large circles of friends, spend increasingly large amounts of time in their company, communicate with them increasingly often when apart, and increasingly regard them as of equal or greater importance than relatives and partners. The American poet Robert Bly blames this on what he defines as 'the sibling society', a culture of semi-adults who reject responsibility and maturity for a narcissistic self-indulgence sanctioned by allegiance to fellow siblings.[166] One of the most popular TV sitcoms of recent times was called simply *Friends*, and promoted the idea of friends as the new family; where the old unit was demanding and troublesome, the new version provides wacky group fun forever – no one need grow up or leave the fold.

So the siblings require constant communication – and technology is happy to oblige with mobile phones, Skype, texting, chat rooms, email and social networking websites. It is beginning to seem as though everyone is friends with everyone else and everyone is in constant communication with everyone else. One of the new reality TV celebrities in the USA, Tila Tequila, famous for putting her affections out to competitive tender between 16 straight men and 16 lesbians in *A Shot at Love with Tila Tequila*, boasts of having 1,771,920 friends.[167]

The trend is to have more and more friends and to share more and more with them. So little remains private. Until fairly recently, sexual practice was unmentionable in public. Now, last night's sex is discussed as casually as last night's TV – one reason why the power and the glory of sex have so diminished. And the last of the taboo private matters, money, is also increasingly public, though in this case any diminishment of the power and the glory of the subject is welcome.

And this leisure phenomenon has its work parallel in the worship of 'collaboration'. This new idol is celebrated in a recent slew of books such as *Crowdsourcing; We Are Smarter Than Me; Here Comes Everybody; The Wisdom Of Crowds; Wikinomics: How Mass Collaboration Changes Everything* and *We-Think: Mass Innovation, Not Mass Production* (by Charles Leadbeater and 257 other people). This form of collaboration is an extension of the team ethos of the last century. According to its visionary advocates, the entire population of the world will eventually be one giant team collaborating happily on a multitude of exciting new projects. Already television is increasingly collaborative, with the outcome of many reality shows decided by the public. And online TV is based on the concept of collaboration, with the audience directly influencing the content of drama shows and even participating in them.

All this has brought about a curious development in late individualism – a diminishing of faith in the individual.

Yet the advice from all the thinkers is that redemption comes not from others but from within the individual. And, to find strength from within, it is necessary to spend time alone. Here is Rilke: 'The essential thing is only this . . . to be solitary, in the way one was solitary as a child, when the grownups went back and forth around us absorbed in things that seemed important and grand because they themselves looked so businesslike and we children had never the slightest idea of what they were doing.'[168] The solitary child knows intuitively that the busyness and babble of the Big Ones are absurd, but grows up, is sucked into busyness and babble and forgets about enchantment. The world demands continuous, total immersion – but there is a form of happiness that depends on holding back something vital, as the child protects a secret self from nagging, intrusive parents. And this withholding is nurtured and strengthened by solitude, when the clamour and the years fall away and something like the old childhood rapture may be experienced once again. Contemporary disapproval may actually make solitude even more exciting – forbidden, illicit, transgressive, like snorting coke but entirely free from concerns about expense, dangerous criminals, the police or a disintegrating nose.

A secret self is such a protection against the world and its vicissitudes, armour all the more effective for being interior and invisible, the chain mail providing greater security on the soul than the body.

Then there is stillness. 'Teach us to sit still,' [169] T.S. Eliot prayed – but his prayer went unanswered. Instead the age has been

increasingly dominated by the superstitions of activity and movement. Mere activity has always been worshipped, but the
obsession with movement is new, driven by restlessness and
facilitated by cheap transport. 'I want to *travel*,' people say nowadays, with a solemn, mystical, faraway look. But, if you respond
with, 'Where to and what for?' the mysticism dissolves into irritated incomprehension. For there is no burning desire to see
anything in particular, merely to get going, to be on the move.
Like sharks, we must keep in motion to stay alive and, as with
sharks, the grin is false but the teeth are real. American culture is
permeated with this worship of movement as the universal
redeemer and renewer. Any failure may be erased by going elsewhere and reinventing oneself as the Great Gatsby. Even if there
is no Gatsby rebirth, the movement itself will be exhilarating, for
movement is the physical expression of potential.

No wonder 'dynamic' has become one of the highest terms of
praise. Dynamic is wonderful. Static is terrible. So buildings have
a serious problem in being mostly chunky cuboids obviously
rooted to the spot. Contemporary architects get around this with
designs that create the illusion of movement. The sexiest new
buildings look as though they are stretching, leaning, twisting,
turning, falling apart, about to burst into sail, about to take off,
already in flight or even dancing, like Zaha Hadid's Dancing
Towers in Dubai, which resemble three inebriated clubbers late
on a Saturday night. The obvious next stage is a building that is
not an illusion but actually moves – and the appropriately named
Dynamic Group has proposed a tower for Dubai where each of
the residential floors turns on its axis so everyone can be on the
move even while watching TV at home.

Perhaps the mania for holidays is really only an excuse for
movement – as is perhaps the mania for second homes. There
is, of course, the colonist's thrill of filling the virgin territory of
a second home with all the possessions in the first, but the unconscious pleasure may be the obligation to move constantly
between the two. And a common vision of bliss is life as a

permanent holiday or, more precisely, an endless succession of holidays. With so many striving towards this ideal, tourism has had to become increasingly resourceful. So there is Sex Tourism, Adventure Tourism, Eco-Tourism, Space Tourism, Drug Tourism, Slum Tourism and now Dark Tourism, which is defined on the website for Lonely Planet guides as 'travel to sites associated with death, disaster and depravity'. Now Heart of Darkness Tours will transport you in comfort to the German concentration camps, the Cambodian killing fields and the slave dungeons of West Africa.

Then there is the superstition of busyness, where the equivalent of 'I want to travel' is the mantra, 'I like to be active'. Activity is another means that has become an end because it provides relief from anxiety, and the illusion of significance and meaning. But thinkers have always extolled the plenitude of inactivity, for instance Cicero quoting Cato, 'Never is a man more active than when he does nothing, never is he less alone than when he is by himself.'[170] Yet the version for the T-shirt is, surprisingly, by a contemporary American, the poet Charles Wright: 'Don't just do something, sit there.'[171]

And when people are obliged to sit there they sometimes enjoy it. Waiting areas are often surprisingly serene, given the raging impatience of the times, even those in hospitals and airports where the wait can stretch into hours. More encouraging still, hardly anyone looks at the inevitable screen.

But it is harder to resist the assault on silence. As far back as the 1880s the French poet Jules Laforgue cried out in despair: 'the modern world has embarked on a conspiracy to establish that silence does not exist'.[172] What would he have made of a world with constant music in bars, cafés, restaurants, hotels, department stores, boutiques, supermarkets, buses, trains, foyers, lifts and toilets? It is becoming difficult to enjoy even a quiet ruminative pee. Nowhere is safe now. I visit my dentist where, for decades, the only distraction has been dog-eared old magazines with missing covers, and find a music centre going behind the reception desk, a television on in the waiting room and a radio playing in the surgery. No sanctuary is beyond assault. Even the fish in the oceans are being driven mad, according to *The Journal of the Acoustical Society of America*: 'Since the 1960s there has been a tenfold increase in underwater ocean noise.'

But the ultimate abomination is canned music in *bookshops*. Imagine trying to browse Chinese poetry about sage recluses having deep thoughts on mountain tops – only to be deafened by loud music. And the nature of this background music has also changed. At first public places played only muzak, created to be blandly unobtrusive, and the occasional bookshop might have baroque music noodling harmlessly in the background. Now there is thumping soul, rock or drum and bass (an example of the contemporary fondness for music with no beginning, middle or end, that just seems to go on and on). This destroys not only attention, but music itself. Anything played as background becomes only background, as meaningless as the humming and singing of a refrigerator.

Also obsolete is the idea of libraries as havens of solitary reading in silence. Imagine being a librarian, increasingly faced with uninhibited talk, laughter and mobile-phone use in the library, and then attending a library conference to hear the government Culture Secretary, *the Culture Secretary*, declare that libraries are far too 'silent and sombre' and should be full of 'joy and chatter'.[173] This Culture Secretary believes that 'libraries should be the places where real social networking happens'. They should offer shared learning, family history research, foreign language lessons and, of course, reading groups. Now people can't even read a book without network support.

But the Culture Secretary need have no fear of sombre silence. The last time I went into my university library it sounded like a bar on Saturday night.

Even the office is no longer a sanctuary. The colleague I share with puts on music the moment I leave and refrains in my presence only from the fear that I will rip out my workstation

keyboard and batter him to death with it. Not that his fearful forbearance makes much difference: the guy in the office next door
plays music constantly and the partitions are made of thin card-
board. And one of the most shocking stories I have ever read in
a newspaper was on the installation by the BBC of a 'chit-chat
machine that provided soothing artificial office noise for employees working in a quiet office'. This device was installed after staff
complained that their office was 'so silent it was hard to concentrate'.

Then, after a stressful day, I get home to find the television
blaring in the living room and the radio blaring in the kitchen.
Who? *Who?* My niece, currently in the bathroom taking her
second shower of the day. She comes home, switches everything
on and makes for the bathroom. Later, like so many students, she
has to have a radio playing while she studies. Claims it helps her
to concentrate. And other adult guests turn up in dressing gowns
as I prepare for bed. There is no radio in the guest room and they
can't get to sleep without it. *Could I possibly . . . ?*

So employees are unable to work without noise, students are
unable to study without noise, guests are unable to sleep without
noise.

Of course the ubiquitous background music is not music in the
traditional sense. It is not meant to be enjoyed, or even properly
heard. Its only function is to abolish silence. And silence must be
abolished because it is a reminder of the silence of the void –
cold, remote, inhuman and terrifying. So people arrive home and
switch on televisions and radios as automatically as they would
heating in winter and for the same reason – to keep out the cold.

And those who enjoy silence must also be cold, remote and
inhuman. At least these cranks can draw comfort from the poets,
for instance the Spanish poet Juan Ramón Jiménez: 'Unity is the
noble daughter of silence; dispersion, the mad stepchild of
noise.'[174]

How Jiménez would have suffered in contemporary Spain!
Two families are sharing a holiday home at a resort in Spain. My

friend wants to discuss a thesis he is planning to write but, of
course, there is noise everywhere in the house. We go out to find
a quiet bar. It's eleven o'clock in the morning so many are
empty – but all throb with loud music. Eventually we find a silent
bar, order coffee and settle down. But, just as I open my mouth
to speak, I'm drowned out by thunderous disco pop. The proprietor has switched on his sound system. My friend rushes up to the
bar, grimacing. Could he turn it off, we're trying to talk. The man
refuses, outraged. We have to abandon the coffee and leave. The
significant thing is that the bar owner would rather lose customers than please them by turning off the music presumably
intended to please them in the first place – because music in bars
is normal and these customers are cranks.

The tragedy is that he has a point. Even those who hate music
in public places begin, unconsciously, to register it as normal and
its absence as abnormal. I go into the London Review Bookshop,
one of the last to preserve sacred silence, and the atmosphere
seems unnatural, tomblike. Other customers may well feel the
same – there are fewer of them. This beautiful shop may well
close, validating the music policy of other bookshops and reinforcing the customers' belief that universal canned music is
natural. So the age, relentlessly, inexorably, imposes its will.

What to do? Let it go – or quarrel with colleagues and relatives,
and complain to dentists and managers of bookshops? This way
lies the self-indulgent crankiness of Schopenhauer who, enraged
at having his marvellous thoughts interrupted by a seamstress
chattering outside his door, rushed out and threw her downstairs.
This episode is instructive in another way, illustrating not just the
intolerance and aggression of the despisers but the benefits of
what they so violently despised – the enlightenment demand for
universal rights. The seamstress took Schopenhauer to court, won
her case and obliged him to pay her a quarterly stipend for the
rest of her life.

And Juan Ramón's obsession with silence was also cranky, even
farcical. He continually moved apartments to escape noise that

would scarcely even register with many contemporary city dwellers – the landlady singing below, Cuban ladies playing the piano above, street vendors, trolley lines and troublesome sparrows outside. In one apartment he attempted the Proust solution of soundproofing a room – hiring carpenters to insulate a wall with a cushion made from sacking and esparto grass. It failed to work so he had to move again. On another occasion he was driven wild by a cricket kept in a cage by the concierge's son. This time he offered to buy the noisy pest to get rid of it. The boy considered this but failed to understand the cranky motive. As far as he was concerned, noise was good. 'For twenty-five pesetas,' the boy said, 'I will bring you five of the finest crickets imaginable.'

8

The Rejection of Difficulty and Understanding

It is shocking and profoundly regrettable, but, apparently, sales of oranges are falling steadily because people can no longer be bothered to peel them.[175] As soon as I read this I began buying oranges more frequently and eating them with greater pleasure. Now I peel an orange very slowly, deliberately, voluptuously, above all *defiantly*, as a riposte to an age that demands war without casualties, public services without taxes, rights without obligations, celebrity without achievement, sex without relationship, running shoes without running, coursework without work and sweet grapes without seeds.

Even the favourite clothes of the age, the T-shirts and tracksuits and fleeces, are lazy, as easy to pull on as to throw off, imposing little constraint and requiring little maintenance. No wonder ties have gone out of fashion. Who, if not obliged by a dress code, would have the energy and patience to knot a tie? I've forgotten how to do a Windsor knot myself.

On the intellectual level the news is even more shocking. The last bastion has fallen. Even France has succumbed. The Finance Minister of the country that gave the world the legendary sentence, 'I think, therefore I am', has addressed its National Assembly as follows: 'France is a country that thinks. There is hardly an ideology that we haven't turned into a theory. We have in our libraries enough to talk about for centuries to come. This is why I would like to tell you: Enough thinking, already.'[176] And this minister's boss, the President, proudly declared to a television interviewer, 'I am not a theoretician. Oh, I am not an intellectual! I am someone concrete.' To prove the point he poses in dark glasses with the much younger model and singer who has replaced his first wife.

The President is merely doing what is necessary. As the world's problems become ever more complex and intractable, the world's leaders are required to make their jobs seem more effortless. Though frequently this is not an illusion – Ronald Reagan genuinely abhorred effort. For a contemporary leader, appearing relaxed is as important as having a full head of hair. (When was the last time a bald man got elected to significant office? Silvio Berlusconi was reinstated as Italian President only after a major hair transplant.)

Difficulty has become repugnant because it denies entitlement, disenchants potential, limits mobility and flexibility, delays gratification, distracts from distraction and demands responsibility, commitment, attention and thought.

So, what is the latest work of a French intellectual to be translated into English? Another impenetrable slab of postmodern theorising? No. *How to Talk About Books You Haven't Read* by Pierre Bayard, a university professor of French literature who boasts of teaching books he has never even opened.[177]

Of course, the cultural world has always been almost entirely peopled by chancers, but brazen bragging about ignorance is new, and reveals the extent of the rejection of difficulty and understanding. And open hostility to intelligence itself is new. Now intelligence is satanic and only fools can be holy. One of religion's greatest triumphs was to portray reason as arrogant and overweening, Lucifer's sin of intellectual pride. The modern, or rather postmodern, version of this is that reason is elitist and oppressive. But, to think in order to see the self as it really is – a puny, deformed, fearful thing – and to acknowledge the world as it really is – in all its objective abundance and complexity rather than as a theme park for the gratification of the self – these are surely acts of liberation and humility.

Besides, I have never known a fool who struck me as even remotely holy, nor a fool who, as William Blake claimed, became wise by persisting in folly. Nor a thinker who suffered fools gladly. The Old Testament prophets directed much of their wrath at fools, as did compassionate Christ and even benign Buddha ('If one were never able to see fools, then one could be forever happy'[178]). The nineteenth-century thinkers were even more scathing, but my favourite quote is from Ecclesiastes: 'For as the crackling of thorns under a pot, so is the laughter of the fool.'[179]

Rational thought has been successfully discredited – and Francis Wheen, in his book *How Mumbo-Jumbo Conquered the World*, has catalogued many of the monsters brought forth by the sleep of reason. Can it really be true, as Wheen claims, that the UK government hired a feng shui consultant called Renuka Wickmaratne to advise on improving inner-city council estates and that the advice they got for their money was: 'Red and orange flowers would reduce crime and introducing a water feature would reduce poverty. I was brought up with this ancient knowledge'? That, as a presidential aide put it, 'virtually every major move and decision' made by Ronald Reagan, including the signing of the Intermediate-Range Nuclear Forces treaty, was first cleared by a San Francisco astrologer called Joan Quigley, who also provided an astrological analysis of the character of Mikhail Gorbachev? That 48 per cent of Americans believe in UFOs, 27 per cent in alien visits to earth, and that 2 per cent (3.7 million people) claim to have been the victims of alien abduction?[180]

How have such irrationality and credulity come about? As always, there are many causes, overlapping and interacting, in both high and low culture. There is the postmodern promotion of epistemic relativism, which not only rejected reason but also truth, objectivity, meaning and even reality and fact; the age of entitlement's demand for qualifications without the tedium of difficult study; the preference for presentation over explanation and image over content; the hatred of science, so cold, remote, inhuman, arrogant and oppressive; and the replacement of rational argument by emotion, so warm, human, humble, positive and liberating.

Thinkers themselves, especially Nietzsche and Sartre, must take some of the blame. Nietzsche's strident denunciations of morality planted the seeds of relativism and Sartre's hatred of philosophical systems caused him to reject, along with systems, the reason used to develop them – he denounced reason as an 'iron cage'. This is like blaming a collapsed house on the builders' tools – but the idea was enthusiastically taken up and extended by the postmodern project, which used reason to attack reason in an attention-seeking vandalism like that of rock musicians destroying their own instruments on stage.

Once reason has been discredited anything goes. Truth becomes merely relative – everyone has a different version of truth and they are all equally valid. So historians began to argue that anyone's version of events is as good as anyone else's, and literary critics that a 'text' means anything a reader wants it to mean. The great advantage of these approaches is that they render unnecessary the difficult business of establishing meaning and truth.

So science has been derided for its claim to objective truth – and the valid point that science is influenced by the culture in which it operates has been extended to a dismissal of it as merely one more fictional narrative among many. And the fact that modern physics is strange has been used to justify any wacky belief – if science can be weird then anything weird can be science.

And science has been blamed for bringing disenchantment to the human world and devastation to the natural world – despite the fact that scientists tend to regard their discoveries as a source of wonder, and that it was scientists who first issued warnings on the dangers facing the planet and are now attempting to find solutions. But the prize for most ingenious attack on science must go to the philosopher John Gray who claims that science is not based on reason at all: 'The origins of science are not in rational enquiry but in faith, magic and trickery. Modern science triumphed over its adversaries not through its superior rationality but because its late-medieval and early-modern founders were more skilful than them in the use of rhetoric and the arts of politics.'[181] And: 'As pictured by philosophers, science is a supremely rational activity. Yet the history of science shows scientists flouting the rules of scientific method. Not only the origins but the progress of science comes from acting against reason.'[182] What Gray seems to be suggesting is that rejecting the prevailing orthodoxy, which is often how discoveries are made, is 'acting against reason', whereas this is the most important use, the very triumph, of reason. Though, in a rare moment of gratitude, Gray acknowledges some benefits of magic and trickery: 'Anaesthetic dentistry is an unmixed blessing. So are clean water and flush toilets.'[183]

As well as being derided from above, science is being eaten away from below. It has come to be regarded as the ultimate difficulty, the most forbidding test of understanding. So the numbers of those willing to study it drop year by year. Why submit to mathematical rigour when you can do a degree in Surfing and Beach Management instead? A few years ago, during a university meeting to devise new courses sufficiently undemanding for contemporary youth, I proposed Pizza Studies, a multidisciplinary and highly academic degree requiring students to learn the history of the pizza and at least twenty words of Italian. But life as usual exceeded me with the announcement by McDonald's that it was awarding academic qualifications. The joke of Pizza Studies was outdone by the reality of Hamburger Studies.

Education's abandonment of difficulty is a consequence of developments over several decades. As a boy growing up in Catholic Ireland I experienced one educational extreme where arrogant and snobbish, but largely philistine, teachers routinely insulted and beat pupils. This was appalling, a consequence of Ireland remaining in the nineteenth century until the mid-1960s.

I could never have taught in such an environment, but when, in the early 1970s, I came to London to teach, I discovered that English education had gone to the opposite extreme. Instead of being insulted and beaten, pupils were flattered and indulged. Of course there were worthy motives for this – to bring into education those formerly excluded, to attempt to compensate for family and social problems, to give hope to the despairing and initiative to the helpless. And who is to say that this project has not been a success? A proper debate of the issues would require a separate book. But there have certainly been prices to pay. One is the collapse of teacher authority. No pupils enjoy being insulted and beaten but neither do they respect an appeaser. Another price is the rejection of difficulty. The fundamental axiom of teaching is that anything worth saying can be said simply. But expressing difficult ideas simply is itself difficult. How much easier to avoid the difficult altogether. Another axiom is that enthusiastic teaching should inspire pupils to become active rather than passive learners. But, faced with the exhausting business of coaxing pupils to show initiative and work for themselves, how tempting simply to tell them what to do, or even to do it for them. So more and more assessment is by coursework, with assignments regularly brought to teachers for correction of errors and detailed instructions on what to do next. A third teaching axiom is that understanding involves paying attention to explanations. But obliging pupils to listen in silence means exhausting authority battles. So much less stressful to let them talk as they wish and are used to. And teaching means raising pupils to the level of the teacher – but lifting dead weight is arduous and frustrating; it is so much easier to come down to the level of the pupil. The result of all this is an inexorable lowering of standards, which no one in education is allowed to admit.

Then pupils carry these assumptions with them to university and are shocked at being expected to listen in silence rather than chatter as usual, and outraged when lecturers decline to read coursework in advance ('just to see if I'm on the right lines').

There has been a gradual change in attitudes to understanding over the years. Once, when students failed to understand, they would ask to have the explanation repeated. Then they began to suggest, often with considerable resentment, that if they had failed to understand, the explanation must have been at fault. More recently, there has been another subtle shift. Now many students do not even mention understanding or its absence. Instead they laugh in a relaxed, tolerant way at the absurdity and redundancy of the entire enterprise, bestowing a smile of amused pity on their ridiculous, obsolete lecturers. Here is another absurd reversal: once teachers patronised students; increasingly it is the other way round.

It is not so much that difficulty and understanding have been rejected as that these very concepts have ceased to exist. In fact, the concept of concepts – the idea of an abstract, underpinning theory that must be understood to grasp a subject – has ceased to exist. Now understanding is instrumental – it is necessary to know how to operate technology but not to know how it works.

So the human animal, long since out of touch with the earth, is now losing touch with the machine. People once opened the backs of television sets and raised the bonnets of cars and understood the technology well enough to carry out repairs (I am not claiming to be one of these – looking at the insides of machines gives me vertigo and nausea). But the built-in obsolescence of gadgets has made the concept of repair also obsolete. Now, hardly anyone understands how anything works. If it breaks down, just dump it and buy the new model. And, with the growth of communication technology, the machines doing the work are often no longer even visible, but somewhere out in the ether, as intangible and mysterious as the mind of God. All that remains is the interface, the screen. So image triumphs over content, presentation over understanding, description over analysis.

For many years I was responsible for supervising postgraduate project students, many mature and in professional jobs, who were required to identify a business problem, analyse it and propose a solution. But, increasingly, what they produced was merely description. In a version of the 'location, location, location' mantra, I would repeat 'analysis, analysis, analysis', warning that a Masters level project would be failed if it did not have original analysis (actually untrue). So they withdrew huffily and returned a few weeks later (glowing with pride at having finally satisfied this maniac) to hand me thirty more pages of description. Of course, it was beautifully presented description, full of impressive illustrations expertly cut and pasted – but all image and no content.

So face value becomes the only value, and there is no longer any awareness of anything beneath the surface. In fact, the concept of 'beneath', like those of difficulty and understanding, is ceasing to exist. There is no longer a beneath, there is only the surface; no longer a complex machine, only a bright interface. The result is astonishment and shock when the affable colleague or neighbour is revealed to be a terrorist or a serial killer: 'Oh, but he was always so polite and friendly . . . always smiled and said good morning.' Likewise when the vibrant interviewee turns out to be a monster of incompetence, resentment and malice, or when the loving romantic who sends roses, chocolates and a teddy bear mutates into a rapist: 'Oh, but he was so *nice*.'

And when these gullible people suffer personal difficulties, for instance from a career or relationship betrayal, their lack of perceptiveness, foresight and understanding means that the response is shock and outrage. And their lack of a personal 'beneath' means that they have no inner life to put the problem into perspective and provide strength and defiance. There is nothing to fall back upon, only depression to fall into.

I was made to understand the new power of the image when I attended the launch of a government publication called 'Images'. This was when the Northern Ireland conflict was at its most murderous and the purpose of the initiative was not to understand or address the problems, but to counteract them with expensively produced images of all the good things going on in the province: eel fishermen happily lifting a catch; bearded folk musicians ecstatically fiddling; and solemn potters mystically moulding clay on wheels. To help spread this positive message, anyone involved with culture or the media had been invited to the launch. And indeed many had turned up for the free drink and canapés. Suddenly a tremor passed through the crowd – the Minister for Northern Ireland had arrived. A mere politician; we returned to our booze and snacks. But, a while later, there was a disturbance that sent a tsunami through the room. Everyone turned – and remained turned. It was a newscaster . . . *a newscaster from News at Ten*. Officials rushed to express gratitude, surrounding him and abjectly babbling thanks for deigning to turn up to such an unimportant function. This spectacle brought a shocking revelation – *those who read the news are now more important than those who make it.*

Then came a lesson in self-image. I approached a science-fiction writer called Bob Shaw, who struck me as one of the most unhappy-looking people I had ever seen, but was the only face I recognized. I assumed he would be pleased to hear that I had read one of his novels – but not a bit of it. He grunted and looked fretfully around at other groups, focussing eventually on an approaching photographer, who assessed us with a swift glance and moved on by.

I laughed. 'We're not famous enough.'

But Bob did not laugh. With a grunt of outrage he pursued the photographer and caught his arm. 'Excuse me, I'm Bob Shaw *the world-famous science-fiction writer.*'

Nor did the photographer laugh. Instead, with a repentant, apologetic expression, he turned and raised his camera. Bob began to pose – then looked in disgust at this nobody by his side who was about to benefit from the proximity of a world-famous writer. Uttering another grunt, he walked to a group nearby and, with a final triumphant and contemptuous glance at me, turned to the camera for the transfiguring flash.

The transfiguring power of celebrity was also behind the most shocking abandonment of reason for emotional indulgence in recent memory – the death of Diana, Princess of Wales. Here was a woman of average looks who, if not illuminated by celebrity, would have passed unremarked in the street, now suddenly worshipped as the most dazzling beauty since Helen of Troy; a woman living a life of pampered indulgence suddenly pitied as the most downtrodden of victims; a woman who had left her husband for the playboy son of a wealthy man, suddenly revered as the greatest saint since Teresa of Avila. But anyone who even attempted to suggest any of this was attacked and reviled as a heartless cynic. It seemed as though the entire country – the entire Western world – had lost its mind. Even my wife, whom I had always regarded as a rational sceptic, was swept away on the tide of emotion and went to worship at the flower mountain outside Kensington Palace. And she, too, refused to listen to any attempt to put the death into perspective. It was one of the most disturbing episodes I have ever lived through. In this case the emotion, grief, was harmless, but it was easy to imagine less benign emotions – panic, hysteria, hatred, rage – sweeping aside rational argument in the same way.

Most of these dangerous emotions are based on fear – and a hedonistic culture, concerned as much with the avoidance of pain and difficulty as the pursuit of pleasure, is always fearful. The citizens of Western democracies have never been more healthy and safe – and have never felt more unhealthy and unsafe. We now fear the air we breathe, the food we eat, the water we drink, the people who smile at our children, the local streets we walk on, the public transport we take to work and the buildings we work in, which may be sinisterly and toxically 'sick'. The less visible the threat the more frightening it becomes.

This is not an argument against emotion. Without emotion there would be no possibility of happiness, compassion or love. Even rational decision-making would be impossible. But emotion must be balanced by thinking. And the negative emotions are so much more powerful than the positive that it takes a constant effort of understanding to keep them at bay.

The alternative to thinking is not emotion but thoughtlessness. Failing to think may sound like a harmless form of abdication – but Hannah Arendt was vouchsafed a profound insight while attending the trial of the Nazi Adolf Eichmann in Jerusalem. Attempting to understand his motivation, she considered – but was forced to reject – the traditional idea of evil as a positive, demonic force i.e. the original sin or Manichean explanation. Then came the insight: Eichmann's most notable characteristic was not ideological conviction, nor was it evil motivation, but *thoughtlessness*. In the Israeli court he functioned, as he had done in Germany, by sticking to the clichéd, conventional language that protects against reality and renders thinking unnecessary. Arendt's conclusion: 'Could the activity of thinking as such, the habit of examining whatever comes to pass or to attract attention, regardless of results and specific content, could this activity be among the conditions that make men abstain from evil-doing or even actually "condition" them against it?'[184]

So thinking may make the difference between good and evil. It may even make the difference between life and death. Primo Levi, the concentration camp survivor, has written that the one quality survivors had in common was intellectual curiosity.[185] Even the extreme suffering of the camps was an object of study for the active mind, and attempting to understand it conferred a crucial sense of worth. Wholly bourgeois people, reliant only on status and possessions, had no such resource and were the first to die. So curiosity may have killed the cat but it has saved many human lives.

And the Levi experience is just one example of how understanding can not only ease but *make use of* adversity, as the Stoics and existentialists advised. Anyone not consumed by self-pity, anger and blaming can try to turn to advantage whatever happens. For those willing to learn, pain is an excellent teacher.

But Hannah Arendt's 'thinking attention' and thinking 'regardless of results and specific content' refer to undirected mental activity rather than thinking in the generally understood sense of purposive thought i.e. thinking with a specific goal, such as establishing a truth, making a decision or choosing from a range of options. Thinking attention is a purely enjoyable form of thought. But directed thought, while frequently necessary, has always been difficult and is becoming increasingly so. How to establish anything as true without the support of theology or tradition, in a culture of epistemic relativism? How to make crucial life decisions in a culture without constraints and almost unlimited personal freedom? How to choose anything when the range of options is huge and constantly changing and growing? Sartre, who insisted on the necessity of choice, also acknowledged that it was 'agony'. The price of autonomy is the agony of choice.

The psychologist Barry Schwartz has studied choice and reached sobering conclusions. We all believe we love choice and demand as much of it as possible but we actually hate having to choose. We demand the widest possible range of options but, in fact, the wider the range, the longer and more stressful the choosing and the lower the possibility of eventual satisfaction; we are exhausted by evaluating trade-offs and haunted by the missed opportunities of rejected alternatives. Frequently we become so confused that we no longer even want to make the choice – the fate of the holiday restaurant menu reader who is thrilled by the first menu, intrigued by the second, interested in the third . . . but by the tenth is too bewildered to decide and is no longer even hungry. And we prefer decisions on choice to be reversible but, in practice, we rarely reverse them and are nearly always less satisfied with a reversible choice.[186] This is evidence for Sartre's view that we can be happy only in finitude – making choice final and following through.

It is not surprising that our soft times have embraced a new theory on hard choices. Once, decision-making was understood to be entirely rational. Then it was shown to involve emotion. So now theory has gone to the opposite extreme with the claim (advanced in books such as *Blink* and *Gut Feelings*) that decision-making is entirely intuitive. This approach is obviously exciting for an age that hates to have to think – but it fails to acknowledge that intuition is itself the product of thought. The most rigorous analyst will also be the best intuitive judge, even if unable to explain the intuition. And the emphasis on gut feeling conveniently blurs the line between intuition (usually reliable) and impulse (usually unreliable). Other recent research on snap decisions suggests that they are less reliable than those based on rational deliberation.[187]

The only alternative to difficult thought is surrendering autonomy to a higher authority. This is the attraction of fundamentalism, which sheds the burden of freedom and eliminates the struggle to establish truth and meaning, much of the trauma of life's decision-making and all the anxiety of doubt. There is no solution as satisfactory and reassuring as God.

Directed thought is hard work but there is also a fun form of thinking – Hannah Arendt's 'thinking attention'. When thought has no specific goal, no urgent need of a conclusion, then thinking itself is the only end and uncertainty may not only be tolerated but relished, even treasured. Chuang Tzu, a Taoist from the fourth century BC: 'A sage steers by the bright light of confusion and doubt.'[188]

Even scientists are not exclusively concerned with absolute truth. Recently I watched a television documentary on gravity, which featured a physicist who, in a search for a highly elusive particle known as a graviton, had just spent eight years smashing matter by colliding it at high speed with other matter in a tunnel several kilometres long. At the end of this period there was so little sign of the graviton that the physicist was beginning to doubt its very existence and the theory on which this was based. Was he in despair at this disappointment, the waste of so much time and effort, the expense of building a huge tunnel in the Louisiana swampland? Not at all. Beaming with satisfaction, he chuckled, 'Scientists are happiest when they're confused.' Science is no different from any other human endeavour. It is the striving that matters, not the outcome. The search for meaning is itself the meaning.

Hannah Arendt argues (and herself italicises the passage to emphasise its importance): '*The need of reason is not inspired by the quest for truth but by the quest for meaning. And truth and meaning are not the same.*'[189] To oblige the mind to establish truth is to put it into harness and blinkers and whip it along the road to town. But the mind can also be allowed to roam free, in other words to speculate rather than to prove, to romp among the questions that can never be answered and so are usually dismissed as a waste of time by the practical: 'Behind all the cognitive questions for which men find answers, there lurk the unanswerable ones that seem entirely idle and have always been denounced as such. It is more likely that men, if they were ever to lose the appetite for meaning we call thinking and cease to ask unanswerable questions, would lose not only the ability to produce those thought-things that we call works of art but also the capacity to ask all the questions upon which civilisation is founded.'[190]

This kind of thinking is undirected, a form of pleasure in pure being, the mental equivalent of pleasure in the body. Aristotle considered such thinking divine: 'The activity of God, which is supremely happy, must be a form of contemplation; and therefore the human activity that is most like God's will be the happiest ... So happiness is the partner of contemplation.'[191] And, since God is tireless as well as omniscient and omnipotent, He did not need a seventh day in which to rest. No, He needed the seventh day for contemplation. He needed the seventh day in order to ruminate.

The benefits of rumination have been recognized by some therapists, for instance Anthony Storr, who treated depressives by encouraging them to practise what he described as 'active imagination'.[192] This is a kind of detached reverie, which benefits patients suffering from loss of identity as a result of too long and too complete immersion in the world. In the course of 'active imagination' they reconnect with aspects of their personalities that have been lost, develop an identity deeper than that required for the world – in other words a secret self – and frequently become less egotistical and less career-driven.

Storr spoke of a 'technique' but privacy is the only requirement – and even that may be snatched during a boring conversation or meeting. The idea is simply to free the brain network from distraction, then power it up and let it run to see what connections it can make. Of course, on bad days the network may refuse to power up because it is overwhelmed by practical issues, disabled by ill-health, paralysed by despair and dread or merely suffering from a hangover. At other times it thrums feebly to no apparent purpose. But, just as athletes know when they are 'in the zone', there are times when the network is perfectly attuned, is itself aware of this and hums with a thrilling vibrancy that promises imminent new connections, the winning combination when the dollar signs line up and the fruit machine shudders in ecstasy and coughs out a jackpot. This is the sublime eureka moment, the orgasm of the mind.

Like most thinkers before them, neuroscientists have been more interested in purposive thought, or the connections between thought and feeling and thought and memory. But recently they have taken an interest in the eureka phenomenon and sought insight on insight.[193]

Their conclusion is that the brain has two hemispheres, the left and the right, with very different functions, and that these are coordinated by the prefrontal cortex, the executive controller. The left brain is responsible for normal consciousness, the ceaseless babble of fretting and fussing over health, bills and career, and for many specific functions including language comprehension, visual processing and linear, rational thought. The right brain has fewer specific functions and a greater connexity that permits it to make new associations (including understanding themes, metaphors and jokes) and to see the big picture rather than the detail. So the left brain sees the trees and the right brain sees the forest. Or, the left brain is a nagging realist and the right a detached dreamer.

When a problem is solved by analysis it is probably the left brain that is doing the work. But, to facilitate insight, the prefrontal cortex must change strategy, order the left brain to shut up and set the right free to associate – a strange form of concentration that involves encouraging the mind to let go and wander. The brain must be entirely relaxed to make the connection that provides the insight – which is why insight rarely occurs when it is being consciously sought, but rather at some unexpected moment such as in the shower or at 4 a.m. on the way back to bed from a pee. And, if a winning combination comes up, the insight is immediately, blindingly, obvious, because it is recognized by the prefrontal cortex which lights up like a fairground. This also happens on recognition of someone else's insight, and the illumination of the prefrontal cortex stimulates the right brain to new understanding of past experience and new perceptions of future behaviour. An insight, one's own or another's, is a glorious flash of incandescence that lights up the brain and the universe, the self and the world, the past and the future – but, most of all, the sublime present.

Of course, original insights are rare, but, even without eureka moments, it is intensely pleasurable to silence the chattering, obsessive, nagging, humourless left brain and encourage the right brain to take over. This is surely what Spinoza meant by his many expressions of relish for the working of the mind: 'When the mind considers itself and its power, it rejoices, and rejoices the more, the more distinctly it imagines itself.'[194] And although such rumination can look like mere daydreaming, an escape from, or even denial of, real life, it is in fact the most profound expression of gratitude for life. Hannah Arendt does not often provide T-shirt maxims – but here is one: 'thinking is thanking'.[195]

The beauty of ruminating is that it requires no expertise or training, no ritual or jargon, no special location or conditions. It is possible to ruminate anywhere, at any time. Even solitude is not essential. I have ruminated successfully during meetings at work (though a sudden, unexpected question can be tricky). But, for best results, seek peace and quiet and a comfortable sofa. A view of a tree also helps – a single tree, exiled in the city, rooted in concrete, isolated and assailed by delinquent, spiteful urban wind, but taking this and making use of it to rustle, ripple, shimmy, sway.

9

The Atrophy of Experience

It is getting towards the end of the afternoon of a heavily overcast day at the end of November. Light has long since abandoned the struggle and the rain, which threatened all day but could never summon up the energy to fall, can only hang in damp irresolution in the grey. In the doorway of a dying business the proprietor looks out in resentment and bewilderment at a world that prefers supermarkets to the overpriced and understocked Dave's Deli. On the pavement before him schoolboys wrestle and shove, though without conviction, more from habit and a desire to postpone returning to dreary homes. Two mothers with pushchairs approach from opposite directions and come to a halt.

'It's closed,' says one in outrage. 'Some problem with the toilet. A health and safety thing. Don't know why they can't use the toilet in the main Centre.'

'They couldn't be bothered,' the second says peevishly. 'My Tyler is potty trained but he's always messing himself when he's there. I said to them, "He's potty trained but you need to remind him to go" and they said, "Why don't you remind him yourself?" I said, "What are drop-in staff for? I mean, what are they being paid for?"'

The other nods grimly. 'This is what you're up against.'

They fall silent, regarding the children so capriciously deprived of drop-in facilities. One is asleep and the other, though awake, slumps back and girns continuously, albeit in a low feeble tone without hope of salvation or even concern. Imperceptibly the sky darkens. But on the billboard across the street a handsome sports star lolls in a deckchair in bright sunshine, his sculpted-teak torso glistening with oil, golden thighs parted to present a substantial beasthood snug in tight white briefs.

As the November sky grows dark, a terrible truth becomes clear. Here, nothing is happening or going to happen. Life, in its radiance and glory, is off somewhere else.

Everyone has days like this – and for many it is November afternoon all year round. The feeling is of insubstantiality, impotence and worthlessness. The world becomes grey and dull and the buoyant heart turns to lead

One source of such feeling is habit. Repetition and familiarity deaden perception and diminish experience. The problem is that habits are necessary. Some, for instance the rituals of employment, are unavoidable. Others have to be adopted because no one is capable of constantly making it new. To live entirely without habit would be as terrible as living entirely within it.

But the contemporary dramatization of potential intensifies the devaluation of familiar experience. It was Schopenhauer who first perceived the tendency to live, without being aware if it, in a constant expectation that is endlessly disappointed and endlessly renewed – and he understood how such an attitude makes it difficult to appreciate the present.

The siren voices of the age exacerbate this tendency to live in expectation – which runs forever ahead of realization like the hare at the racetrack pursued by slavering dogs that never catch it up or recognize it as a fake. It is increasingly difficult to avoid being constantly distracted by anticipation. Desires are ever more quickly forgotten, annulled by gratification or habit and overwritten by urgent new wants. It takes an enormous effort to recall why something was coveted so desperately. I spent many years in second-level teaching aching to move up to the third level, to the reduced timetable, longer holidays and increased intellectual satisfactions of university teaching. And, of course, snobbery was also involved. I yearned for the status of lecturer and grieved at the ignominy of being a mere teacher. But, when I finally moved up, more by luck than application, the wonder of this civilized new world began to wear off after a year or two and I found myself whingeing with everyone else about the laziness of the students, the venality of the management and the relentlessly increasing admin burden. It took a conscious and prolonged effort to recall the desire that had been so constant and intense and to realize that the reasons for this desire remained valid. *I had been taken up into paradise.*

And direct experience is also devalued by the many opportunities to live at a meta-level. Thanks to technology it is now possible to meet, befriend, have sex with, work for and kill people without ever having laid eyes on them. This diminishes reality and encourages delusion. It is not surprising that, given also the contemporary emphasis on potential and expectation, there is increasing recourse to fantasy.

Of course, Hollywood has been selling fantasy for almost a century but, whereas in the past the movies featured something like real people in an approximation of the real world, the trend now is for comic-book characters and imaginary worlds, as in the *Star Wars*, *Lord of the Rings* and *Narnia* series. The conclusion is that film fans would be happy in the known world if they could be superheroes but, otherwise, would like to go through the back of a wardrobe into an entirely new world.

Another significant development is the huge and continuing growth in user-directed fantasy through computer games, which encourage the gamer to blow away legions of badasses, and websites where it is possible to enjoy sex in a new custom-built body and genitals. The aim of 1970s' liberation was to become one's self – but, since this has proved to be unexpectedly difficult, the new liberation is to become someone else.

The enormous revenues from the games industry have guaranteed its respectability, with prestigious universities providing degrees in games programming, and serious newspapers reviewing new games as solemnly as art-house movies from European auteurs (the quality most prized seems to be 'immersiveness', which is the ability of a game to distract from real life). Apart from sport, children's games and movie tie-ins, these games are mostly based on fantasies of power, violence and destruction, with the weapons of choice usually swords or machine pistols (though 'innovative slaying' is also admired and one *Guardian* reviewer was greatly impressed by a game hero with a chainsaw instead of a right arm).

So there are sword fantasies (*Broken Sword: The Shadow of the Templars, Prince of Persia: Rival Swords, Dragon Swords*), war fantasies (*Warlords Battlecry, Warhammer, Dawn of War*), omnipotence fantasies (*Dark Messiah of Might and Magic, Overlord, Demigod*), revenge fantasies (*Dark Vengeance, Command and Conquer 3: Kane's Wrath, Assassin's Creed*) and, of course, end-of-civilization fantasies (*Resistance: Fall of Man, Mortal Kombat: Armageddon* and *Eternal Darkness: Sanity's Requiem*).

But this is the age of collaboration so, for those requiring more authentic interaction, the next step is websites such as World of Warcraft where 'in Azeroth the Horde and the Alliance are locked in a struggle for control' and users join one of the races of the Horde (Orcs, Tauren, Trolls, Undead, Blood Elves) or the Alliance (Humans, Dwarves, Gnomes, Night Elves, Draenei) and set about whacking as many as possible of the enemy. Getting whacked oneself is of course never a problem. 'Death has no lasting consequences. You will immediately be able to release your spirit as a ghost, at which point you will be transported to a nearby graveyard where you must run back to your corpse to revive yourself.'

If fantasy sex is more exciting than violence, there is the passive option of pornography, now widely available and often free, or the interactive option of websites such as Second Life, where users can create a new existence with an open-plan beach house on a tropical island and, of course, a comic-book glamour body – youthful, slender, tall, narrow-waisted, broad-shouldered or basketball-breasted as appropriate – skimpily clad to display these assets, and adorned with exciting accessories such as tattoos and piercings for her, and, for him, perhaps a samurai sword and a couple of Uzi machine pistols. I have often wondered why fantasy so often combines the extremely primitive and the ultra-advanced, a weird pick 'n' mix of medieval and space age, but it must be because both offer escape from the contemporary world – they are pre- or post-civilization. So, no one in Second Life is over forty, short, fat, afflicted by skin or teeth problems, short-sighted, lame or bald. In this dream world there is only one real thing – the money needed to purchase the fakery. The default 'avatars' have no sexual equipment and the must-have accessory of a virtual penis costs $5. I would have undertaken fieldwork but for the constant need to apologise for having no genitals.

But what is wrong with indulging in a little harmless fantasy now and then? For Kierkegaard the desire to become someone else was a symptom of the most extreme despair.[196] And this extreme despair is a modern phenomenon. In traditional societies life was entirely determined by gender and class. There was no possibility of becoming someone else, so no one dreamed of it. But the continuing development of individual freedom has encouraged the notion that anyone can be anything. Even gender has become a matter of choice, and celebrity has now been decoupled from the tiresome prerequisites of talent and hard work. There appear to be no barriers to a more exciting and fulfilling life. And the images of such apparently fulfilling and exciting lives are everywhere. So the temptation to fantasize is overwhelming. But indulging in fantasy exacerbates the very despair it is meant to assuage. Reality and the self are so disappointing that they encourage escape – but the fantasy makes reality seem even more disappointing and intensifies the need to escape. This is why fantasy is so addictive. Millions of people now spend up to fourteen hours a day on games or fantasy websites.

Second Life is certainly the only place where two heterosexual men can enjoy a lesbian affair – but the saddest aspect of the fantasy world is that it is coming to resemble the real world. Apparently, Second Life subscribers are becoming bored with fantasy sex on the 'mature' islands and increasingly turning instead to business – selling virtual land, homes, accessories and services. So the fake lesbians are increasingly outnumbered by the real capitalists fleecing the fantasists, just as they do in reality. As if anyone needed *virtual* estate agents! The only encouraging news is the appearance of a rival website called Get a First Life, which offers radical advice such as 'Fornicate with your actual genitals'.

Sometimes the virtual lovers attempt this. A woman meets a man in the new ballroom of romance, an internet dating site, and they fall in love and gambol for a time in the enchanted glades of cyberspace. Of course, these are two mature people with many failed relationships behind them so they are taking no chances. They have examined each other naked by webcam, with close-ups of both sets of genitals. And they have established that both sets are in working order. She has brought herself to climax with a vibrator on camera and he has jerked off to the performance. Finally, they agree that they are perfectly matched and agree to meet in real life. She chooses Waterloo station, not because it is convenient, but because it is the most romantic place for lovers to meet. He will, of course, arrive bearing sixteen white roses and she will be waiting in new lingerie from Agent Provocateur. Everything is perfect. No – there is one terrible omission. As the woman laments to a friend, 'If only we had someone to *film* us meeting.'

In the modern world, an event has not really happened unless it has been photographed or filmed. This failure of primary experience means that the photograph or the film becomes the reality instead. One of the earliest examples of this was after the first moon landing when the astronauts had returned safely to earth and, after the debriefing, emerged to learn of the media frenzy surrounding the event. Buzz Aldrin, who had just been one of the two men to walk on the moon, turned to his fellow moon-walker Neil Armstrong and wailed, 'Neil, we missed the whole thing.'[197]

The tyranny of screen life is becoming total. Screens are ever larger, with ever higher definition, and becoming ever more numerous and widespread, colonizing more and more public space, and constantly reinforcing the suspicion that life is else-where. The reality on screens is infinitely more real than the reality around them and the screen people more real than the viewers absorbed in them. There is something unassailable about images on a screen. And, as the screens become larger and brighter, their viewers become smaller and duller. Finally the viewers are like the inhabitants of Plato's cave: shadowy creatures in a permanent gloom, with true perfection only in the bright world on screen.

As well as growing larger, screens are also becoming smaller. The mobile, personal screen was an inevitable development. As well as personal phones and music players, people need personal screens – and the three will soon converge into a single gadget. Already there are screens embedded in eyeglasses and the techies predict that there will soon be screens embedded in nanobots on contact lenses, operated by eye movements. What hope for poor reality when Disney World is not only in your line of vision or even in your face but *permanently camped on your eyeballs?*

Screen images are vibrant, dynamic, bright, rapidly changing. Reality is moribund, static, dull and shuffles along on odorous, misshapen, sore feet. So, to be truly real, it is necessary to become an image. Only those who appear on screens truly exist.

All screen behaviour is heightened. The crises in the soaps are more intense and dramatic, the laughter in the sitcoms more fre-quent and hysterical, the banter of the chat-show hosts more relentless and bright, the concern of the reporters in famine-stricken Africa more grave, the outrage of the interviewers at venality more righteous. Even the ordinariness of the ordinary people on screen becomes a heightened ordinariness – they are radiantly ordinary, attractively unattractive and eloquently banal.

But the crucial difference is that screen life is faster than real life and, with ever more frenetic editing, is becoming faster all the time. Screen changes happen much more rapidly than in reality and each triggers the orientation response to a possibly dangerous new environment, interrupting attention to establish new bearings.[198] The response is physiological and lasts from four to six seconds – but advertisements, music videos and action dramas trigger it every second so there is never time for the brain and body to recover equilibrium. The system is in a permanent state of red alert. This is why it is difficult to tear your eyes away from a screen and dauntingly difficult to switch off a television. The long-term consequences are that it becomes difficult to pay attention to anything static, slow moving or requiring prolonged concentration on a single topic or task. And, of course, reality becomes impossibly sluggish and dull.

Experience is nothing other than what we decide to attend to, so the quality of experience depends on the quality of attention. But passive, stimulus-driven attention tends to notice only the most dramatic details – the bright colours and loud bangs – whereas active purposeful attention, the Buddhist practice of mindfulness, is more likely to register an entire scene. There is evidence that cultural conditioning has created Eastern and Western forms of attention. When Americans and Japanese were asked to study an underwater environment for twenty seconds and then describe what they had seen, the Americans said things like 'big blue fish', and the Japanese 'flowing water, rocks, plants and fish'.[199] The Eastern reality was wider, fuller and richer.

TV news also diminishes reality. Back in the 1930s cultural critic Walter Benjamin observed that modern man was 'increasingly unable to assimilate the data of the world around him by way of experience'.[200] The novelty, brevity and unconnected nature of news items in the daily press made it impossible for them to enter tradition, and Benjamin described the consequence as 'the atrophy of experience'. How quaint to be alarmed by newspapers! What would he have made of ubiquitous screens with rolling twenty-four-hour news?

As Benjamin implied, the breakdown of traditional communities, with their rituals to give the year structure and meaning and their webs of close connections to provide rich human contact, has also greatly impoverished experience. It is easy to become nostalgic for communities, but necessary also to remember why people were so desperate to break out of them. When I was growing up in a traditional society I could hardly wait to escape the boredom, oppression and conformity. But there is no doubt that an independent life involves a significant loss of richness. There is always a price to pay. Freedom is thin.

What communities once provided as the reward for conformity, the free individual now has to earn. So how to enrich thin experience and re-enchant the dull world?

Walter Benjamin offered a contrast to ephemeral news items, 'the story, which is one of the oldest forms of communication. It is not the object of the story to convey a happening *per se*, which is the purpose of information; rather, it embeds it in the life of the storyteller in order to pass it on as experience to those listening.'[201] Benjamin was referring to traditional storytelling – but this tradition is alive and well in literature.

Literary reading revitalizes personal experience by revealing that what appeared so drab and dreary was in fact mysterious and extraordinary – and it provides new experience by communicating life in a way that feels as though it has actually been lived. And not only does it renew past experience, its urgent command to pay attention, like the Buddhist concept of mindfulness, makes the present incomparably richer. And reading, though solitary, does not imply a rejection of others. Again, detachment, paradoxically, brings deeper engagement. Reading increases empathy, and therefore compassion and patience, by inspiring understanding for unsympathetic and even atrocious characters. And it creates a new network of intimate friends, the writers. Finally, last but by no means least, reading is itself a significant experience.

In the last century the two great enrichers of experience were James Joyce and Marcel Proust. Joyce recreated the strange texture of everyday life and Proust revealed its equally strange psychology. One of Proust's major themes was the psychology of expectation and disappointment. So the narrator of *À la recherche du temps perdu* lives an endless cycle of feverish desire and anticipation followed by disillusionment and despair.

The society world of Proust is now as lost and remote to us as the civilization of the Incas but the narrator's lifestyle is strikingly contemporary – networking, parties, infatuations, casual sex, capriciousness, impulse buying, celebrity worship and celebrity stalking. And the aristocrats, whose company the narrator craves, are the precise equivalent of the modern celebrity, special only by being thought special, living entirely in a bizarre, enclosed world designed to pander to their narcissism, violently glamorous from a distance and utterly tawdry at close range.

Proust is also one of the funniest writers. Better still, he is funny not by exaggeration, by resorting to caricature and farce (the laziest and most common approach to comic writing), but by concentrating intensely on what people actually do and say. The satirical scenes in the society salons have the ferocious accuracy that causes winces and groans along with the laughs because the failings are so recognizable. This was Proust's avowed aim: 'In reality, each reader is reading his own self. The writer's work is merely a kind of optical instrument which enables the reader to discern what, without this book, he would possibly never have experienced in himself. And the recognition by the reader in his own self of what the book says is the proof of its truth.'[202]

The beauty of lessons learned in this way is that they are absorbed more fully than by abstract instruction. After reading Proust you know, in the marrow of your bones, in your DNA, the craziness and absurdity of living perpetually in expectation.

But the novel which does most to re-enchant everyday life is

Joyce's *Ulysses*. As Proust's intention was to make every reader an interpreter of his own self, so Joyce's intention was to transform every reader's insignificant days into adventures as strange, rich, heroic and mythical as those in Homer – to turn every day into an Odyssey. Firstly, the stream-of-consciousness technique revealed the richness of the average ruminating mind with its endless flickering phantasmagoria of observation, perception, memory, imagination and desire. Then the inclusiveness of Joyce's vision and the beauty of his style lifted up into literature much that had previously been rejected as too boring or sordid. Even now, almost a century after it was written, there are scenes in *Ulysses* which startle by the ordinariness of their everyday squalor. Even in the age when anything goes, few novelists would devote several pages of loving attention to a man reading *Titbits* on the toilet: 'Quietly he read, restraining himself, the first column and, yielding but resisting, began the second. Midway, his last resistance yielding, he allowed his bowels to ease themselves quietly as he read, reading still patiently, that slight constipation of yesterday quite gone. Hope it's not too big to bring on piles again. No, just right.'[203]

We all yearn for renewal but imagine that it may be found only in novelty – a new place, a new lover, a new job. More effective, and much cheaper, is to see the familiar with new eyes. And a few writers offer just such transfiguring eyes. They smash the crust of habit and permit us to see life anew. In the contemporary world, such crust-smashing is both more difficult and more necessary. Once there was no crust at all and most people were exposed to hunger, cold, disease and violence. Experience was unavoidably immediate and real. But now most are increasingly protected from the old dangers, and the new danger is that, as the crust becomes thicker and stronger, the life it shelters is more likely to wither and die in its shell.

So seek out the crust-breakers and the eye-openers. Read authentic writers – and then begin a new job in your current post, enjoy a holiday where you actually live and, most thrillingly, plunge into a tumultuous affair with your own spouse.

Of course, it is true that writers like Proust and Joyce are difficult – but it is also true that difficulty increases satisfaction. Reading is always assumed to be easy because the technique learned so long ago has been forgotten and we now do it unthinkingly all the time. So, if a book appears too difficult, it must be the fault of the book rather than the reader. But, like learning to play a musical instrument, reading is a skill with levels of difficulty. What makes Proust and Joyce seem hard work is the absence of plot, the device most novelists use to drive readers forwards through a book. Plots are effective – everyone wants to know what happens next – but the *dénouement* of plot-driven novels is often implausible and disappointing. *Is that all it was?* This is because there are no plots in real life – only a complex web of continuum and connexity – so the reader has the unpleasant sensation of having been conned. And plots are instantly forgettable. Try explaining the plot of the thriller you read only last week. The pleasure of plot is all expectation and sensation, illusory and short-lived, so plot-driven novels leave no residue of beauty. Whereas a novel that reproduces the texture and feeling of life will be harder to read, but provide richer satisfactions and live longer in the memory. The bad news is that such novels are rare. Proust and Joyce showed how to succeed triumphantly without plot but this lesson has been forgotten by the age of potential. It is common now for reviewers to rate novels as 'well plotted' or 'poorly plotted', as though plot is an essential feature, and to express astonishment and consternation at the absence of plot.

So literary reading can deepen and extend experience by improving understanding of the self, the world and other people. One of the greatest gifts in a writer is the ability to create characters who behave atrociously but are entirely sympathetic. The supreme example is Falstaff, who is a compendium of everything most contemptible in human nature – he is a thief, a coward, a liar, a braggart, a glutton, a drunkard and, worst of all, a callous mercenary happy to send men to their deaths for money. Yet everyone loves him. As an exercise in intellectual and moral discipline, I once listed Falstaff's faults before going to see *Henry IV: Part II* and was determined to disapprove but, like everyone else, laughed and loved the old reprobate. And when Prince Hal was about to become king and rejected his former drinking companion as, of course, was essential – such a corrupt man could never be allowed anywhere near power – like everyone else I ached for poor Falstaff and loathed Hal for being a cold-hearted prig. Hal's six words of rejection are among the most grievous in literature: 'I know thee not, old man.'[204]

So, although there can be no prescriptions for writing, as there can be none for living, here is a prescription nevertheless. A work of fiction should be plotless but compelling, surprising but inevitable and full of appalling characters who are entirely sympathetic.

And there is such sensuous pleasure in lifting a book in the left hand to feel the satisfactory heft, then allowing it to fall voluptuously open and release its unique fragrance, and finally taking a group of pages in the right hand and allowing them to riffle past the right thumb, with a pause now and then to permit the leisurely perusal of a random page. This is the sovereign, ruminating pleasure of the sultan. And the reading itself is as sensuous. Reading is a contact sport – physical, strenuous, a grappling with another of superior strength, trickery and speed. Another who may become a close friend. Postmodernism attempted to remove authors and make literature only a set of 'texts' – but true readers agree with Proust that reading is friendship. Writers are such friends, a secret social network extending throughout time and space.

And the stereotype of the reader as a dysfunctional, short-sighted, body-hating, effete wimp unable to face the world is disproved by the regular and extensive surveys of readers carried out by the National Endowment for the Arts in the USA. According to the NEA, readers are more likely than non-readers to take exercise, become actively involved in sport, go to museums, theatres and concerts, engage in voluntary work and vote in elections.[205] The beauty of the contact sport of reading, according to Proust, is that this form of contact provides the benefits of conversation with none of the tedium, because it is 'a communication with another way of thinking, all the while remaining alone, that is, while continuing to enjoy the intellectual power that one has in solitude and that conversation dissipates immediately'.[206] It is an encounter of depth with depth, undistracted by social conventions and froth, and more rewarding than any encounter in the flesh (which is why meeting writers is usually disappointing).

This is also why skipping is acceptable but skimming is not. Skipping is disengaging for a breather, but skimming means that the challenge is proving inadequate, that the contact is with a superficial, lazy, coarse, uninteresting mind. Any book that encourages skimming should be immediately thrown away. And our brains seem to understand this. Brief skim-reading causes more severe eye strain than long, concentrated reading.

The reading experience has been investigated by neuroscientists, who also seem to have a thing for Proust. There is even a book called *Proust was a Neuroscientist*.[207] And, in *Proust and the Squid*, Maryanne Wolf explains that reading, unlike speech and vision, is not genetically programmed and therefore must be learned by each individual, and that this learning process creates in the brain distinctive connections, which depend on the language used. Doctors treating a stroke victim bilingual in English and Chinese found that, as a consequence of specific brain damage, the patient could no longer read English but could still read Chinese. So, in a real, even physical, sense, 'we are what we read'. And, when children are learning to read, major areas of both brain hemispheres are involved but, as reading skill improves, activity is mostly concentrated in a small area of the left hemisphere, though the right may be activated anywhere in unpredictable ways. In other words, the left hemisphere develops a dedicated reading function and the more parallel right hemisphere, which produces insights, is set free to speculate and associate, to romp and gambol like the mind of God. 'The secret at the heart of reading,' Wolf concludes, is 'the time it frees for the brain to have thoughts deeper than those which came before'. And the problem with skimming is that it loses this 'associative dimension', 'the profound generativity of the reading brain'.[208]

This potential for 'Aha!' insight distinguishes reading from viewing. The pace of reading may be varied by the reader, but the pace of viewing is set by an editor (and this editing has become increasingly frenetic). Viewers do not have the luxury of looking raptly into the far distance while the right brain performs its associative magic. If they hold a screen on pause, it is usually to get another beer from the fridge.

Deep reading creates attentiveness; heavy viewing destroys it. And this may have consequences at both ends of life. In early childhood, heavy viewing inhibits the development of brain networks for attention and reflection[209], and heavy viewing in later life encourages brain deterioration and Alzheimer's disease.[210]

So, reading is not only intensely pleasurable in itself, but is also crucial in developing and maintaining the associative brain. And it is so much more satisfying if it also enhances experience. Flaubert: 'Do not read as do children, to amuse yourself or, like the ambitious, for the purpose of instruction. No, read in order to *live*.'[211]

10

The Loss of Transcendence

Unusually for an ageing rocker, Bruce Springsteen has retained both creative and performing vitality so that his new songs are as good as his classics and he belts them out for a generous three hours with undiminished gusto and relish. But the young couple next to me sit in what appears to be frozen misery. In the row in front, four men suddenly stand up and leave with grim I-demand-to-see-the-manager expressions. Are these people genuinely disappointed? What more could they want? And those who appear to be still in good humour talk, laugh and drink beer all through the performance, as though they are out for the evening in a bar and the music is on a high screen in a distant corner. It is true that The Boss is indeed a long way off – this is a stadium concert – but, of the many thousands standing in the playing area, closer to the stage and with plenty of free space, few are disposed to dance. Compare and contrast this with the early days of rock and roll when audiences went crazy, smashed up theatres and ran riot in the streets. This evening is summed up by a family a few rows in front, all with bleached blonde hair and new designer leisurewear, who are entirely ignoring the performance to photograph each other on mobile-phone cameras.

It is easy to understand why so many commentators talk of the flattening tendency of contemporary culture. Constant exposure to entertainment has left many incapable of sustained interest, never mind transcendence.

And there is an equivalent indifference in high culture, caused by the neutralising effects of relativism, which makes everything equally meaningful and therefore equally meaningless. To praise writers, musicians or artists extravagantly is considered naive, childish, certainly embarrassing. For a critic to express simple liking would be unforgivably gauche. In popular culture the tyranny of cool has the same deterrent effect. The language is different but the strategy is the same – to pass off indifference as the height of sophistication. Enthusiasm is not acceptable because it is an affront to indifference.

As well as chronic general indifference there is chronic general ingratitude – an inevitable consequence of the era of entitlement. If everything is deserved there is no reason to be grateful. Yet gratitude is the basis for affirmation and transcendence.

But what *is* transcendence? The term covers a wide range of imprecisely defined and overlapping beliefs, feelings, attitudes and states, including religious faith, mysticism, exaltation, joy, ecstasy, zest and delight, on down to humble enthusiasm and absorption, and then right down to drinking a pitcher of margaritas and dancing on the table on Saturday night.

The common factor in various forms of the feeling is escape from the self – and this can range from a spiritual desire to lose yourself in God to a more materialistic desire to get out of your head at weekends. The paradox is that the most intense experience of the self is loss of the self. This is why transcendent states have to be short-lived. Being out of your head is fun but not practical – and the longer you stay out the harder it is to get back in. So, the more intense the experience, the shorter the duration. Low-level loss of self in absorption can last for hours; ecstasy is sadly brief (though adepts of tantric sex may disagree).

Transcendence is important because it seems to be necessary to escape every now and then from the burden of self-consciousness. Even the earliest cultures sought this escape. In 'primitive' societies around the world there were remarkably similar rituals involving face painting and group dancing to rhythmic accompaniment.[212] Complicated circle and line dances were especially common – and it is heartening to know that, when my in-laws have one of their 'big nights' culminating in the hokey-cokey and a conga, I am participating in a ritual at least ten thousand years old. Western observers of the 'primitive' dances were often alarmed by what they interpreted as abandonment and frenzy intended to work up a mood for orgies – but most of the rituals were carefully planned, tightly disciplined, chaste and took place only at certain periods in the calendar as a reward for community endeavour. Primitive cultures understood that there were no easy, free highs. The ecstasy had to be learned and earned.

In Europe this ritual ecstasy persisted into the carnivals of the Middle Ages but was ruthlessly suppressed by both Calvinism and the Counter-Reformation. Dancing, originally a group practice, diminished to an activity for couples in the nineteenth century and by the late twentieth century was almost entirely a solo performance. Now you have to become your own shaman and invent your own shamanic dance.

In the modern world theistic religion became the acceptable form of transcendence – and when this faded in the twentieth century there was the secular religion of international socialism. But it has become increasingly difficult to believe in a paradise above the world or a Utopia ahead of it.

An alternative is to locate the transcendent ideal not above or ahead but in the world itself – pantheism. To escape the wrath of the faithful, pantheism has often pretended to be a version of monotheism – but it is essentially pagan. For instance, the Sufi tradition, a version of Islam that flourished in Persia at the end of the first millennium CE and still has a contemporary presence, justified its pantheism by claiming that God created the world in order to be known through it, explaining to His prophet, 'I was a Hidden Treasure and I desired to be known, so I made the

Creature that I might be known.'[213] Perhaps craving for recognition is not so modern after all – God may have created the world to be worshipped as the ultimate celebrity. For the Sufis, everything in the world was an epiphany and the world was not merely enchanted but divine – a belief that inspired the poet Jelaluddin Rumi to create the dance of the whirling dervishes and poetry with an equivalent wildness.

> There's a light seed grain inside.
> You fill it with yourself, or it dies.
>
> I'm caught in this curling energy! Your hair!
> Whoever's calm and sensible is insane.[214]

Spinoza was also a pantheist and spoke of 'that eternal and infinite being we call God or Nature'[215], though 'God' may have been added to the phrase to placate believers. And poets from Wordsworth to Rilke have espoused forms of secular pantheism, which inspires the most ecstatic affirmation, because the escape from self is into a mystical unity with everything.

The most intense and lasting forms of happiness seem to derive from pantheism. I should found a Church of Latter-day Pantheists with, as prophets, Rumi, Spinoza, Wordsworth and Rilke. This religion would have the advantage of constant, serious difficulty. No one would find it easy to feel divine presence in a multiplex foyer or a departure lounge – and only Rumi himself could believe the Beloved immanent in a shopping mall. These places are more likely to encourage a Manichean belief in man as a fallen creature and the world as the realm of eternal darkness.

Naturally, our own age prefers the fast and easy route to transcendence – drugs. According to neuroscience, the problem is that the feel-good drugs – cannabis, cocaine, heroin, Ecstasy – do not replicate exactly a natural high, but produce equivalent effects by prolonging or suppressing other effects, and these prolongations and suppressions permanently damage the brain network.[216] The minor short-term gains result in major long-term losses – a physiological demonstration of the truth that there is no easy, free way to paradise. On the other hand, the earned, natural highs create beneficial new associations that endure.

The other popular form of transcendence – falling in love – is also believed to produce a high without effort, but it, too, has long-term complications (see Chapter 12 for details).

For me, as a non-believer, the high of highs is exaltation, better even than sexual ecstasy, though this is a close-run thing. Fortunately, these two supreme excellences are not mutually exclusive. It may even be possible to experience both simultaneously, and those blessed with such grace will not only mystically merge in the Great Chain of Being but also be one with God in eternity and paradise.

But exaltation is elusive and rare, one of a group of heightened experiences that includes artistic inspiration, epiphany (in the sense of a mystical but secular significance, as described by Joyce and Proust), insight, problem solving and intuition. These experiences cannot be willed, arrive abruptly out of the blue, provide absolute certainty though no explanation, and are intensely pleasurable but brief. They seem entirely random and gratuitous – but the apparently unearned gift is usually the reward for persistent hard work and patience. For artistic inspiration this hard work is the discipline of learning and practising the craft. For insight and problem solving it is prolonged but unconscious thought. For intuition it is observation and analysis of experience. For epiphany it is the habit of intense attentiveness to the physical world. But what prepares the mind for exaltation, an experience that provides the ecstasy of revelation without a revelation? My hypothesis is that the brain offers exaltation as a reward for previous endeavours – a sort of buy-six-get-one-free loyalty-card deal. In return for concentration in the past, the brain will grant the eureka feeling without a eureka product. So, in a way, even exaltation has to be earned.

Naturally, the era of entitlement would like a longer-lasting version of the experience at no cost. And an American neuro-scientist, Jill Bolte Taylor, did indeed have such a durable experience, though it was not exactly free.[217] One morning she woke up in a mood of extreme euphoria. This was the good news. The bad news was that she was also partially paralysed and incapable of speech. She had just suffered a stroke that knocked out her left-brain hemisphere but left the right side unimpaired. This left hemisphere operates more serially, is responsible for analysing the past and preparing for the future, and maintains the constant brain chatter that constitutes consciousness. So the stroke provided Taylor with natural transcendence, taking her out of the self by disabling the brain site of the self. The right hemisphere, until recently thought to be purposeless and inert, processes information in a more parallel way and provides coherence and meaning for the sensory data of the present. It is this combination of lighter workload and greater ability to make new connections that allows the right side to produce mystical experience, epiphany, inspiration, insight and intuition. And the fact that the right side also processes sensory data from immedi-ate surroundings means that the eureka incandescence can also make the outside world sublimely vivid. This is why mystical experiences are so similar to inspiration and insight and why the more intense the experience the stronger the accompanying pan-theistic awe. Taylor described her euphoria as a profound sense of unity with all things.

But, as her left brain responded to her recovery regime, it reactivated the circuits for negative left-brain emotions such as anxiety, fearfulness, envy, resentment and anger. As psy-chologists have discovered, these are more powerful than positive emotions. But Taylor was not prepared to surrender her new-found sense of oneness and well-being and fought to suppress the mean left-brain effects, arriving, via a stroke and neuroscience, at a conclusion reached by the Stoics several thousand years earlier: 'Nothing external to me had the power to take away my peace of heart and mind . . . I may not be in total control of what happens, but I certainly am in charge of how I choose to perceive my experience.'[218] Her technique is to permit these instinctive reactions of the old reptilian brain their natural ninety seconds of life, but then to use detachment and analysis to identify them and prevent them from colonizing her mind. And she adds that, when she tries to teach her students this technique, they complain vehemently that it requires far too much mental effort – another example of the rejection of difficulty.

Taylor's reaction to her misfortune is also the classic Stoic strategy of turning to advantage whatever happens. She is probably the only stroke victim to enthuse about the experience. But how to liberate the right brain without being paralysed by a left-brain stroke?

One possibility is meditation. There have been several brain-scan studies of experienced meditators and the research teams have reached similar conclusions – meditation increases activity in the prefrontal cortex, the executive controller responsible for focussing and maintaining attention, and decreases activity in the left brain.[219] But there is no mention of increased right-side activity (although meditators themselves have often spoken of heightened awareness of immediate surroundings). This may be because meditators focus intensely on a single thing – a mantra, an image, breathing – and succeed in suppressing the fretting self on the left, but fail to make use of the liberated dreamer on the right. So rumination may be meditation plus, not only a curtailment of the nag but an encouragement of the dreamer. If I devised a suitable ritual and jargon I could make my fortune as a guru peddling Transcendental Rumination (TR).

Another possibility is that, if transcendence is accompanied by here-and-now oneness, then the reverse may also be true, and paying intense attention to the immediate environment may facilitate lift-off. This is the kind of attentiveness encouraged by writers like Joyce and Proust.

For those of an active disposition, or those who distrust anything mystical and aesthetic, there is a lower-level transcendence of self in absorption.

The American psychologist Mihaly Csikszentmihalyi uses the term 'flow' to describe a deeply satisfying state of mind achieved by intense and prolonged concentration on difficult activities requiring a high level of skill.[220] The experience is similar for a wide range of apparently unrelated activities, including competitive sport, mountain-climbing, professional work, playing an instrument, artistic creativity, dancing, martial arts and sex. Again the phenomenon is well known and really only a special case of happiness as by-product.

As with other methods of transcendence, this satisfaction has to be earned. Skill must first be acquired, slowly and frustratingly. There is no immediate gratification. Indeed, there may never be any. The learner may not have the aptitude or the discipline. But when the skill becomes automatic the miracle may occur – an absorption so complete that it shuts out self, place and time. Hours, even days, can go by unremarked. The self dissolves and disappears. And something strange happens. The activity seems to become not only effortless but *autonomous* – to take over, to assume control, to be running itself. So the musical instrument plays itself, the sword wields itself, the poem writes itself, the dancer does not so much dance as permit music to enter and take over the body, and the lovers do not so much make love as surrender to the vertiginous movement of the earth.

There are many paradoxes in this. Intense effort is needed to produce the sensation of effortlessness, intense consciousness to lead to unconsciousness, total control to experience the total absence of control. And only those fully in possession of the self can fully surrender it. In fact, the stronger the sense of self, the greater the rapture in escaping its tyranny.

As in meditation, the flow experience is a consequence of persistent, concentrated attention – and 'attention' is a key word both for Csikszentmihalyi and Zen Buddhism. The concept of flow is also familiar to Zen. Here is D.T. Suzuki, explaining how the master swordsman Takuan instructed novices: 'Takuan's advice is concerned with keeping the mind always in the state of "flowing", for when it stops the flow is interrupted and this interruption is injurious to the well-being of the mind. In the case of a swordsman it means death.'[221]

This repeated intense focus on a difficult activity is exactly what creates or enhances brain connections. And the pleasure of the flow high is so intense that it reduces the attractions of power, status and celebrity and, above all, of passive entertainment, encouraging instead a desire to experience a similar satisfaction in other activities. This is why theoretical physicists play the bongo drums.

The trick is to understand that the attention and difficulty are what bring the reward. When Csikszentmihalyi surveyed teenagers, he discovered that those with least flow activity, who watched lots of television and hung out in shopping malls, also scored lowest on all satisfaction ratings, whereas those who studied or engaged in sports scored highly on every rating – or on all except one. They believed that the mall rats and couch potatoes were having more fun, too influenced by the tyranny of cool to realize that they themselves were the blessed. This is an instance of a general rule – youth rarely realizes the value of what it has.

And how thrilling to learn, from another of Csikszentmihalyi's surveys, that the more expensive, bulky and complex the hobby equipment, the less enjoyable the hobby. Perhaps there is a just God after all. Much more satisfying are walking and dancing, where the body is its own equipment and instrument. Walking and dancing, rhythm regular and ecstatic, the prose and poetry of the body.

The humblest flow activity, walking, is also an effective way of creating readiness for exaltation. There is a theory that bipedalism is the source of the superior human intelligence. When the human animal got up on its hind legs, the front legs became free for gesturing, which evolved into sign language and eventually speech – and this rich new verbal language massively increased brain size. Certainly, using the four limbs as pistons seems to fire up the brain.

Nietzsche, the philosopher of exaltation, was a fanatical walker. So was his arch-enemy Christ. Only the iconography shows Christ at rest; Leonardo da Vinci has him seated at the Last Supper – but a good teacher never sits. He would have been moving round with a word of reassurance here and a word of inspiration there. And most representations of the Sermon on the Mount show the customary static pose with sorrowful eyes and submissively out-stretched arms. But Pier Paolo Pasolini's film *The Gospel According to St Matthew* has Christ storming up the hill throwing freshly minted beatitudes over his shoulder to disciples scrambling, both physically and mentally, to keep up. Not the Sermon on the Mount but the Sermon on the Hoof.

Nietzsche often walked for six to eight hours a day and had some of his best insights on these walks. And he was also obsessed by dancing: 'I could believe only in a God who knew how to dance.'[222] Nietzsche himself regretted that he was unable to boogie: 'I know how to utter the parable of the highest things only in dance – and now my greatest parable has remained unspoken in my limbs.'[223] And he described himself as the last disciple of the philosopher Dionysus, the horned god of ecstasy and original Lord of the Dance, the presiding deity of early rituals and worshipped under a variety of names including Bacchus, Pan, Faunus, Osiris and Shiva. Dionysus (known in Ireland as Satan) even turned up near my hometown in the 1960s – in a dance hall, of course. An ordinary Saturday night in the Mecca was galvanized by the appearance of a strikingly handsome stranger, dressed all in black, who could jive with astoundingly languid ease. All the women yearned to be with him; of course, he chose the most lovely. This girl danced all night in ecstasy and agreed to go out-side but, as they were leaving, glanced down and saw, just in the nick of time, *the cloven hoof*. There could be no mistaking the iden-tity of the stranger. Though, when I heard the story I wondered how, if he was resourceful enough to look like Cary Grant, dress like Johnny Cash and move like Elvis, he could fail to have disguised that stupid hoof. In an earlier era, women would have gladly followed the god into the woods but, in 60s Ireland, they remained at home – and the Mecca was obliged to close down.

More than any other thinker, Nietzsche devoted himself to the pursuit of transcendence in all stages of intensity – zest, intoxication, joy and exaltation – and this is both his strength and his weakness. Nietzsche is the great aerator of life, the tonic in the G & T (Schopenhauer is the slice of lemon). Nietzsche effervesces, dances, leaps but, when the fizz dies away, there is nothing left. There is little to retain and use. Nietzsche's main function may be as a non-pharmacological mood enhancer, a thinker more to be snorted than studied. He himself used books as illegal stimulants. The aim was not to learn but to get high and stay aloft. So his famous *Will to Power*, a book title chosen not by Nietzsche himself but posthumously by his editors, was really only a form of personal intoxication: 'The first effect of happiness is the feeling of power.'[224] Note the key phrase 'the *feeling* of power'. I have come across this phrase nine times so far in his work – but I have yet to find him praising the *exercise* or *wielding* of power. Indeed, he had nothing but contempt for those who sought worldly supremacy: 'They all strive towards the throne: it is a madness they have – as if happiness sat on a throne! Usually filth sits on the throne.'[225] He despised those who had struggled to gain power over others and admired the saints and ascetics who had struggled to gain power *over themselves*. What he sought was a purely personal transcendence.

His mistake was to try to make a temporary condition permanent. He went mad, if not *from* then certainly *in* euphoria. Perhaps God, annoyed at being written off as dead, decided to show this so-called Übermensch who had the livelier sense of humour and made the lifelong denouncer of pity embrace in tears a dying horse being whipped by a coachman in the street.

The other thing to remember is that Nietzsche was frequently *play-acting*, being outrageous merely in order to shock. And, from the Marquis de Sade to William Burroughs, the standard way to shock has been to extol cruelty. But no one genuinely cruel would make such a public profession. You do not have to pretend to be what you are. The Nazis, whom Nietzsche is accused of inspiring, never boasted of being cruel. Instead they boasted of being the benefactors of mankind. But the danger with play-acting is that it is interpreted literally by the naive. Nietzsche himself foresaw this misunderstanding: 'The high spirits of kindness may look like malice.'[226]

Nietzsche is like the Zen masters who jolted their disciples into attention with koans, combinations of paradox, illogicalness, surprise and shock – one of the most famous, attributed to Linji, is: 'If you meet the Buddha kill him.' Sometimes the jolt was not just mental, as in this koan of Toku-san's, which I would love to use to bring instant enlightenment to my own students: 'Thirty blows of my staff when you have something to say; thirty blows just the same when you have nothing to say.'[227]

Nietzsche is the only Western thinker to have the key Zen quality of zest – and this alone makes him worth reading: 'Early in the morning, at break of day, in all the freshness and dawn of one's strength, to read a *book* – I call that vicious!'[228] This 'vicious' at the end is so unexpected but perfect that it provokes the rare and wonderful thing – a laugh of sheer delight.

Another lower form of transcendence, zest is more an attitude than a state, so it can be cultivated. It requires first detachment and then the paradoxical engagement that detachment can facilitate, a combination of curiosity, attentiveness and analysis. Zest loves the world but refuses to take the world at its own valuation and finds this usually solemn and self-important valuation ridiculous. So zest is essentially subversive. It is a gleeful delight in the absurdity of the human condition and an ironic acknowledgement of the infinite comic genius of God.

The quintessentially zestful character is Puck in *A Midsummer*

Night's Dream – an intermediary between his ridiculous squabbling fairy masters and the equally ridiculous squabbling humans, Puck is a mere functionary, an administrator with little power to initiate or control – and, as is frequently the fate of administrators, he is given incomplete knowledge and then blamed for inappropriate action. Yet he never complains. Indeed, an example to all resentful employees, he enjoys both his work and his unsocial hours, relishing the absurdity of humans ('Lord, what fools these mortals be!'[229]) and absurdity in general ('And those things do best please me that befall preposterously'[230]).

Puck is a sophisticated and ironic Lord of Misrule, the character in medieval carnivals who mocks and satirizes the established order. And satire and mockery were often features of the early ecstatic rituals. Zest has long been a feature of transcendence and has always involved irreverent humour.

How to become blessed with zest? Seek it out – it is found most often in art forms that favour short bursts. This is why it is rare in philosophy (Nietzsche turned increasingly to aphorisms) and also rare in novels (though there is Terry Southern's classic short novel, *The Magic Christian*, which has a perfect Lord of Misrule for the capitalist age in billionaire prankster Guy Grand).

Zest is most at home in poetry and jazz – and it is no coincidence that both are rhythm based. But the spontaneous directness and brevity of good poems and jazz solos make them seem easy. It looks and sounds as though anyone could do it. So anyone and everyone tries, with the result that 99 per cent of poetry and jazz is depressing crap. It takes time and energy to seek out the real thing.

Good jazz solos are especially hard to find. So I went to a legendary New York club more in a spirit of pilgrimage than in the hope of being inspired. And the club was indeed dispiriting – a dank, dark, shabby basement selling overpriced wine that tasted like antifreeze laced with gall. The musicians were heavy, disabused, middle-aged black men, required to invent and astonish twice nightly, with three shows at weekends. Who could? So they coasted along, desultorily supported by a white-haired drummer who had once played with several of the long-dead greats and was now obviously reconciled to going through the motions for a living. The audience, sparse and white, responded with as little enthusiasm, and the musicians acknowledged the thin applause with weary nods. This is life. You make do. You get through.

But, towards the end of the final set, one of the saxophonists suddenly stepped forward, spread his legs, drew breath and, rising up on the balls of his feet, blew ferociously, searingly, mockingly, *superfluously*. It was an electric shock that jolted everyone out of the mood of torpor and competence. That slumber of habit and routine was not life. *This* was life – complex, surprising, defiant and zestful.

This time the audience response was sincere – but the soloist was deaf to it. He threw himself down on a banquette and listened to the sweetest applause, from within. Though it must have been sweet too when the old drummer, hitherto Mount Rushmore grim, leaned across with the sticks to tap lightly on his arm.

PART IV
The Applications

11

The Absurdity of Work

Solemnly, in the fading light of late afternoon, a group of people form a loose circle standing a few feet from each other and turn expectantly to their leader, who produces a giant ball of twine and, taking hold of the loose end, throws the ball to one of the circle, crying, 'Mike, I thought that idea of yours was pretty good.' Holding on to the twine to maintain a link, Mike tosses the ball across the circle, saying, 'Jo, I thought you presented really well.' Jo also takes firm hold of the twine before throwing the ball on to Chris with a glowing comment on his performance. So the ball, gradually diminishing, and accompanied always by praise, travels from Chris to Jill to Dave to Sue to Bob to Jen to Zak and so on around the circle until the last person throws back what remains to the leader, who grasps an end of the twine firmly in each hand, like a set of reins, and proudly regards this complex web of affirmation, declaring, 'I'm just *so lucky* to have such a *wonderful team.*'

This ritual, known as 'the web', closes the ritual of 'the away day'. Both are new rituals of the religion of work, a relatively late addition to the great world religions, but one rapidly gaining converts and with a growing number of fundamentalists.

So nowhere is detachment more necessary than in the workplace. But nowhere is detachment more difficult to achieve. For this is what pays for the house and the car, the dinners in restaurants with big, heavy spoons and starched napkins, and the holidays in bougainvillea-smothered villas in Provence. The alternative could well be socializing round a fire built in an oil drum. And the massive investment of time and energy in work creates a desperate need for an adequate return – so there is a tendency to overestimate the value of colleagues, the work itself and one's own contribution. It is easy to develop the illusion of being an indispensable member of a great bunch of guys doing a great job of work.

In fact, the great victory of the work religion has been to increase the pressure to conform while almost entirely removing any awareness of conformity. Once people worked in order to live; now working *is* living. As with shopping and travel and communication, the means has become the end. Your job is your identity and status, your life. Long gone is the notion of work as a tedious necessity that supports the true life. Now everyone wants a job. Kings, presidents, assassins, priests, poets and prostitutes – all claim to be merely workers getting on with the job. And so the religion of work grows in confidence. How laughable the twentieth-century predictions that technology would permit everyone lives of leisure – and the fears that we would be unable to occupy adequately all this free time (Hannah Arendt agonized about the future of a society of workers deprived of work). How shocking to think that, in the Middle Ages, people worked only for part of the week and half the year, whereas 70-hour weeks with few holidays are now common in major US and UK corporations. As Erich Fromm remarked, 'There is no other period in history in which free men have given their energy so completely for the one purpose: work.'[231]

The secret of successful religions is benign paternalism. In return for surrender of freedom, the religion provides the appearance of loving care and the ability to satisfy all needs. So the corporations have become self-contained worlds with their own shops, cafés, bars, restaurants, gyms, hairdressers, massage rooms and medical facilities. The workplace is the new village, a community offering not merely employment and status but all essential services, a rich, varied social life and fun, fun, fun, fun.

The sibling society needs social networks – and the workplace is a ready-made, obliging social network. Why look elsewhere for company? Or romance? The taboo on workplace relationships is weakening. According to the job-search website CareerBuilder, the percentage of workers who feel it necessary to keep an office romance secret is falling steadily: 'You might have heard the warning, "Don't dip your pen in the company ink", but, for today's worker, that advice is considered outdated.'

The New York Times offers this typically heart-warming story: 'Soon after word spread that Sarah Kay and Matt Lacks were conducting an office romance, Ms Kay found herself in the office of the director of human resources. There was a time when such a meeting would have signalled a death knell for the relationship, and even jeopardized the employees' careers. Yet as Ms Kay, 29, cheerfully recounted, the human resources director told her, "We're just all really glad that you made a friend".'[232]

Who now wishes to bear in mind that colleagues are never chosen and that, if we encountered them away from the job, in the majority of cases we would run a mile? The work environment imposes a work persona – amenable, shallow, cheerful, gregarious and facetious. Often this persona is reinforced by conferring a new name, usually a monosyllabic diminutive – so the modern workplace is the habitat of Jo, Chris, Jill, Dave, Sue, Bob, Jen and Zak. Needless to say, I am known in work as 'Mike'. As with the renaming of nuns and monks, the new workplace name signifies a renunciation of the old self and a dedication to the values and practices of the new community. Like Sister Perpetua and Brother Benedict, I was reborn as Colleague Mike. But, unlike religious rebirths, this was never officially decreed. No one announced that, henceforth, I would be known only as Mike. Nor was there any organized campaign of enforcement. In fact, it is likely that no one else was even aware of the imposition. The phenomenon was a perfect example of 'anonymous authority', almost impossible to oppose because there was no overt command or source. So I resisted 'Mike' for several months, but eventually gave in. And the new name did have benefits. It made me constantly aware that I was two different people.

Nicholson Baker's novel *The Mezzanine* captures the unique atmosphere of the contemporary office complex – a vast, corporately anonymous space inhabited by people desperately anxious to be friendly:

> There are always residual people in an office who occupy
> that category of the not-introduced-to-yet, the not-joked-
> about-the-weather-with: the residue gets smaller and
> smaller, and Bob was one of the very last. His face was so
> familiar that his ongoing status as stranger was really an
> embarrassment – and just then, the certainty that Bob and I
> were gradually going to be brought closer and closer to
> each other, on his down and my up escalator rides,
> destined to intersect at about the midpoint of our progress,
> twenty feet in the air in the middle of a huge vaultlike
> lobby of red marble, where we would have to make eye
> contact and nod and murmur or stonily stare into
> space . . . filled me with desperate aversion.[233]

Another pressure to conform is the recent development of constant visibility. Increasingly, employees occupy open-plan or glass-fronted offices so that there is nowhere to enjoy a moment of solitude or privacy except in the toilet – and even here the stalls have been cut away at top and bottom to minimise seclusion. Nicholson Baker points out that the only place in the corporate world where privacy may still be enjoyed is in an elevator – and in *The Mezzanine* his characters make the most of this rare luxury:

> Some of the elevator cars were filled with passengers; in
> others, I imagined, a single person stood, in a unique

moment of true privacy – truer, in fact, than the privacy
you get in the stall of a corporate bathroom because you
can speak out loudly and sing and not be overheard. L.
told me once that sometimes when she found herself
alone in an elevator she would pull her skirt over her
head. I know that in solo elevator rides I have pretended
to walk like a windup toy into the walls; I have pretended
to rip a latex disguise off my face, making cries of agony; I
have pointed at an imaginary passenger and said, 'Hey pal,
I'll slap that goiter of yours right off, now I said *watch it*.'[234]

Certainly the idea of a secluded office is obsolete. Now there is
nowhere to be alone and out of sight, nowhere to protect and
nurture the secret self, nowhere to ruminate. Indeed, rumination
has become so alien to the workplace that a ruminant expression
is likely to be interpreted as a symptom not of pleasure but grief.
Such detachment is so unusual and disconcerting that colleagues
can explain it only as a consequence of grievous affliction.

In the end this constant exposure makes a desire for privacy
seem cranky, old-fashioned and even perverse, as though anyone
wishing to be alone could only be jerking off to a child pornography website or worse. And, as for a few minutes with a
book ... though there is a simple but ingenious ploy in Joshua
Ferris's novel about a Chicago advertising agency, *Then We Came
to the End* – an employee who is an avid reader arrives at work
before his colleagues, photocopies all of a library book and then
spends the day at his desk reading what appears to be a work
document.[235]

But it is increasingly difficult to avoid being exposed. Any
attempt to block glass-office frontage, for instance with filing
cabinets, posters, calendars or notices, will be spotted and forbidden by zealous safety staff – often the colleagues most likely
to be Pharisees. It must be the petty and largely prohibitive
nature of safety monitoring that attracts the small-minded and
mean-spirited.

I had a wonderful encounter with a safety guy after leaving a building heavily covered in scaffolding. He positioned himself directly in front of me. 'You weren't supposed to come out of that exit. There's danger from falling building materials.'

'Well,' I said, 'I've come through it and lived to tell the tale.'

'No. No. You'll have to go back and leave by *the designated exit*. There was a diversion sign.' And he shifted forward a little.

'Now, let's see if I understand this correctly,' I beamed with demented affability. 'In order to protect me from falling materials you want me *to walk back under the falling materials*. Or have I missed something?' And I beamed even more insanely.

There was a long silence.

Finally, he said, 'I want your name and staff number.'

And the pressure to conform is maintained by team-building breaks and away days. As if it were not enough to see colleagues all week at work, it may also be necessary to bond with them by exploring an abandoned mineshaft together over the weekend. At the very least there will be an away day, where a venue is hired, at considerable expense and usually more difficult to access than the workplace, so that everyone has to consult maps and timetables and make expensive new travel arrangements, only to end up in a conference room identical to those at work – the same dog-eared flip chart, pull-down screen, front workstation and corporate seating, and, of course, the same people dominating the proceedings with the same talk for the sake of talk. In the religion of work, those who insist on talking in every meeting are the equivalent of the righteous faithful who always sit at the front of the congregation in church. The workplace is the habitat of the contemporary Pharisee.

On an away day there is only the free lunch to look forward to, but even this is depressingly familiar – the standard corporate cold buffet, with the same tasteless sandwich quarters and Asian finger food for exotic effect, and the same fresh-fruit platter with pineapple and melon slices and the two strawberries no one ever has the nerve to eat. Yet a manager will sit down at the front workstation and, with a meaningful eye roll, cry fervently, 'It's *so great* just to be *out of that place.*' For, of course, the real point of this exercise is to give the impression that no one present is bound to the workplace and that, since the cheerful harmony persists in the outside world, *it must be authentic.*

Then, as the long, sluggish afternoon drags on and, in desperation, you seize and devour one of the two strawberries, the company is split up into small groups for 'breakout sessions' of SWOT analysis to identify Strengths, Weaknesses, Opportunities and Threats. Each group draws up lists, brings them back and reports to the plenary session.

As the presentations continue, an eager new recruit leans over and asks me, with genuine interest, 'What do they do with all these reports afterwards?'

The mini Danish pastries have been finished, some bastard has even eaten the other strawberry, the remaining coffee is lukewarm and stewed, and ahead lies the ritual of 'the web' – so I am possibly a little blunt: '*Fuck all.*'

He pulls back, profoundly shocked.

These are supposed to be cynical times – but there is surprisingly little cynicism in and about work. The Joshua Ferris narrator says disapprovingly: 'We didn't have much patience for cynics'[236], so even the mildest scepticism about redundant meetings or unnecessary admin or the futility of throwing a ball of twine around is likely to be dismissed as outrageously cynical. Similarly, there is little overt despair at the prospect of spending so much of life in a partition-board cubicle trying to keep the number of unanswered emails to fewer than five hundred. There is of course always whingeing – about overwork, poor support services, misguided management and so on, but this frequently has a ritualized, cosy feel, as though there is no real sense of grievance behind it. Even the whingeing is a form of happy bonhomie.

Only rarely are the unconscious adaptations revealed. In work I drink cheap instant coffee, whereas at home I grind French beans and then use an Italian machine to make strong espresso with a proper, thick crema. The instant stuff has always tasted fine at work and once, when I was out of beans, I tried it at home. It was absolutely undrinkable, shockingly vile. But back at my desk next day it was once again acceptable. So at work even my taste buds renounced complexity and depth.

The problem is that work involves not just the activity for which we are paid but the maintenance of the simplified persona, a constant performance, ceaseless *acting*. This is why colleagues spotted outside work, for instance in the lunch hour, so often seem shabby, diminished and furtive. They are temporarily off the set, so the artificial vibrancy has been extinguished and only a husk remains. Worse, we are acting *without even being aware of it*, even believing this to be natural behaviour – and entirely sub-limating all negative feelings. This may explain why so many professionals with well-paid and apparently satisfying jobs are suddenly and for no obvious reason struck down by depression. The problem is the loss of identity involved in surrender to the group – the mask has fused into the face. The staff in the ad agency in Joshua Ferris's book are all mad about each other ('Most of us liked most everyone'), all clever, creative, witty, lively – and all on antidepressants ('We fought with depression . . . We took showers sitting down and couldn't get out of bed on weekends. Finally we consulted HR about the details of seeing a specialist, and the specialist prescribed medication').

Once I devised a course with the skills employees *really need* for advancement. There were four core modules:

1. Professional Humour
2. Theory and Practice of Professional Esteem
3. Neology
4. Mentoring

Professional Humour (PH), a more sophisticated form of Professional Cheeriness (PC), is the key core competency, a uni-versal facilitator and lubricant, but confusing to the untrained because, although the jokes must always be rewarded by hearty laughter, they must never be actually funny. This is because Professional Humour is not humour but facetiousness. Humour is a way of engaging with reality; facetiousness is a way of evading it. For instance, Professional Humour should always sound wickedly subversive while offering no threat whatever.

Established Colleague (with hearty roar): 'Are you
  behaving yourself?'
New Colleague (lamely, not yet facetiousness-trained):
  'Yes.'
Established Colleague (with even heartier roar): 'What a
  shame!'

And it should sound like savage abuse while remaining entirely innocuous.

First Colleague at meeting: 'So I attended that
  conference . . .'
Second Colleague (incredulous): 'You mean they *let you
  in?*'
Third Colleague (even more incredulous): 'You mean we
  let you out?'
Entire meeting, but especially the First Colleague, laughs
  uproariously.

And Professional Humour should always make the workplace seem intolerable chaos made endurable only by the bright insouciance of the employees. Support staff for once provide crucial support by decorating their workstations with posters and cards:

You don't have to be crazy to work here – but it helps!
Blessed are the cracked for they let in light!
Situation Worsening – Please Send Chocolate!

I cherish all of these – but this is my favourite: Only Robinson Crusoe got it all done by Friday!

A key book for the PH module would be *The Levity Effect: Why It Pays to Lighten Up* by the employee motivation consultants Adrian Gostick and Scott Christopher. As Gostick tellingly explains, 'We define levity as more of a lightness, more being fun than being funny.'[237] The goal is a 'lighthearted workplace'. Another set book would be *Fish! A Remarkable Way to Boost Morale and Improve Results*. This expounds 'the fish philosophy' of 'lightening up' by adopting the practice of Seattle fishmongers, who maintain high morale by throwing fish at each other.[238] Real fish would, of course, be too smelly for the office so the corporate equivalent is throwing around a soft toy called Percy the Perch.

And Professional Humour may itself offer a career path. Some organizations have an official Levity Manager and Levity Team, for instance the advertising agency Iris North America, whose LM defines his team as 'the Smile Squad' and their function as promoting 'general well-being and serendipitous happenings'.

The module Theory and Practice of Professional Esteem (TPPE) is largely about flattery which, like Professional Humour, is more complex than it appears. Many believe that anyone can easily kiss ass. But bosses are connoisseurs of flattery. They receive it constantly every day and are unlikely to be impressed by anything crass – which may well produce annoyance rather than gratitude. It is important to remember that flattery is an art. Firstly, it requires attention, understanding and perceptiveness to identify *exactly* the praise each boss yearns to hear. Next, it requires delicacy and tact in choosing the right moment to deliver this customized praise. Then, it requires language skills to phrase it properly. And finally, of course, it needs facetiousness to disguise the flattery as banter. All this is necessary for successful flattering upwards. Though just as important is flattering down. The common mistake of bosses is attempting to wield naked power. But, in the contemporary workplace, where everyone is a buddy, flattery is infinitely more effective than intimidation. Rather than issuing a command, an astute boss will gain more cooperation by hand-wringing and wailing, 'Mike, I hate to dump this on you – but it's important and I just can't trust *anyone else here* to do it properly.' This fosters the illusion employees cherish most – indispensability. Ferris's narrator admits: 'Each and every one of us harbored the illusion that the whole enterprise would go straight to hell without our individual daily contributions.' In fact, no one is indispensable. Every worker is replaced and forgotten as swiftly as the anonymous slaves who hauled blocks for the pyramids.

The Neology module studies the creation and use of the new terms, titles and language constantly required by all specialists – and the discipline's own revered specialists will be known as neologians. It is crucial to be able to impress meetings with statements like, 'We need to get out of these vertical silos and provide more opportunities for synergy and cross-fertilization'. 'Synergy' and 'cross-fertilization' are among the most currently exciting workplace terms because they imply new forms of collaboration, cooperation and communion. 'There's so much talent in this organization. If only people could break out of their silos and get together.'

'Innovation' is another key concept and itself constantly needs innovative terms such as 'pushing the envelope', 'thinking outside the box', 'blueskying' and 'reaching beyond the low-hanging fruit'. But there are always new terms for every occasion – 'There's no smoke without salmon', 'We'll just have to Box and Cox', 'It's not my home competency' (so much more satisfactory than saying, 'I know nothing about that').

Finally, the development of resonant new titles is crucial in maintaining morale. One of the most successful title changes in recent times has been the rebranding of 'Personnel' as 'Human Resource Management', though, in conversation, the HR guys describe themselves facetiously as 'the people people'.

The last of the four modules, Mentoring, is about selecting and bonding with those most likely to offer career advancement and, when this is accomplished, becoming a mentor in turn to those most willing and able to provide useful service. The essential tactic is drinking with the potential mentor after work and making use of recently acquired flattery and facetiousness skills. It may also be necessary to develop new interests and sporting activities. I once ruined my prospects by admitting to a sailing-obsessed boss that I was comfortable only around canals where the water had been stagnant for at least a century.

Surviving work requires hypocrisy. Many thinkers have attacked this vice – and none more consistently and vehemently than Christ. But Christ never had to earn a living or endure colleagues (disciples are very different). Honesty at work is a dangerous luxury. It would be foolish to reveal one's true feelings – and even more foolish to become involved in the great eruptions, the disputes and feuds and simmering animosities. It is useful to remember the Stoics on the futility of anger and especially Seneca who wrote extensively on the subject.[239] Quarrelling is a form of emotional involvement that establishes a relationship – and there should rarely be a genuine relationship at work. But an attitude of surly superiority is just as bad – professionally untenable, damaging to the character and far too revealing. The secret of workplace detachment is to understand your colleagues while preventing them from understanding you. One technique is to use all the cheerful conventions but with an elaborate, ironic courtesy so that you are neither breaking the rules nor playing by them. This creates useful uncertainty. *What is his game?*

A paradoxical form of detachment is manic engagement, an alarming collusive zest entirely different from the mandatory cheerfulness. The film *Cool Hand Luke* has a scene in which convicts are spreading gravel on a dirt road and, as usual, working as slowly as possible. Suddenly Luke (Paul Newman) begins to go at it with crazy zest. The others in the gang are at first puzzled but one by one begin to copy him. This bewilders and angers the guards – *what are these clowns up to?* Hurling shovelfuls of gravel like men demented, the convicts work so frantically that they eventually run out of road to cover. Then they lie about laughing hysterically while the guards impotently rage.

But the human creature likes to live in expectation and to establish differentials over others. So it is difficult to detach from hunger for promotion. And, in the era of entitlement, everyone believes that promotion is *deserved*. Even when a post requires specific qualifications and experience, those without either will confidently apply and be outraged if rejected. 'I *deserved* it,' they rage in bewilderment – though it is inadvisable to enquire about the reasons for their entitlement. Or to ask the successfully promoted whether the extra money justifies the extra responsibility and stress. Promotion is self-evidently good.

The key determinant of work satisfaction is not money or even status but the degree of personal responsibility. Yet workers rarely acknowledge this. In a lifetime of employment I have never heard a colleague value autonomy, either as a key feature of a current post or a desirable feature of a new position – and often moving up the ladder involves a loss of autonomy. Come to think of it, I have never even heard anyone use the word. Yet autonomy is the one thing that makes professional life more fulfilling.

Management, of course, understands how promotion excites employees – and that promotions are often insufficiently numerous and frequent. So Performance Related Pay was developed as a permanent and universal incentive. Won't people do anything for an extra few cents? Actually, no. The psychologist Frederick Herzberg, who spent the second half of the twentieth century studying work motivation, concluded that there are two sources of satisfaction in work – what he called 'hygiene factors', things like pay and conditions, and 'motivation factors' such as degree of control and the challenge of the work itself. But the hygiene factors are capable only of causing *dissatisfaction*. Poor pay will demotivate employees, but financial incentives will not have the opposite effect. Motivation may be increased only by greater employee autonomy and more challenging tasks.[240] So in work, as in the rest of life, personal responsibility and difficulty are necessary for fulfilment.

And Herzberg identified two other flaws in the PRP theory. The first is that performance can be objectively and accurately measured; this is often difficult or impossible, leading employees to suspect that the true measure is the ability to curry favour. The second is the assumption that if one aspect of work is changed everything else will remain the same. In fact, everything is connected to everything else so, if one thing is changed, everything is changed. And the most important consequence of Performance Related Pay is the loss of goodwill. So, the very thing management hope to achieve – an increase in voluntary work – is often the very thing forfeited. The employees not receiving extra pay suddenly ask themselves why they should continue to take on extra work if their efforts are not recognized.

Introducing a financial incentive can actually destroy the natural satisfaction of doing a job well and *reduce* motivation. The psychologist Edward L. Deci asked two groups of subjects to solve a series of puzzles – but paid only one group for correct solutions. When time was up, both groups were allowed to continue working. The fascinating and heartening discovery was that the unpaid group worked on for twice as long as the paid.[241] And Deci has also produced a survey of over one hundred other studies with the same conclusion – that extrinsic incentives are counterproductive.[242]

Equally heartening – and one of the most exciting episodes in my own working life – was the ignominious failure of a PRP scheme for lecturers. When the offer was first announced, managers smugly sat back awaiting a flood of applications. But teachers understood that teaching could not be accurately evaluated and that introducing rankings would be divisive. So they agreed that no one would apply. I was certain that a greedy few would find the temptation irresistible – but the agreement held and no applications were submitted. Then management, taken aback, invited certain people to apply – but this merely confirmed the suspicion that the extra money would go to favourites. So the favourites declined to apply for fear of being forever identified as management toadies. Finally management, in desperation, actually paid extra money into the bank accounts of the chosen – but the chosen, rather than keeping quiet as expected, withdrew the money, pooled it and shared it out equally among all the staff. The scheme was withdrawn, never to return – a victory that gave me new respect for colleagues, new pleasure in going to work and indeed new faith in the human race.

It is possible to upset the promotion machine by simply failing to apply for promotion. Of course, in many jobs, such a blatant lack of ambition would result in dismissal – but in public sector employment such as teaching it is perfectly feasible. If you have reached a position that pays sufficiently well and provides a fair degree of autonomy, why seek unnecessary stress? This is another way of refusing to play by the rules without actually breaking the rules. It removes the only leverage managers understand and makes them unsure of how to play the autonomous employee.

But there is also contemporary culture's encouragement of change for its own sake. Employees now move jobs more and more frequently, not merely for more money or status, but because movement itself is considered to be necessary. The perception is that anyone who stays more than a few years in a job is a hopelessly boring old stick-in-the-mud. But it takes a year or two to become fully established in a new job, to learn the arcane rituals of a new workplace and be consistently competent long enough to inspire trust. So the irony is that people leave jobs just as they are about to enjoy the benefits of establishment and suffer instead the equivalent of being abruptly teleported to a strange city without a map, knowledge of the language or any clear idea of the reason for being there. As Nicholson Baker explains in *The Mezzanine*, there is only one place where a new recruit will feel at ease:

For new-hires the number of visits can go as high as eight or nine a day, because the corporate bathroom is the one place in the whole office where you understand completely what is expected of you. Other parts of your job are unclear . . . but, in the men's room, you are a seasoned professional; you let your hand drop casually on the flush handle with as much of an air of careless familiarity as men who have been with the company for years. Once I took a new-hire to lunch, and though he asked not-quite-to-the-point questions as we ate our sandwiches, and nodded without comprehension or comeback at my answers, when we reached the hallway to the men's room, he suddenly made a knowing, one-man-to-another face and said, 'I've got to drain the rooster. See you later. Thanks again.'

Yet people put themselves through the torments of a new job on a regular basis – and Baker does not even mention the agony of trying to work out how to do double-sided copies on a new machine with a baffling control panel, while behind you is a growing line of colleagues just barely containing photocopier rage. Habituation is surely beneficial at least in the workplace where it allows routine tasks to be completed without thought. So habit, the curse of private life, is the blessing of work.

Then there is the vexing question of how much effort to put into work. Christ's advice to imitate plant life was both impractical and unwise: 'Consider the lilies of the field, how they grow; they toil not, neither do they spin.'[243] Work-ethic Protestants have obviously not been paying attention to the Good Book's unequivocal incitement to shirk. But there are objections to shirking beyond the obvious dangers of being despised by colleagues or being sacked. Firstly, since everything influences everything else, shirking in one area will leak into others. But, more importantly, shirking brings no satisfaction. As Buddha, Spinoza, Rilke and Frederick Herzberg have observed, we are born not to be lilies of the field but to seek out the difficult and strive for it constantly. This is why so many employees will undertake extra work without being asked and are insulted by the idea that financial reward is a necessary incentive. And it is often possible to enjoy the flow experience at work, the incomparable satisfaction of release from self and time. As Christ should have said, blessed are those paid to do what they enjoy, for theirs is the kingdom of heaven.

It is possible to enjoy almost any task. In Aleksandr Solzhenitsyn's autobiographical novel *One Day in the Life of Ivan Denisovich* prisoners in the Soviet Gulag are marched out in subzero temperatures to build a wall, without knowing where or why, but they throw themselves wholeheartedly into it and realize at the end of the day that they were happy at this task.[244] So, if it is possible to be happy at freezing forced labour in the Gulag, it might even be possible as a cubicle serf sticking Post-it notes on a screen in an open-plan office. And a sensible work strategy might be: surrender to the task but not to the taskmaster, become absorbed in the work itself but never absorb the work ethos.

How then to resist surrender to the taskmasters? There is no easy answer. It was difficult enough when they wanted to be lord and master – and is even more complicated now that they want to be your buddy as well. But it is useful to bear in mind the thoughtlessness that Hannah Arendt identified as the cause of Adolf Eichmann's behaviour and the psychology experiments on conformity, which show how easy it is for authority figures to command obedience, even for obviously sadistic acts like delivering electric shocks.

Similar conformity experiments on workplace compliance were undertaken by a team of Dutch researchers investigating the 'administrative obedience paradigm'. Participants were instructed to administer a selection test to people described as job applicants (but who were actually researchers' accomplices) and told that these 'applicants' would get the job only if they passed the test. The participants were also told that this oral test was intended to measure ability to work under stress. So, in the course of asking test questions, the participants (now addressed as 'administrators') were told to increase the pressure on 'applicants' with remarks critical of performance and personality; they were to begin with the relatively mild 'That was really stupid of you', and work up to intense personal hostility and abuse. As the test progressed, applicants showed symptoms of discomfort and stress and even protested – but any administrators who tried to desist were urged by an authoritarian researcher to continue. The apparently distressed applicants gave more and more incorrect answers, failed the test and, as far as the administrators knew, were not employed. Yet, despite increasing evidence of applicant distress and failure, 91 per cent of administrators complied with the urging of the researchers and continued the abuse to the end. Though, when a comparable group of 'administrators' were surveyed on how they might respond to such an experiment, over 90 per cent were adamant that they would never comply. So the degree of compliance was almost exactly the opposite of what participants predicted. And the results were the same when actual Human Resource managers, supposedly trained in the sensitive treatment of employees, were used as 'administrators'.[245] So much for 'the people people'.

If an unknown researcher will be blindly obeyed, how much more overwhelming the desire to submit to an imposing boss in a grand office with power over livelihood?

Part of the answer is to remember that the boss may not be so imposing: according to Fromm, 'The lust for power is rooted not in strength but in weakness. It is the expression of the inability of the individual self to stand alone and live. It is the desperate attempt to gain secondary strength where genuine strength is lacking.'[246] This is another application of the rule that you don't have to pretend to be what you are – power-seekers need the appearance of strength because they are not actually strong. The imposing figure behind the huge desk may well be as much of a fraud as the authoritarian researchers in the psychology experiments. And understanding this will make any boss less intimidating. Conversely, an unimposing figure behind a desk may be genuine. The best managers are often people who had no great desire to be managers. And who would want to manage the human creature, contrary at the best of times, and now impossibly so – feeling entitled to have everything but obliged to do nothing?

In the worst case, the boss is a bully and, therefore, more dangerous but also even weaker than the ordinary power-seeker. The classic bully mindset is kiss up and piss down – and the craven subservience of the kissing up should expose their extreme weakness. When it comes to pissing down, bullies attack only the most obviously vulnerable, so absence of fear is often sufficient protection. The most appropriate attitude is contempt, though this should be circumspect because bullies are vindictive. Hannah Arendt has argued that revolutions occur when contempt for bad governance becomes so widespread and corrosive that the system simply collapses – a theory demonstrated by the fall of communism.[247] So it may be useful to spread and intensify contempt for the bully boss by slyly fomenting sedition in the photocopying room.

Considering the centuries of sweat expended on the earning of daily bread, it is surprising how little guidance has been offered on the conduct of this near-universal necessity. Of course, thinkers have been remarkably successful in evading the burden of paid employment and have refused even to soil their minds with the problem. But literary writers have also largely avoided the subject of work, even though most of them have work experience to draw upon and the workplace is a stage where disparate, incompatible people are forcibly confined together for long periods and suffer violent emotions such as power-hunger, greed, lust, hatred and rage. It may be that the experience of work, with its shocking expenditure of time and energy, is just too appalling to contemplate. Or that the deadening effects of habituation make it impossible to raise to the level of the imagination. But it is a curious and significant fact that there are hardly any novels set entirely in the workplace.

This is what makes *The Mezzanine* so valuable. It is full of perfectly observed details that provoke instant recognition and remind the reader that the workplace is not at all dreary, but instead rich and strange, full of human oddity and absurdity. Here is the narrator describing a secretary's cubicle:

> In the shadow of the shelf under the unused fluorescent light, she had pinned up shots of a stripe-shirted husband, some nephews and nieces, Barbra Streisand, and a multiply-Xeroxed sentiment in Gothic type that read, 'If You Can't Get Out Of It, Get Into It!' I would love someone to trace the progress of these support-staff sayings through the offices of the city; Deanne had another one pushpinned to a wall of her cube, its capitals in crumbling ruins under the distortion of so many copies of copies; it said, 'YOU MEAN YOU WANT ME TO RUSH THE RUSH JOB I'M RUSHING TO RUSH?'

Unfortunately, *The Mezzanine* covers only a lunch hour. Extended to a full day, it could have been the *Ulysses* of the workplace, and its privileged readers could have felt like Homeric heroes on the morning train. This book is determined to celebrate even work – and quotes with delight from Marcus Aurelius: 'Manifestly, no condition of life could be so well adapted for the practice of philosophy as this in which chance finds you today!' There is even a tip on how to enjoy private exuberance and zest at work:

> One time, while I was locked behind a stall, I did unintentionally interrupt the conversation between a member of senior management and an important visitor with a loud curt fart like the rap of a bongo drum. The two paused momentarily; and then recovered without dropping a stitch – 'Oh, she is a very, very capable young woman, I'm quite clear on that'. 'She is a sponge, a sponge, she soaks up information everywhere she goes'.

'She really is. And she's tough, that's the thing. She's got armor'. 'She's a major asset to us'. Etc. Unfortunately, the grotesque intrusion of my fart struck me as funny, and I sat on the toilet containing my laughter with the back of my palate – this pressure of containment forced a further, smaller fart. Silently, I pounded my knee, squinting and maroon-colored from suppressed hysteria.

12

The Absurdity of Love

What is more appealing than an intimate candlelit dinner for two? But first there is the choice between eating locally and going into town. Staying local restricts the range of restaurants but requires no travelling and permits an aperitif in the comfort of home. Town provides more eating options but involves a journey on public transport and an aperitif in a noisy, expensive city bar.

This evening, the couple decide not to travel. But the local restaurants are just *so last century*. How many decades since Italian, Chinese and Indian were happening cuisines? And these stick-in-the-mud local restaurateurs seem never to have heard the term 'new wave'. What the area desperately needs is a good Vietnamese restaurant.

Then *he* wants to choose in advance and make a reservation, while *she* argues that this may mean the horror of *an empty restaurant*.

'What's wrong with an empty restaurant?'

The question is so *unbelievably obtuse* that she turns her eyes to Heaven for patience and strength, eventually finding the heroic forbearance to say calmly, 'We'll just stroll along and find some-where.'

So they stroll and, frowning, peruse the familiar local menus. Knowing that *his* secret desire is for Chinese, she says coldly,

'Everything will be doused in gloop.' Knowing that *her* secret desire is for Indian, he issues a harsh laugh: 'You put on four pounds just by reading the menu.'

There remains only the Italian, which neither of them really wants and which exposes them once again to the appalling maître d' who is simultaneously obsequious and domineering. Once this man actually tried to seat them *in the basement*. And now he asks if they have a reservation when he knows perfectly well they do not. She requests the window table and the maître d' explains with an utterly insincere hand-wringing apology that this table is reserved. What is the man thinking of? Not only should a sophisticated and attractive couple be placed in the window, they ought to be *paid* to sit there and attract something other than a clientele who make the place look like *a retirement home canteen.*

Instead, they must squeeze round a tiny table between two other occupied tables, where anything above a whisper can be heard by all three sets of diners. So much for intimacy. And he had been hoping to make the romantic suggestion of watching a porn movie later, not, of course, anything crass but that woman-friendly, tasteful production he spent so much time searching for. She, on the other hand, had been hoping to discuss her diminished libido.

Already moving into the wall seat with a view of the room, she says, 'Do you mind?' He laughs bleakly: 'I'm used to looking at walls.'

Now here are menu and wine list. He points out the considerable gap in price between the house red and the others. She reminds him that house red is invariably vinegar. He orders the expensive Chianti Riserva, which the waiter brings and pours, reminding them of another problem here. The waiters invariably rush forward to pour wine, robbing the diners of autonomy, forcing them to drink too fast and unjustly rewarding the greedy who drink fastest. To make a fuss or to accept this annoyance?

As for food, in the interests of good theatre, an essential part of the eating-out experience, she likes them to order different dishes and romantically share forkfuls. But they usually like the same dishes – it is a symbiotic union after all. So he has adopted the strategy of choosing and announcing his choice in a nanosecond. Now, understanding his ploy, she says with cold contempt, 'So this is your new approach.'

'Why can't we both have the same thing if that's what we want?'

Like so many of his questions, this is not worthy of an answer. Instead, she forgoes her first preferences, orders a starter and main different from his and slams the menu shut.

And only now, when the waiter has left, do they notice that their table *has no candle*. Every other table has its billowing flame. So this waiter insists on pouring wine, which is not only unnecessary but infuriating, and then neglects the one essential thing. *Bring a candle, asshole.*

But, even by candlelight, romance is not easy.

Indeed, so numerous and varied are the illusions, difficulties, demands, resentments, burdens and strains that beset contemporary relationships that the wonder is not that so many fail but that any survive at all. Yet never have so many sought relationships so urgently or entered into them with such high expectations. For, as the actual relationships have become more like short-term business transactions, the belief in eternal love as an essential prerequisite has grown stronger. In the romantic 1960s 40 per cent of women were willing to accept marriage without love but, by the hard-headed, money-obsessed 1980s, only 15 per cent would countenance loveless financial security.[248] There seems to be a weird and catastrophic inverse effect – the less tolerant the practice, the more demanding the theory. The lovers expect more but are willing to give less. Yet the inevitable disasters rarely chasten these romantics. Cyberspace teems with seekers of love entirely undaunted by constant past failure. In any other area of endeavour the bewildered and frustrated would give up, or at the very least ask searching questions. But the magic of potential, the key facilitator of the age, is strongest in sexual attraction. Love, or rather the expectation of love, is indeed blind.

The primary illusion is that establishing a relationship is easy. This is built into the very language: to 'fall in love', as though it is merely a matter of passive acceptance; to 'be in love', as though the passive acceptance leads to a definitive, final state. Erich Fromm addresses the problem at the start of his classic work *The Art of Loving*: 'This attitude – that nothing is easier than to love – has continued to be the prevalent idea about love in spite of the overwhelming evidence to the contrary.'[249] And, in order to fall in love and be in love, it is simply a matter of finding the right person, who will immediately remove difficulties, insecurity and loneliness by providing eternal, protective love.

This belief that it is only a matter of finding the right person is further encouraged by the refusal of personal responsibility, the tendency to look outward in demand rather than inward in obligation. It is up to the other to provide love so, when the relationship breaks down, it must be the fault of the other. This was not the right one after all and the solution is to resume the search with greater urgency. It is astonishing how those with a string of failed relationships rarely accept that they themselves must be at least part of the problem. Even more astonishingly, the succession of failures does not make another failure seem more likely. The series of disasters is, in fact, a *guarantee of success next time*. Because, after so many painful failures, success is *deserved*. The sense of entitlement is strengthened by grievance: *I really deserve this to work this time*. So instead of caution there is recklessness. The distraught singleton plunges back into the game like a gambler betting ever more heavily to recoup heavy losses.

And when singletons find partners they fling themselves into the relationship with desperate abandon, believing that love is the ecstatic surrender of self and fusion with the beloved, a kind of mystical unity. They shower each other with flattery, promises, gifts and sexual favours, introduce each other's relatives, colleagues and friends, are rarely out of each other's company and, when separated, bombard each other with romantic messages – a total abandonment and immersion that encourages a sadomasochistic relationship to develop without either party being aware of it. In fact, this dependency is often initially exhilarating, a release from the burdens and anxieties of freedom. So the domineering one thinks that the control will be permanent and the submissive one that all needs will always be met by the controller. And, when problems and tensions arise, each lover is baffled – *how can this be going wrong when I've given myself so completely?* But the surrender that was meant to ensure love has actually made it impossible. The result is bewilderment, anger and impatience – and the conclusion that this was not the right person after all.

Because the relationship, for all its intensity, will also have been unconsciously provisional – there is no longer any permanence even in marriage. And, though reversible decisions appear attractive, such choices satisfy much less than the irreversible and permanent. So there is a self-fulfilling prophecy – a relationship understood as potentially less than final will more than likely turn out to be less than final.

There is also the problem that, in contemporary cities, the couple relationship may be the only source of connection, structure, meaning and enchantment. In traditional societies there were religions to confer meaning and magic, rituals to structure the year, communities to offer strong connections and extended families to provide support. Now the poor groaning 'relationship' has to provide all of this, to take upon its weakened back the entire burden of living. No wonder it collapses under the strain.

And there is the problem that the initial phase of the relationship is always more exciting, especially in an age fond of fantasy and bewitched by the glamour of potential. In fact the early and later stages are so different that they deserve different names. It would be more accurate to describe the initial stage as infatuation and the later stage as love. And the crucial misconception is that everyone claims to be seeking love but is usually seeking only infatuation.

This is hardly surprising. Almost all so-called love stories are really infatuation stories. Is there a novel or film that portrays mature, happy love? Everyone claims to want such bliss but no one wants to read about it or see it portrayed.

In fact, the Western notion of romantic love is frequently based on the *impossibility* of cohabitation. Dante barely even met Beatrice. Abelard was swiftly separated from his nuts and so spared the tedium of actually living with Heloise. The treacherously slain Tristan never went house-hunting with Iseult. The courtly love of the troubadours was reserved for unattainable married ladies – they could not even *touch*, much less shack up with, the beloved. Romeo and Juliet died after one night together (the notion of the single night of ecstasy is perennially popular in infatuation stories, from *Tristan and Iseult* to the novel and film *Cold Mountain*). *Young Werther* gets the hots for Charlotte who is conveniently engaged to another man – and avoids messy developments by shooting himself. In *Wuthering Heights* Cathy and Heathcliff get their kicks from thwarting each other. And the classic analysis of infatuation, Stendhal's *De L'Amour*, was based on an unrequited passion for a woman called Mathilde Dembowski.

Stendhal described falling in love as a process of crystallization of the beloved. As a bough thrown into an abandoned salt mine becomes studded with 'scintillating diamonds', so love 'draws from everything that happens new proofs of the perfection of the loved one'.[250] In other words, the lover creates a fantasy that has little to do with the actual person and falls in love with this entirely personal creation: 'In love one enjoys only the illusion one creates for oneself.'[251] So the love is really self-love, a form of narcissism. And it flourishes mostly in anticipation. As Stendhal remarks, meeting the real lover may even become an unnecessary embarrassment. The world also shrinks and the beloved expands until they merge into one overwhelming image that eclipses

everything else. So infatuation is a way not of accepting responsibility but of actually escaping it – lovers are entitled to avoid the
tedious obligations of life beyond the beloved. In the legend of
Tristan and Iseult the influence of potions excuses the irresponsible behaviour of the lovers – and, in the modern world, the
sanction is infatuation's involuntary, even irrational, nature. It's a
clinical disorder. The lovers can't help it.

But infatuation may appear irrational only because the forces
driving it are not understood. It may be a delirious matching of
pathologies, as when sadist meets masochist. Or the beloved may
be unconsciously chosen to re-enact some murky childhood business. There may even be an unconscious social motivation. For
instance, working-class young men who become educated are
fatally attracted to middle-class princesses – the very type most
likely to despise and deride them.

The infatuated like to believe that they are the random victims
of Cupid's arrows – but are more likely to be victims of neediness,
loneliness and insecurity, keen to surrender responsibility, and
with a talent for fantasy rather than for self-awareness or understanding. But what does this matter if they are overwhelmed by
an ecstasy that invests life and the world with such radiance?
Don't the infatuated have great sex – and more fun all round? The
problem is that infatuation does not last. There is general agreement that the maximum duration is two years, though it is more
likely to be much less, with an average duration of somewhere
over a year (and, like the average attention span, this is probably
shrinking). But the infatuated themselves are blissfully unaware of
a time limit so the disenchantment comes as a nasty shock.

Why must it come to an end? Infatuation is a transcendent
state, a loss of self, and transcendent states cannot last. The tran-
scender always comes back to earth. Reality and the stubborn self
always re-establish their dominance.

Recent neuroscience research has confirmed the distinction
between infatuation and love. The anthropologist Helen Fisher
uses the terms 'romantic love' and 'attachment' for the two phases

and has identified 'romantic love' in all of the 175 cultures she studied. To investigate how the old black magic actually works, she set up a team of neuroscientists to scan the brains of those in the different stages of love. These scans revealed that 'romantic love' and 'attachment' involve entirely different brain circuits and neurotransmitters. Romantic love is associated with increased levels of dopamine and lower levels of serotonin, while attachment is associated with oxytocin in women and vasopressin in men, both neurotransmitters involved in pair-bonding in animals. And the brain pathways and dopamine levels prominent in romantic lovers are similar to those in users of all the major addictive drugs. Fisher concludes that romantic love is indeed a form of addiction.[252] This confirms Stendhal's insight that such love, which presents itself as the most selfless activity, is in fact largely selfish. The lover is in love not with a person but with a high. The beloved is indeed thrilling – but only as a line of coke is thrilling to an addict. And this also explains why infatuation never lasts. Addiction creates tolerance – with ever higher dosages required to produce the same effect. But infatuation cannot increase the dosage beyond a certain point, so the high finally wears off. Another team of neuroscientists has investigated the time span of the love high and concluded that the popular perception is correct – infatuation usually lasts between twelve and eighteen months.[253]

What to do when infatuation fades? One option is stoic acceptance – by this time the couple may be married and have children. This was a solution common in traditional societies. The prince in Giuseppe Tomasi di Lampedusa's *The Leopard* describes love as 'a year of fire followed by thirty years of ashes'[254] and goes to prostitutes for his pleasure. In the contemporary world, a popular alternative would be adultery, the adventure tourism of the middle-aged middle classes. Another option is a different kind of acceptance – to understand that the guttering flame is a signal to find a new partner. Why live among ashes if fire can be rekindled elsewhere? Why not skip the disillusionment and enjoy only serial infatuations? This, too, is popular, but depends on not wanting to bring up children and on being always attractive to new partners, an attribute that diminishes with time. The twilight of the serially infatuated is likely to be as bleak as that of the hedonist.

The final option is to attempt the transition from infatuation to love. So, while the infatuation story ends with 'Reader, I married him', the love story begins with 'Reader, I suddenly realized I would have to spend the rest of my life with him'. There are not many such love stories. One is Tolstoy's *Family Happiness*, in which a couple falls madly in love, marries and enjoys a happy life of intimate suppers, music and laughter. But, over time, infatuation wears off. As the wife explains, 'We had long since ceased to be the most perfect people in the world for each other, and now we made comparisons with others, and judged each other in secret.'[255] She knows that her husband is a good man, kind and gentle, an excellent partner and father – but comes to find his wisdom predictable, his perpetual calm irritating and his appearance old and unpleasant. Depressed and angry, she longs for movement, excitement and danger and, like Emma Bovary, attempts to recreate romance by a hectic society life of parties and balls. But this excitement also wears off, and its only consequence is to drive the couple further apart. Unlike Emma, though, this wife wants the marriage to be meaningful. She confesses her feelings to her husband and discovers that his calm is not just a ploy to infuriate her, but the product of a detachment that has foreseen and understood their problems. He explains that there was no alternative to working through the experience: 'All of us . . . must live through all life's nonsense in order to return to life itself; it's no good taking someone else's word for it.' She understands and begins the journey back to life: 'From that day my romance with my husband was over; the old feeling became a dear, irrevocable memory, but my new feeling of love for my children and for the father of my children laid the beginning of another but now quite different happy life.'

Unfortunately, Tolstoy does not explain the nature of this 'quite different happy life' or how it was achieved, other than to suggest that the process is long and painful. And, in fact, the transition from infatuation to love is difficult because the two are opposites in many ways. Infatuation is transcendent; love is down to earth. Infatuation creates a fantasy; love accepts a reality. Infatuation is an addiction; love is a commitment. Infatuation craves unity; love cherishes separateness. Infatuation evades responsibility; love wholeheartedly accepts it. Infatuation is effortless; love is hard work.

And just when down-to-earth realism is most needed, there is often the most disastrous form of expectation – planning the perfect wedding. Another bizarre development is that, as investment in marriage has declined, investment in weddings has shot up, so that the average UK wedding now costs much more than the average annual wage.[256] This is another example of the emphasis on image over substance – planning not for the reality of a life but for the symbolism of a day. As with most pageantry, the idea is to suggest solemn tradition by means of historical locations, costumes and accessories – castles and country houses, tiaras and top hats, horse-drawn carriages and vintage cars (though the significant requirement these days is a disposable camera on every table). So a contemporary wedding is like the Olympic Games, a spectacle of stupendous complexity and ruinous expense, which requires years of detailed research and preparation but lasts only a short time. Even if it all goes according to plan, a wedding is over in a day, much of it spent being ordered around by photographers, and when the audience is gone and the costumes returned to their boxes (never again to be taken out), an ordinary man and woman look at each other and think: 'Is this all it is?'

It may well be that an analysis of figures would reveal a law – the duration of a marriage is inversely proportional to the cost of the wedding. Or, to put it another way, any union celebrated with personalized toasting flutes is doomed.

After the dream wedding, reality makes a shocking return and the problems suppressed by the spell of potential are suddenly all too apparent. Because not only is no one the 'right' person, no one is easy to live with, much less capable of enveloping a partner in instant, enduring, unconditional love. This is a fundamental axiom: *no one is easy to live with*. There are only degrees of difficulty – and it is essential to realize that the other is encrusted, not with scintillating diamonds, but with irritating beliefs, habits, superstitions, neuroses, moods, ailments, indulgences and bad taste, not to mention appalling relatives and inexplicable friends. And living together exposes all this banality and squalor. The lustrous hair that gleamed so seductively in candlelight becomes a matted wad in the shower plug, and the member that was so thrillingly erect becomes a flaccid, shrunken fillet dribbling urine over the toilet seat. If there is ever compatibility it is a hard-earned end product rather than a natural precondition. But, while the infuriating habits of the partner will eventually become apparent, it is more difficult to recognize the equivalent in oneself. Many, especially those with doting parents, seem to believe that their eccentricities are sanctioned by the natural law and that even that their most revolting habits are charming and endearing.

No one is easy to live with – and there is no such thing as a final, definitive state of love. Like happiness, love is an ongoing process, a kind of never-ending joint creative project. And, as with happiness, the striving for fulfilment becomes itself the fulfilment. Also, as with any creative endeavour, love is subject to the cycle of exhaustion and renewal: the exhaustion essential for the joy of renewal. The project requires time and patience. It takes a lifetime to learn any worthwhile skill properly – and love is no exception.

It is not surrender and immersion but autonomy and detachment that are necessary. The growth of the partner, often perceived as a threat, may be a source of renewal. What benefits the individual and appears selfish may also benefit the couple. The converse is also true – one partner's failure to develop may inspire contempt and terror in the other: dear God, the prospect of a lifetime of *this*. And contempt is the most dangerous development in any relationship, either with a person or a group. Dictators fall because contempt for them becomes widespread and extreme. Marriages fail because contempt is an acid so corrosive it dissolves any bond. But an autonomous, independent partner, while more difficult to live with, is much less likely to inspire contempt. So a couple will grow together more surely if each encourages the other to grow separately – and the paradox is that, in mature love, detachment encourages attachment. As Rilke puts it: 'A person in love thus has to try to behave as if he had to accomplish a major task: he has to spend a lot of time alone, reflect and think, collect himself and hold onto himself; he has to work; he has to become something!'[257] This is radical advice – to succeed as a lover, spend more time alone.

So the process is not passive and dependent but active and independent.

And, as Rilke suggests, love, like happiness, cannot be achieved directly but is a by-product of living productively. Fromm: 'It is an illusion to believe that one can separate life in such a way that one is productive in the sphere of love and unproductive in all other spheres. Productiveness does not permit of such a division of labour. The capacity to love demands a state of intensity, awakeness, enhanced vitality, which can only be the result of a productive and active orientation in many other spheres of life. If one is not productive in other spheres, one is not productive in love either.'[258]

So the Buddhist concept of 'mindfulness' is also necessary for love. But it is necessary to remember why Buddha and other thinkers were frightened by love – there is also the wildness, the lunacy.

Love is supported by a tripod whose three legs are liking, respect and desire. If any leg buckles, the whole thing crashes down – but only liking and respect are subject to sweet reason. Desire is the joker in the pack, the dark force that renders everything volatile, complex and unstable.

Like weather and the stock market, marriage (or any live-in

sexual relationship) is a chaotic system. This is a system driven by forces too complex to understand, and subject to long runs of similar behaviour which cannot be explained by randomness. So good or bad weather tends to go on being good or bad and a rising or falling market to persist in the trend. Similarly, in marriage, calm will tend to lead to more calm and quarrels to more quarrels. But another feature of chaotic systems is that the lengthy runs are abruptly terminated by something unpredictable and frequently trivial – a tiny change in input produces what seems a massively disproportionate change in output. This is the cliché of the butterfly fluttering its wings in South America causing a storm in northern Europe. For a marriage it means that everything can appear to be going well until one partner utters one wrong word and all hell breaks loose.

In other words the system goes into turbulence, where none of the normal laws applies. On his deathbed, the physicist Werner Heisenberg said that he had only one question for God: *why turbulence?*[259] Deceased lovers might be inclined to ask God the same question. How can everything turn instantaneously into its opposite – love into hatred, kindness into cruelty, the desire to please into the desire to wound, and the desire to look upon the beloved forever into the desire never to see this loathsome face ever again? A marital row is a strange and frightening phenomenon, a sudden cyclone that whips both parties off the ground, hurls them around the sky insanely for a time and finally dumps them back on earth, exhausted, drained and bewildered. *What the hell was all that?* But the dynamics of the process are impossible to explain. Although every couple since Adam and Eve has had this experience, there are few convincing descriptions in literature of the authentic marital explosion. Like most writers, John Milton evades the problem, saying of Adam and Eve's first quarrel, 'Thus they in mutual accusation spent/The fruitless hours, but neither self-condemning.'[260]

The explosive factor is sex. Any sexual relationship is inherently unstable. The problem is inordinate need combined with utter powerlessness over the object of this need; the result is a desperation that can make love instantaneously flip over into its opposite – a uniquely ugly hatred compounded by shame, disgust and rage at helplessness. So, the overwhelming urge to possess becomes suddenly an equally overwhelming urge to annihilate. An American judge has remarked that he is more concerned for his safety with divorcing couples than with violent criminals and that he and many other judges have panic buttons in their chambers for use when marital rage gets out of hand.[261]

Tension is at the heart of every sexual relationship because the animal and emotional needs are painfully urgent but never fully understood or under control. Yet the tension is central to the relationship. What threatens to blow it apart is also what makes it live. Although companionship is essential and companionable sex is one of the great consolations of maturity, a sexual relationship can never slip too far into mere friendliness. Equilibrium and stability may be tempting but they are the equilibrium and stability of death. There must always be an element of danger and risk. Every lover has to be a demon lover.

But demons are easily bored. When a relationship is in trouble, sex is usually the first thing to go. Frequently this falling-off is the first warning sign. So sex is the canary in the mineshaft: if it sings all is well; if it dies the atmosphere is becoming poisonous.

How to keep the canary singing? How to keep the demon involved? One of many problems with sex is that it is rarely about sex but often really about any number of other things including vanity, power, control, reassurance, habit, novelty, keeping up with fashion and getting what everyone else appears to be getting. And nowadays it is increasingly a branch of the entertainment industry – there are already sex theme parks in several countries. I may well belong to the last generation for whom sex is a mystery, a miracle, an inexhaustible source of wonder. Merely to be in the presence of a woman is to be touched by the sublime. Once everyone was thus ensorcelled, enraptured, enchanted. But now sex is just one more form of idle amusement.

Modern love is photographing yourself being sucked off and, with the help of the obliging technology, immediately circulating the photograph to your large circle of friends.

And we are jaded now. We have tested and tasted too much, urged on by advice endlessly stressing the importance of novelty, repeating that the secret of a successful relationship is making the sex varied and fresh. As with its political predecessors, the sexual revolution has become a kind of tyranny.

The original manual for the liberated age, *The Joy of Sex*, was published back in 1972[262] and, though a revelation in its time (introducing the world to gourmet delights such as the flanquette, the Viennese oyster, and birdsong at morning), has had to be revised and extended to include over a hundred new positions and to acknowledge the growing importance of BDSM and the emergence of the anus as a major new heterosexual resource.[263] In fact, the contemporary lover needs not just one but an entire collection of manuals – to include reference works on erotic furniture (love swings, smothering boxes, queening stools), erotic jewellery (nipple clamps, cock rings, butt plugs) and, of course, the rapidly evolving technology (the vibrating Rabbit strap-on, the multi-speed turbo bullet, the Teledildonic Sinulator). Already it must be time for a Museum of Sex Toys, where couples of a certain age weep bitter-sweet tears at the sight of the original Non-Doctor Vibrator in its 1970s packaging showing, on the front of the box, the heavily lipsticked and mascaraed model with backcombed, flicked-out, lacquered hair. The heartbreaking simplicity of it all in the old days! Now having sex is like putting on a Broadway musical – it requires an original script, costumes, props, a stage set, special lighting and, of course, a fit, energetic and enthusiastic all-singing and all-dancing cast of athletes and acrobats. Now everyone has to be a circus in bed . . . no, a circus all over the home.

And to guide bewildered lovers through all of this there is a growing army of therapists and counsellors, frequently offering advice on prime-time television. These men and women are bright-eyed, fervent believers on a contemporary quest for the Holy Grail of the G spot, a site as legendary, rich and difficult to find as the buried city of Atlantis. In fact, the G does not stand for Grail, but for the original G-man, Ernst Grafenberg, a German gynaecologist who speculated that there must be an erotic zone on the front wall of the vagina because the stimulating effect of doggy-style sex 'must not be explained away . . . by the melodious movements of the testicles like a knocker on the clitoris'.[264] And the new high priests of sex also worship a Holy Trinity. A conventional orgasm is not bad, concedes a radiant TV therapist, but much better is the 'bigasm' which involves both clitoris and G spot, and the ultimate goal is of course the 'trigasm' in which the Holy Trinity all participate – clitoris, G spot and anus uttering hosannas in unison. *More*!

The problem is that sex is losing touch with physical appetite and the body's natural cycle and capability. Even sexual identity has become uncertain and fluid. Few are entirely sure of being straight, gay or both. There is always the haunting thought of missing out on fulfilment in some other identity. And, in losing contact with physical identity and needs, sex becomes increasingly cerebral, driven by concept and image, with the concepts supplied by fantasy and the images by pornography. And the fantasy is driven in turn by novelty and transgression, hence the fascination with anal sex – the anus is the new vagina – and the transgressive thrills of BDSM. It is certainly ironic, and possibly significant, that the age of liberation is increasingly turned on by bondage. One of the most popular products in the Ann Summers chain of sex shops is the Bondage Starter Kit. And the latest BDSM kick for the jaded is paying to have yourself kidnapped: as you walk along the street, a van suddenly screeches up and several burly men in balaclavas jump out and bundle you away to a basement where they inflict all the indignities specified in the contract. (Apparently there are national differences in abductor preference – the English love to be seized by American Deep South hillbillies.) The ingenious feature of this service is that it plays not just on the desire for bondage but also on the contemporary thrill of expectation – the customer never knows where or when the 'customized abduction' will happen, and has days or even weeks of delicious anticipation. And the waiting period can be further enhanced by surveillance and stalking, so that attention is added to expectation. Finally, the satisfied abductee is presented with a souvenir DVD of the experience (because an experience hasn't happened unless it is captured on film). The genius who created this service should be a candidate for entrepreneur of the century.[265]

But where is the harm in such play-acting? The men in balaclavas are limited to specific contractual instructions; the Ann Summers handcuffs are lined with pink fur. The problem is that transgressive pleasure always requires more to reproduce the original kick. So one minute you're being delightfully spanked with a silk slipper and the next minute you're having your scrotum nailed to the floor.

And transsexuals are a new fascination because they embody maximum potential by combining identities, functions and equipment – human Swiss Army knives. They are not only concepts made images but made images of flesh and blood. A trannie is a walking, talking, living, breathing sex toy. And the concept is also exciting to consumers because it is a 2-for-1 offer – buy one gender, get one free.

Another new factor is that the images that fuel all this, pornographic movies, once expensive, difficult and embarrassing to access, are now available free in the comfort of home. Porn certainly perks up the canary but its distortions are legion. Ironically, for the age of expectation, porn omits the most thrilling expectation of all – foreplay, the intoxication of proximity and fragrance, the electricity of worshipful touch, the enchanting glide of zips and the yielding of buttons, the stirring rustle and slither and soft fall of garments. Instead, porn cuts straight to naked pumping and sucking. The action must always be dramatic and visible. So, instead of tender union there is frantic driving, and it is always the man pumping madly, whereas to achieve orgasm the woman needs to control the rhythm and make it more gentle (although not at the end). And instead of orgasm within, there is always the money shot of ejaculation over the woman. Hence the new sweet nothing murmured by male lovers: 'Can I come in your face?'

But the orifices and positions and combinations are limited. Soon everything human bodies are capable of will be available for viewing in everyone's living room. Where then will we turn for transgressive excitement? Visionaries are already working on this problem. David Levy, an artificial intelligence researcher, promises that by the mid-twenty-first century, 'love with robots will be as normal as love with other humans, while the number of sexual acts and love-making positions commonly practised between humans will be extended, as robots teach more than is in all of the world's sex manuals combined.'[266]

This contemporary obsession with variety as the way to prevent habituation is misplaced. In an experiment on appetite two groups of volunteers were invited to attend a laboratory once a week for tests, which were in fact a sham – the real experiment was the snack offered as a reward. One group was allowed to choose all their snacks in advance and so opted for variety; the others were given their favourite snack every week. When satisfaction ratings were compared at the end of the study, those on the same snack turned out to be more satisfied than those with variety.[267] The explanation is that the time-lapse of a week was sufficient to renew the appeal of the old favourite. So rarity may be better than variety at beating the habituation trap, and the spice of life may not be variety but having what you enjoy most at appropriate intervals.

Also misplaced is the idea that love is the consequence of sexual fulfilment. It may well be the other way round. The most satisfying sex is an expression of tenderness, not a mastery of the techniques in the manual.

The deepest pleasures are those that have been earned, and it is no different with sex. So the most intense experiences come after difficulty, pain, anger and turbulence – in other words, after violent quarrelling. Reconciliation sex is the most sublime experience available to the human creature.

Of course, this is a rare bounty. For regular pleasure, here is a radical suggestion, to be implemented only at suitable intervals – the sex of simplicity, the sex of less, Zen sex. Let the lovers lie in bed at night, touching and marvelling, at intervals seeking each other's mouths for silent but profound communication of gratitude. Eventually, moving slowly as one, they assume the missionary position and tenderly conjoin. Then, in sweet silence and practically motionless (with the minimal movement directed by the woman), they lie still and permit an autonomous ecstasy to steal slowly over them.

Perhaps this would be the ideal way to depart from life? There would also be the exquisite absurdity of simultaneously coming and going. But a lifetime of responsible and considerate behaviour would never permit leaving a lover with the nuisance of a corpse. That would *so* ruin the sweet, silent, still afterglow.

13

The Absurdity of Age

How can I be this old when I was always the youngest boy in the class? Ageing is counter-intuitive . . . shocking . . . *absurd.*

The physical changes are obvious. But there are also mental and psychological developments.

1. Memory Loss: Actually, it is not so much that information is lost as that the retrieval time gets longer and longer until eventually it exceeds the remaining lifespan. So, at some point, you may wake shouting that the guy who had a hit with that great number 'Chantilly Lace' was of course The Big Bopper . . . but the attempt to punch the air in triumph reveals that you are in a wooden box six feet beneath the air.

2. Shrinkage: Everything shrinks – the body itself and all its component parts (brain, liver, dick and especially heart). The only good news may be a psychological shrinkage. Occasionally the ego also shrinks.

Not so good is the shrinkage of interests and activities. The years bring an overpowering temptation to withdraw from difficulty into a comfort zone. In particular, the effort of thinking is often abandoned as strenuous and futile. The world is becoming increasingly alien, so why bother even trying to understand it? But this surrender is likely to lead straight to senility. The only way to retain life is to be interested in all of it (or everything except rap music and celebrity chefs). Otherwise life will take its revenge. Those who show no interest soon become of no interest.

3. Stinginess: There seems to be truth in the stereotype of the old miser. I've noticed in myself an increasing reluctance to put my hand in my pocket. Is it a consequence of diminishing resources, especially strength, energy and time, which must all be hoarded so a general hoarding instinct develops?

4. The Acceleration of Time: Not only is there little time left, but what remains is no longer content merely to pass and actually begins to *accelerate*. Or, to be more precise, there is a disturbing double effect – time in the short term appears to drag while in the long term it appears to speed up. The psychological explanation is that the time axis resembles a spatial dimension. In a painting with perspective, the distance between two points appears long if there are interesting objects between the points and short if there is nothing between. On the time axis, youth is packed with vivid events, or events more vividly experienced because fresh, a series of first times including *that* first time; the common feeling of the desultory middle years is that nothing at all is happening. So time in the middle years seems to pass more quickly. This also explains why, although it is difficult to remember what happened yesterday, memories of youth remain startlingly vivid.

5. Metaphysical Impatience: Possibly a consequence of the acceleration of time, this is a growing rage at the obduracy and recalcitrance of the world, its persistent and continuing refusal to oblige. Though essentially metaphysical, it can take specific form – for instance, as queue rage or, my own version, escalator rage. When I see people blocking an escalator by standing two abreast I could happily strangle both of them.

6. Uncertainty: Youth is supposed to be the time of indecision and doubt and the middle years the time of conviction. I can only say that, for me, it has been the other way round. Youth was the time of passionate beliefs, enthusiasms and aversions and middle age is the time of growing uncertainty. At one point there came the shocking revelation that I no longer knew what I believed in – or if I believed in anything at all. I no longer even knew what I *liked* or *disliked*. Do I prefer sea bass to salmon? Is William Faulkner any good? Do I even care about any of this?

The middle years made me a castaway on the Greek archipelago of aporia, ataraxia and anhedonia – or, in plain English, perplexity, indifference and joylessness.

7. Bowel Obsession: This is a strange one. I am at a loss for a theory. But there is no denying the phenomenon. I have an octogenarian friend who is that increasingly rare thing, a wise man, so when he offered to give me the meaning of life in one word he had my undivided attention.

After waiting for a moment – his sense of timing was still exquisite – he murmured softly, 'Bisacodyl.'

There was silence. I was every bit as mystified as he wished.

Eventually I said, 'Is that some sort of Viagra thing?'

He grimaced impatiently. 'No, no . . . never mind fucking,' and the frown relaxed and softened into radiant wonder, 'the thing is to *crap* like a young man.'

8. The Death-in-Venice Effect: My octogenarian friend was disingenuous in claiming to have lost interest in the opposite sex. Throughout lunch his eyes kept returning to the waitress. For the beauty of youth, which youth itself seems hardly to appreciate, astounds and dazzles the ageing. Rilke said that 'beauty is the beginning of terror we can still just endure'[268] – and, not only does this terror intensify with the years, almost everyone young starts to seem beautiful and terrifying. Because the life which blooms so gorgeously in the young body is a promise of extinction to the ageing beholder. And yet the urge to look is unbearably strong. Beauty is the headlight that paralyses the grey rabbit, the blazing sun that withers the spent husk. Turn away the failing eyes. *Turn them away*.

On another day I was at a very different lunch with a dentist whose patients included movie stars, television presenters and celebrity chefs. The connection was through our children and wives who had met at a nursery – before the dentist became hugely successful and moved to this large, detached house with pool in an exclusive suburb. Other guests included the affluent neighbours and their wives – attractive women in their forties and fifties who laughed frequently, heartily and knowingly. It was a beautiful April day, full of freshness and promise. Light danced on the still water and champagne flowed as joyously as the torrents of spring. Bottles were popped as frequently and casually as cans of Coca-Cola. It was like one of Gatsby's legendary parties. I had never known the phenomenon of un-limited champagne.

By and by, the wives decided to go for a swim. We are bom-barded relentlessly by sexual images but always of ridiculously slim, youthful models; the magnificently heavy thighs of mature women are a glory rarely seen. Then, just as the swimmers emerged from changing indoors, our host the dentist lifted a lawn chair and placed it right in front of me, blocking the view.

'You seem a thoughtful type,' he said. 'Give me *one good reason* for getting up in the morning.'

This was not the sort of request to be expected from Gatsby. Out of sight behind him, the mature Nereids with girlish cries lowered splendid thighs into the dappled water.

It turned out that, but for his guests, he would probably not have bothered to get out of bed. He slept for most of most week-ends and was on a heavy dosage of antidepressants.

'I was one of Harley Street's first endodontists,' he explained. 'Now there's lots of them . . . all younger, cheaper and most likely better. So I've lost my nerve. I'm terrified of fucking up. My patients are demanding, intolerant, ruthless. They'd ruin me.' He waved at the house, gardens and pool. 'Then what about all this? I'm mortgaged to the hilt and beyond.'

So his story continued – depression, exhaustion, chest pains, loss of libido. There was no need to explain this last symptom. He never once turned to the abundance and plenitude just behind him, not even when the wives emerged and scampered, dripping, towards the house. I tried to look round him but, of course, missed everything. There was only a flash of towels and laughter, mocking, on the air.

Meanwhile, he was regarding me in an intense, thoughtful way that seemed to suggest expectation of wise counsel. But the times do not venerate the sage.

He said, 'Your teeth badly need whitening.'

Nevertheless I persisted. 'What age are you now?'

'I've just turned fifty-four'.

I suggested that he was probably undergoing *the episode*. This is nothing like the cliché of the 'midlife crisis', which is supposed to make men of forty buy open-topped sports cars in fire-engine red and roar off in search of young women with large breasts. As in the case of the dentist, the episode is more likely to encourage the opposite – a complete loss of interest in sex and an over-whelming reluctance to get out of bed. It is also more likely to occur in the fifties and it happens to women as well as men. When my friends and relatives moved into their fifties most of them had episodes, which varied in duration, intensity and style, but had in common an abrupt, unexpected collapse, the symp-toms of which varied from extreme, lasting depression to intermittent panic attacks. This collapse seems to be the result of a sudden loss of nerve, a failure of certainty and confidence, an overwhelming feeling that 'I just can't do this anymore'.

My own episode began with sudden bolts of terror at the prospect of having to deliver large lectures. I had been doing these for years when, out of the blue, came anxiety, chest pains, heartburn, sweating and the shakes. The authority, knowledge and teaching ability acquired over a lifetime disappeared into terrifying blankness, leaving only one certainty: 'I can't do this anymore.'

How did I get out of it? I'm still not entirely sure, but it was probably by a form of Cognitive Behavioural Therapy, though without being aware of the practice or the term. Firstly, I allayed anxiety by meticulous, detailed preparation of material, so that there was no need to remember or improvise. Then I reminded myself that, after twenty years of competent lecturing, this fear was irrational. Finally, I forced myself to establish at least the appearance of authority over the students. It was them or me, and it could not be me.

But what causes the episode? Many factors are involved. There is the awareness of change and physical decline, of personal impotence and insignificance, of a world growing ever more indifferent, demanding and ruthless while one's own strength and energy diminish. There is the loss of faith that brings the feeling of being a charlatan, an old fraud. And there is the certainty of death and of being swiftly forgotten as though one had never existed. But perhaps most significant is the death of potential, the failure of imminence. We live in constant expectation, believing always that something will turn up, some invitation or opportunity, and then we will step forward to seize our destiny and become at last our true selves. But the middle years bring the sickening realization that nothing is going to turn up. There will be no magical deliverance. This is indeed all it is. Worse still, this meagre all-it-is will actually diminish.

So all these termites eat away at confidence, silently and invisibly but relentlessly, until confidence suddenly crumbles and collapses into the dust. The worst fear is that the panic and depression will become permanent – and perhaps even intensify. But most people get through the experience and look back on it with astonishment. I understand it now as a kind of initiation rite: as adolescents are initiated into adulthood and life, so the episode initiates adults into ageing and death. It is the Valley of Poverty and Nothingness, the last valley, that, in Farid Ud-Din Attar's poem, the birds must fly through to emerge and discover themselves as the Simorgh.

The reward is that everything brightens up afterwards. The graph of the set point, the default temperament, is a U shape, with the high mood of youth declining to a minimum low in the middle years but then, surprisingly, climbing back to its earlier height.[269] And the graph of marital satisfaction follows the same shape, dropping steadily in middle age but, if the couple can stay together, rising again in the later years.[270] Even memory follows this curve. Septuagenarians have intense memories of youth, remember hardly anything about the middle period, and have intense memories again about the recent past.[271] All the surveys seem to agree that the middle years are a crock of shit. According to the World Health Organization, depression 'is already the single leading cause of disability for people in midlife'. There is even evidence of a rise in the suicide rate of the middle-aged. In the USA between 1999 and 2004 the suicide rate for the young remained stable, while the rate for those in the age range 45 to 54 rose by nearly 20 per cent and the rate for those in the older age groups dropped by an average of 10 per cent.[272] The U shape of the temperament curve seems to be becoming more pronounced. But at least there is good news – if you can hang on rather than hanging yourself, things may look up.

There are several reasons for this. Ageing involves much involuntary detachment – retirement from a job, departure of children from the home, an easing of sexual appetite. The nature, needs, desires and oddities of the self are better understood and, therefore, more easily controlled. There is greater awareness of what will bring satisfaction and what will not. And, though the circumstances of age may be more depressing than those of youth, it seems to become easier to suppress negative thoughts. In brain scans of younger adults the amygdala reacts both to positive and negative stimuli, but in older adults it tends to react only to the positive.[273] The theory is that the prefrontal cortex becomes better able to control the amygdala. The ego has finally learned to tame the id.

Thrilling sexual adventures and career developments are increasingly improbable. So the siren call of the world becomes easier to resist. There is less need to be like everyone else, as well as less need to be liked and less need to like – and so less compulsion to be accommodating. One of the great glories of later life is contrariness, provided it remains conscious and does not harden into mere eccentricity. One of the most thrilling research findings I have come across is a survey by Howard Friedman of the University of California which concluded that not only is cheerfulness unrelated to longevity, but that the chronically cheerful have a shorter than average lifespan: 'It's bad advice to tell people to cheer up and they'll live longer.'[274] So here is another good thing about ageing – stick around and you may get to dance on the grave of the smiley face.

On the other hand, mindfulness, attention and learning new skills do appear to extend life, as well as improving its quality.[275] So the tendency of age to shy away from the new and difficult may literally be fatal. There is even evidence that the brain, far from being doomed to steady decline, can generate new neurons right up until death, a miracle known as neurogenesis.[276]

Best of all, the failure of imminence, which seemed so catastrophic, may be revealed as a blessing. For the spell of potential is an evil spell that occludes the senses and deranges the mind. When the spell finally lifts it is easier to learn the crucial lesson – that the journey is more important than the destination, the activity more important than the outcome. This is the conclusion that turns up again and again. The struggle to learn is more valuable than the learning itself, thinking with no particular purpose is the most enjoyable form of thought, absorption in a difficult skill – the flow experience – is more rewarding than any recognition, striving to love is more satisfying than being in love. Everything must be its own reward.

It becomes clear that the life being lived is indeed all it is – but, *hey*, it is not so bad after all to be able to see, hear, taste, walk unaided, run up stairs and sustain an erection with merely human rather than chemical assistance. In fact this is *astoundingly good.* The natural world stands revealed in all its sublime abundance and the human world in all its sublime absurdity. But this wealth is on offer for only a strictly limited period, so there is an obligation to appreciate. In what may be the last speech Shakespeare wrote, he said: 'Let us be thankful for that which is.'[277] The strange and unexpected gift of age is gratitude.

Whichever way life is regarded, it seems to assume a U shape. The curve of strength, energy and ambition is an inverted U with a high in the middle; the curve of temperament is a U the right way up with a low in the middle; and progress through life is a U laid flat, a switchback where stops are first passed going out and then again coming back but with less burdensome baggage and more appreciation and gratitude. So the ageing couple can be lovers again but without the exhausting battles of youth and the burdens of child rearing. And it is possible to be a student again but without the tyranny of career, curriculum or examination and with the ability to choose and actually enjoy the study texts. Of course, the final stage of the switchback is second childhood, a phrase that assumes more and more meanings as this stage approaches, though, for once, these are meanings best left unexplored.

The crucial factor on the return leg of the U is acceptance of ageing and mortality – not easy in a culture of eternal youth. Who now would say, like Rilke, 'I believe in old age; to work and to grow old: this is what life expects of us'?[278]

And the cities of the sibling society have banished death. When I was growing up in a small town in Ireland death was a constant presence. Every time I visited my grandfather he listed, with malevolent delight, the contemporaries who had recently died. The local paper had one page of news and several of death notices. Funeral cortèges regularly moved through the streets and all the passers-by stopped, removed hats and solemnly bowed their heads. There were large wreaths on doors and wakes lasting for days to give the entire community time to view 'the remains'.

But now, in the city, death is invisible. There no cortèges, no notices, no mention, no 'remains'. Years can go by without even a trace of death. It is like the flourishing city rats – always close but never mentioned, much less seen. There are no wakes – and, in secular cremation services, most of the mourners never see the corpse or coffin, much less the cremation. It is like a retirement-from-work party but without the retired employee.

People used to say things like 'when I'm gone', 'I won't live to see that' and 'not in my time'. But now no one mentions finitude. As we draw closer to death we should become more aware of it, but the opposite is often the case. The problem is that living is itself as habit-forming as any of the activities living involves. We just get terribly used to being around. As E.M. Cioran put it: 'The more laden he is with years, the more readily he speaks of his death as a distant, quite unlikely event. Life is now such a habit that he has become unfit for death.'[279]

So the new solution to death is to banish it from view and from mind, and to take refuge in habit. But only awareness of transience can give life its savour. Mortality is the spice of life.

In his essay 'On Transience' Freud rejected the argument of a young poet who believed that impermanence devalued everything in life: 'On the contrary, its value is heightened! The value of transience is one of scarcity over time. The limitation of the possibility of enjoyment makes it even more precious.'[280]

Awareness of mortality can provide the focus and intensity so often missing from experience and is another gift of the later years. The time-rich young are as presumptuous and careless as the materially wealthy – if everything may be purchased then nothing has value – but the time-poor old know that very little may now be purchased and so everything is valuable. Sexual pleasure, for instance, is immeasurably enriched and intensified by the knowledge that it may not be available for much longer, cut off by incapacity or the death of a partner. One of the most heartfelt lines I have written is: 'If every time could be the last it's as good as the first.'

Literature, from Homer on, abounds in eloquent reminders to appreciate the miracle of earthly existence. When Odysseus tries to console Achilles in the underworld with news of his renown on earth, the legendary warrior replies:

Let me hear no smooth talk
of death from you, Odysseus, light of councils.

Better, I say, to break sod as a farm hand
for some poor countryman, on iron rations,
than lord it over the exhausted dead.[281]

'To philosophize is to learn how to die' is the English version of
the French of Montaigne who took it from the Latin of Cicero who
took it in turn from the Greek of Plato. Buddha was there before
all of them: 'I do not use magic to extend my life. Now, before
me, the trees come alive.'[282]

To learn to die is to learn to live. Death is the giver of life. As
Elvis warned, 'It's now or never.'

Death may even extend life. The monks in the communities on
Mount Athos in Greece wear black to remind themselves during
every waking moment of mortality, and yet mostly live into
extreme old age. So the secret of a long life may be acknowl-
edging that it is short. And if this acknowledgement does not
extend life, it certainly improves its quality. There are no cases of
Alzheimer's among the Mount Athos monks.

Acknowledgement is everything. Reactions differ, from the
famous rage of Dylan Thomas, 'Do not go gentle into that good
night', to the beautiful acceptance of Marcus Aurelius: 'Observe
how transient and trivial is all mortal life; yesterday a drop of
semen, tomorrow a handful of ashes. So spend these fleeting
moments on earth as Nature would have you spend them, and
then go to your rest with good grace, as an olive falls in its
season, with a blessing for the earth that bore it and a thanksgiv-
ing to the tree that gave it life.'[283] These reactions appear to be
opposites – but both face the unwelcome truth.

And only through this acknowledgement can come the unique
flaring, an incandescence inspired by the prospect of extinction.
One example is the phenomenon of late style, a flourishing
common in the final phase of painters', composers' and writers'
lives. In spite of the many differences in artists and arts, there is
a common wild impatience – verging on frenzy – that is possessed
by obsession, rejects virtuosity, rhetoric and finish, bursts out of

conventional form, transcends technique, surrenders conscious control for instinctive power and is utterly indifferent to audience and reception. So these works often shock contemporaries who dismiss them as childish, crude, fragmentary, unfinished and repetitive, the products of deteriorating minds. Only much later can they be appreciated for their exhilarating vitality, what the critic Barbara Herrnstein Smith defined as the 'senile sublime'.[284] And, paradoxically, by working exclusively for themselves, these painters, writers and composers communicate even more directly and intensely. With no desire to please, impress, charm or reassure, depth can speak nakedly and urgently to depth.

The works of Picasso's last decade, produced in his eighties and nineties, have all these qualities and also a scandalous eroticism. Entirely unreconciled, Picasso could not bear to depart from the paradise of the flesh, and obsessively painted female nudes and embracing couples. The nudes are massive, with monumental limbs, huge wild staring eyes, onion toes and banana fingers, distorted, displaced breasts with large black nipples and, always drawing the eye to the centre, gaping, graffito-crude vulvae. Picasso wanted these women to be so physically present that the startled art lover could smell their armpits and vaginas. 'You have to know how to be vulgar,' he said. 'Paint with four-letter words.'[285] There is a work called 'Woman Pissing' which fully lives up to its title and another of a woman masturbating with both hands. The paintings of couples are crazier still, with the even more wild-eyed heads and bodies of the lovers merged and the man seeming to wish to devour or strangle the woman. Never has sexual fusion been so intensely portrayed. In the final embrace picture, painted when Picasso was over ninety and close to death, limbs are so enmeshed that it is impossible to identify which belongs to the man or woman, though there are two sets of graffito genitals. There are also late self-portraits. One, painted in his eighties, is of his upper body in a striped top. The torso is painted with cursory violence, the stripes of the top whacked on with a loaded brush so that the paint is encouraged to misbehave and splatter, dribble and run. The head is grim, the eyes two black sockets dead to the outer world and seeing only some terrible inner revelation. And, in the same month as the final embrace, there is a final self-portrait – a gigantic head with enormous wild eyes staring in terror at something close and approaching inexorably closer.

When these last works were exhibited they were almost universally derided; the consensus was that Picasso's astounding technique had finally deserted him. In fact, Picasso had merely transcended technique. As he himself put it, he had so much technique it completely ceased to exist.[286] More perceptive views came from outside the art world, for instance from the Mexican poet Octavio Paz: 'He paints out of urgent necessity, and what he paints is urgency itself. He is the Painter of time.'[287] This identifies the key quality of late style – urgency. Picasso: 'I have less and less time and more and more to say.'[288]

Claude Monet's late works contain no nudes or even people, but pulsate with the same sensual frenzy. He could not bear to leave the physical world, represented obsessively by water lilies in paintings that grew bigger and bigger and were worked over with increasing fervour – he regularly rose at four in the morning and worked all day. These works abandon representation almost completely for an abstract orgy of slashes, daubs and swirls, interspersed with areas of bare, coarse-textured canvas. The brushstrokes make no attempt to conceal themselves but are ragged and uneven, beginning in rich impasto swathes and tailing off in broken patches and long, straggly tendrils – he often deliberately used old, worn brushes for a more irregular effect. Paint exults in being paint, and clumps, clots, ridges and drips. In the macro view everything runs into everything else in a welter of fusing colour, which is his vision of the gorgeousness of the world he has no choice but to leave. Standing in front of these late works, mesmerized, exhilarated and terrified, you wonder how an old guy had the balls to be so mad.

In music there are the late quartets of Beethoven, which are more like ruminating aloud than attempts to capture the attention of listeners. And the same could be said about a musician of a completely different style and era – the jazz pianist Earl Hines. About the only things Hines and Beethoven had in common were playing the piano and growing old. In his youth an entertainer, showman and bandleader in a Chicago nightclub owned by gangsters, Hines was forgotten in his middle years and rediscovered only late in life, when he was invited to give a solo concert at the Little Theater in New York. There he came on stage to inform his audience that he intended to play as if he were in his own living room – and proceeded to astound them with boundless audacity and exuberance. After this, he rejected not only bands but even small groups and played almost exclusively solo piano, a rare and possibly unique development for a jazzman. And, in the recordings of these solo performances of long, dense improvisations full of abrupt tempo changes and jolting counterpoint, with each hand playing things not only unrelated but actually *warring*, he seems indeed to be in his own living room, arguing eloquently with himself. But there are always individual qualities in late style. The Hines wildness was an irrepressible jubilation that burst through even on ballads and blues. After his rebirth he said: 'The greatest thing to draw wrinkles in a man's face is worry. Why should I be unhappy and pull down my face and drag my feet and make everybody around me feel that way too? By being what you are, something always comes up. Sunshine always opens out.'[289]

And in literature there is Shakespeare, whose late plays burst out of the constraints of the play form, in particular its unity of time and place. The late works – *The Winter's Tale, Cymbeline, The Tempest, Pericles: Prince of Tyre* and *The Two Noble Kinsmen* – are known as romances but aspire to the freedom of the novel. And their language is equally impatient – urgent, compressed and dense, syntax twisted out of shape by the pressure of new ideas crowding in on the old. Shakespeare just couldn't be bothered with the tedium of padding out sentences. When, in *The Winter's*

Tale, Leontes cries, 'Stars! Stars! And all eyes else dead coals'[290], we have to work out that, in these eight words, he is comparing his wife's eyes to stars and that, in turn, compared to his wife's eyes, those of all other women seem like dead coals.

With Tolstoy, late urgency made him break out of literature completely into works with baldly questioning titles such as *What Is Religion?*, *What Is Art?*, *What To Do?* and, even more relevant in the contemporary world, 'Why Do People Stupefy Themselves?' And, when he did write fiction, the stories are full of bitter, questioning characters bewildered in the face of extinction. *The Death of Ivan Ilyich* is a study of the consequences of denial. Ilyich is a magistrate who has lived only for status and comfort, 'pleasantly' and 'decently', insulated by habit and banality, but is struck down by an unexpected fatal illness and is obliged to die alone, excluded by the conventional life he himself has always espoused. His wife and daughter can't wait to get rid of him to resume their social lives and his colleagues see his death only as a promotion opportunity. Entirely lacking outer or inner resources, Ilyich dies 'after three days of incessant screaming'.[291]

In poetry there was W.B. Yeats whose late subjects included 'A Crazed Girl' and 'The Wild Old Wicked Man', who claimed that only lust and rage could spur the old into song and who posed the rhetorical question, 'Why should not old men be mad?' As with Picasso, Yeats's imagination grew stronger and wilder as his physical powers declined:

> What shall I do with this absurdity –
> O heart, O troubled heart – this caricature,
> Decrepit age that has been tied to me
> As to a dog's tail?
>   Never had I more
> Excited, passionate, fantastical
> Imagination, nor an eye and ear
> That more expected the impossible – [292]

In one of his finest late poems, 'Lapis Lazuli', Yeats ponders on three old Chinese men carved in stone: 'Their eyes mid many wrinkles, their eyes,/Their ancient, glittering eyes are gay'.[293] Always solemn and humourless, Yeats himself could never abandon the grand manner and be gay, but he recognized that gaiety was an inspiring feature of Eastern culture. The Western late style is most often angry, discontented and bitter, even despairing, but the Eastern version, while just as defiantly rejecting convention and cherishing independence, prefers humour, zest and delight.

Here is the painter Hokusai, a major influence on Monet, who owned one of his works and took from him the idea of the obsessively repeated subject (for example in *One Hundred Views of Mount Fuji*): 'At seventy-three I learned a little about the real structure of nature, of animals, plants, birds, fishes and insects. In consequence when I am eighty, I shall have made more progress, at ninety I shall penetrate the mystery of things; at a hundred I shall certainly have reached a marvellous stage; and when I am a hundred and ten, everything I do, be it but a dot or a line, will be alive. Written at the age of seventy-five by me, once Hokusai, today Gwakio Rojin, the old man mad about drawing.'[294]

What an anthology could be compiled of defiant, zestful, self-sufficient Eastern old age! For instance, Tu Fu's 'Returning Late':

Holding a candle in the courtyard, I call for two
Torches. A gibbon in the gorge, startled, shrieks once.

Old and tired, my hair white, I dance and sing out.
Goosefoot cane, no sleep . . . *Catch me if you can*![295]

PART V

The Happy Ending

14

The Happiness of Absurdity

Among the many disturbing discoveries of the twentieth century was the revelation that life is essentially absurd. Kafka was the first to develop this idea. In his quest stories, the quest hero is constantly frustrated, always unable to gain admission to the Castle or the Law, but equally unable to abandon the quest. In other words, the search for meaning will never find meaning but must continue even so.

And, while Kafka was developing this theme in literature, physicists were coming to the conclusion that, at the weird sub-atomic level, nothing exists unless it is observed. So the search for the nature of reality revealed that in fact there was no reality. Werner Heisenberg, discoverer of the uncertainty principle, declared in despair that nature itself was absurd.

In philosophy Camus compared the human condition to the fate of Sisyphus, condemned to push a rock up a hill again and again for all time. An absurd fate – but Camus insisted that Sisyphus could be happy.

Then Beckett added a new twist – a quest saga without a quest. In *Waiting for Godot* his pair of tramps, modern men, are too lazy and incurious to go on a journey in search of meaning. Instead they just hang about waiting for meaning to come to them. Godot was bound to turn up soon, they repeated endlessly, while knowing in their hearts that he never would. For Beckett this absurdity was hilarious.

And mordant laughter seems the only possible response. There is no way back to certainty, simplicity and innocence, only the way forward into confusion, uncertainty and knowingness. The gasp of wonder becomes the sardonic bark of disbelief. Absurdity is the new sublime.

The good news is that, while other resources are dwindling, absurdity is multiplying and flourishing and filling the earth. There are ever more bizarre ways of passing the time while waiting for Godot. For instance car-park attendant Bob Prior honours the quest from the comfort of his own home by devoting all his spare time to making *Star Trek* sets and characters from Rice Krispies packets.[296] It's the Rice Krispies detail that makes this story sublime. Scorning mere scale models, Elvis-impersonator James Cawley has given ten years and $150,000 to building a full-sized replica of the bridge of the *Starship Enterprise* in his garage.[297]

For sporty types demanding engagement and spectacle, there is competitive eating, a new sport but with its own official body, the IFOCE (International Federation of Competitive Eating), which establishes world records and rankings and oversees contests, disqualifying any competitor who has a 'Roman incident' as a consequence of 'urges contrary to swallowing'. As Brazil dominates soccer, so Japan dominates competitive eating and the current world champion is Takeru 'The Tsunami' Kobayashi who has eaten 53 hot dogs in 12 minutes (and 18 pounds of cow brains in 15 minutes). Other top gastro-athletes include Carl 'Crazy Legs' Conti who downed 168 oysters in 10 minutes, Oleg Zhornitskiy who got through four 32-ounce jars of mayonnaise in 8 minutes and Don 'Moses' Lerman who consumed 7 quarter-pound butter sticks in 5 minutes. Just to think about this last feat could give the average eater a Roman incident. But even Competitive Eating has its paradox – all the top eaters are slim. Kobayashi weighs only 131 pounds.

For those of artistic temperament, contemporary art offers splendidly absurd opportunities. Major publicly funded institutions have paid an artist to exhibit his girlfriend's used sanitary towels, another to hire sprinters and organize a series of them running through an art gallery every thirty seconds, and a third to film himself abseiling down a studio wall, naked except for a titanium ice screw in his rectum. Tate Britain has invested over £30,000 of taxpayers' money in 'Monochrome Till Receipt (White)', which is a supermarket shopping receipt for items such as boil-in-the-bag rice, pickled eggs, sanitary towels and swing-bin liners. Though the bin liners may be artist's materials. One of the artist's enigmatic previous works, possibly a self-portrait, was a black bin liner filled with air.

For the politically minded, there is the possibility of becoming the leader of the Western world by saying things like, 'They misunderestimated me', 'People say I'm indecisive, but I don't know about that', 'One has a stronger hand when there's more people playing your same cards' and 'I know the human being can coexist peacefully with fish'.[298]

Who would not rejoice to live in a century where such things are possible? Lord, what fools these mortals be!

Surely business at least is too hard-headed for absurdity? Not a bit of it. Major corporations have paid large sums to a management guru who describes himself as 'the leading world authority on creative thinking' and claims that, 'without wishing to boast', his latest system is 'the first new way of thinking to be developed for 2,400 years since the days of Plato, Socrates and Aristotle'. Known as the 'Six Thinking Hats', this system requires managers to don a red hat for proposing a project, a yellow hat for listing its advantages, a black hat for its disadvantages and so on. But, as well as coloured hats, investors in the system get the aphorisms of the greatest thinker since Socrates: 'You can't dig a hole in a different place by digging the same hole deeper', 'With a problem, you look for a solution' and 'A bird is different from an aeroplane, although both fly through the air'.[299]

Inspired by this wisdom, the entrepreneur can discover many absurd ways to make money. For instance, by selling dirt. Not the figurative dirt of pornography – actual dirt. Alan Jenkins, an Irish immigrant to the USA, has become a multimillionaire by selling 12-ounce plastic bags of Official Irish Dirt. Like all astute businessmen, Jenkins offers substantial discounts for bulk purchasing. For instance, he has provided a Galway-born Manhattan lawyer with enough Irish dirt to be buried in – for the very reasonable round figure of $100,000 – and, for only $148,000, he has delivered to a Corkman several tons of Irish dirt to serve as a secure foundation for his new American home. It seems that the twenty-first century has added a new stage to the immigrant experience: after getting established and sending for the family, send for the native dirt. Jenkins now has a Jewish counterpart in Steven Friedman, founder of Holy Land Earth, which imports Israeli dirt bearing an official seal of approval from Rabbi Velvel Brevda, director of the Council of Geula in Jerusalem. There is an obvious opportunity for importing Islamic dirt from Mecca – but a true visionary will see the global possibilities and set up International Sacred Soil to send dirt from everywhere flying to everywhere else.

And clear-headed science is as absurd as hard-headed business. The search for the nature of reality leads ever deeper into absurdity. It is difficult to know now which is more absurd – the micro or the macro, the physics of the atom or the physics of space.

At first the atom was only a nucleus surrounded by electrons and only the electron was weird. Like a modern bisexual, it could be a particle one moment and a wave the next, depending on who was making eyes at it. And, like a modern celebrity, it did not exist at all if no one was looking. This was disturbing, but at least the nucleus was as solidly dull and dependable as a GP in a market town. Then the supposedly solid nucleus was found to teem with weird particles. It was a particle zoo. No, these were all actually the same particle – the quark. So there are only two elementary particles, the electron and the quark. Except that there are two heavier electrons, the muon and tau, and six types of quark – up, down, strange, charm, top and bottom (sometimes known as truth and beauty). There are also superquarks known as squarks.

And, apparently, atoms, which should be the basis of everything, account for only about 4 per cent of the universe. The other 96 per cent is missing – but it is probably 25 per cent dark matter and 75 per cent dark energy. The scientists explain gravely that there is not enough gravity. Dark matter is certainly no laughing matter.

Even the void, the last cloister, is no longer chaste. It appears that emptiness is not empty and stillness is not still. The firmament is a ceaseless churn of matter turning into antimatter and back again. Even matter itself is incorrigibly unstable and restless, endlessly trying to become its opposite and then dissatisfied with that too.

And the weird micro is weirdly mixed up with the weird macro due to a weird phenomenon known as quantum entanglement, which means that a quantum event on earth may instantly change things in some distant galaxy.

But the galaxies do not appear to be keen on entanglement. Apparently the stars are fleeing from us ever more rapidly. And who could blame them after their first contact with humans in space? The most spectacular and absurd quest in human history was the landing of men on the moon. Not even Kafka and Beckett working in collaboration could have come up with such a sublime fable. This event initiated so many of the key features of the age – the new privileging of image over content (the landing offered no benefits other than pictures, but the pictures were more valuable than the moon rock), of differentials over absolute values (the USA's real purpose was to land on the moon before the USSR), and of means over ends (men went to the moon to show that it was possible to go to the moon).

This was also the first global media event and the apotheosis of modern technology. Almost 600 million people watched on TV, none aware of the frailty of the technology or how close it came to failing. The lunar module overshot its landing site and the navigational computer, which had less power than a contemporary mobile phone, developed a double hernia under the strain, producing the error message '1202', a message no one had ever seen before. Imagine tearing across the surface of the moon, with the fuel gauge reading close to zero, and being offered as the solution 1202. Men with a philosophical bent might have interpreted this message as conclusive proof that God has a great sense of humour. But the astronauts had neither the inclination nor the time for such thoughts. Neil Armstrong had to assume manual control and watch impossibly rocky terrain rush past as the fuel ran out. With just ten seconds of fuel left he found an area flat enough to land on.

The 600 million watched and waited. And waited. Was Neil surveying the terrain, checking the equipment or agonizing over his first words? Perhaps he was overcome by terror at his insignificance in the cosmos? None of these. Neil was doing the dishes, tidying up. An orderly man, he spent the weekend before the flight dismantling and reassembling his dishwasher at home.

Eventually Neil emerged, followed by Buzz Aldrin, who lingered for what seemed like an eternity on the steps of the module. Was Buzz more sensitive than his companion to cosmic terror and awe? No, he had merely paused to enjoy a piss. And this may have been a rebellious act, like deliberately peeing in a swimming pool, because Buzz was originally supposed to be first out and was still unhappy at being demoted. So when he eventually got down on the moon and was ordered to photograph Neil he refused, with the excuse that he was 'too busy'[300] – and the only photograph of Neil on the moon is the one taken by Neil himself showing his reflection in his companion's visor. This is another example of the power of differentials and the negativity bias. As one of his fellow astronauts put it, Buzz resented not being first more than he appreciated being second. In fact, he had achieved unique distinction – he was the first and probably the only man to huff on the moon (and, better still, he got his crap hot in the Sea of Tranquillity).

Buzz had many sources of grievance, for instance the unflattering underwear supplied by NASA. When he got back to earth after coming close to death on the moon, his first words to his wife were, 'Joan, would you bring me some Jockey shorts tomorrow morning?'[301] And, as a consequence of NASA's three-day debriefing, the astronauts missed the media storm, which Buzz presciently understood to be the real event.

The media excitement was unprecedented. A Reverend Terence Mangan published detailed architectural plans for a church on the moon and the Hilton hotel group considered building an underground moon resort (based on a prediction that the moon would soon be the most popular honeymoon destination),[302] while the Nepalese nation was outraged at the violation of the resting place of the souls of the departed and the Union of Persian Storytellers believed that storytelling would never be the same again.

And the Apollo photographs revealed for the first time the insignificance of the earth – a tiny marble lost in an infinity of black. On the moon Armstrong discovered that he could eclipse earth merely by raising his thumb. 'Did it make you feel really big?' he was asked. 'No, it made me feel really small.'[303]

Armstrong remained stable after going to the moon but Buzz Aldrin sank into alcoholism and depression.

Depression is often the fate of the modern personality – greedy, attention-hungry and resentful, always convinced of deserving more, always haunted by the possibility of missing something better somewhere else, always smarting at lack of recognition and always dissatisfied. It is necessary to find again the classical courage and humility of Sisyphus who does not demand gratification but knows how to turn to advantage whatever the gods have decreed, and how to make every activity its own reward. Sisyphus is happy with the absurdity and insignificance of constantly pushing a rock up a hill.

Of course, he grumbles now and then. The rock could have been less jagged and the hill less steep. On the other hand, rock and hill could each have been more harsh. And there is much to be grateful for. Nothing in his sentence obliges him to use a particular path and there is an infinity of paths to match the eternity of the task. So, even as he seeks out the perfect way, he hopes secretly never to find it. Nor is he forbidden sideways motion, when the rock could almost be said to roll itself. And if it all gets too much he can appear to lose footing or grip and let the rock roll back down. Then the heavens will darken and crackle with divine displeasure – but Sisyphus can merely shrug and display empty, roughened palms.

Frequently he pretends to be stuck and turns his back to the rock, apparently to push harder – but really rock and man are supporting each other. At such times he falls into a reverie, often remembering his wife and developing a tender erection. Often, too, he will attack the rock with sudden force, propelling it all the way to the summit in a single, shrieking, manic rush. The gods hate such insolence – but what can they do? And, of course, there is the moment of release on the summit, always anticipated and, if never quite as rapturous as the promise, still a moment to savour. Is there any reason for him to descend as precipitately as the rock? None whatever. He strolls down with provocative insouciance by varying zigzag routes. How the gods glower in impotent wrath! This task, supposedly changeless, in fact has infinite variation.

Even if all variation were forbidden, there would still be his deepening relationship with the rock. As his hands come to know every outcrop and hollow, the rock seems to grow more responsive, more understanding, more cooperative. And who would have believed that frail human hands could smooth away such jaggedness? Of course, there are bad moments when the rock is obdurately unmoving and Sisyphus curses and even strikes it. But, at other times, the rock is blithe, even skittish, rolling easily and playfully, as though teasing him. At these times his touch is a warm, light caress.

All this the gods observe in growing disapproval. They, too, can be cunning and subtle. One day, they say, 'Sisyphus, we have watched your ingeniously varied labours with increasing admiration. And we have decided to ease your heavy burden. Here is a much better rock.' Stupefied, Sisyphus looks back down to see a rock considerably smaller and so smooth and spherical he can almost feel its curves fitting his hands as it rolls effortlessly up the hill. He is unable to speak. The gods wait, in malign assurance, and then add, not without satisfaction, 'Did you believe that eternal hard labour would set you free? No man may escape the agony of choice.' Still Sisyphus does not reply. Now his rock feels heavier, a deadweight, burdened suddenly by its awkwardness, imperfection and bulk. Then, all at once, the glory of the human creature – contrariness – floods his soul with intoxicating vinegar and piss. He can defy. He can refuse. He can say no. Or rather, in arrogance and humility, rebellion and acceptance, absurdity and happiness, with a loving slap, 'This is *my* rock.'

Acknowledgements

I would like to thank Jennifer Iles for giving me the original idea for this book, Emily McLaughlin for advice on quotations, Jennifer Christie, Kerri Sharp, and Kirstie Addis for many invaluable suggestions and my wife, Martina, also a keen student of absurdity, for much crucial research.

And I would like to express my gratitude to an institution – Camden Council Libraries. There are frequent complaints nowadays about libraries failing to stock new books but Camden libraries had almost all the recent books I needed and, when I requested arcane volumes from the Reserve Stock, library staff gladly trudged down to the vaults to fetch them. This is a public service to cherish.

Notes

1 Derek Mahon, *The Yellow Book*, Gallery Press, 1997
2 Quoted from *The New York Times* in the *Observer*, 17 May 2009
3 Jean-Jacques Rousseau, *Collected Writings of Rousseau*, University of New England Press, 1994
4 Hannah Arendt, *The Human Condition*, University of Chicago Press, 1958
5 John Stuart Mill, *Autobiography*, Penguin, 1987
6 Gustave Flaubert, *Extraits de la Correspondance*, Editions du Seuil, 1963
7 ibid.
8 Immanuel Kant, *Groundwork for the Metaphysics of Morals*, Hackett, 1981
9 Friedrich Nietzsche, *Also Sprach Zarathustra*, Ernst Schmeitzner, 1885
10 Sally Brampton, *Shoot the Damn Dog*, Bloomsbury, 2008
11 Erich Fromm, *The Fear of Freedom*, Routledge, 1942
12 Quoted in Henri Troyat, *Tolstoy*, Doubleday, 1967
13 Inge Kjaergaard, 'Advertising to the Brain', *Focus* Denmark, 2008
14 Quoted in Barry Schwartz, *The Paradox Of Choice: Why More is Less*, HarperCollins, 2004
15 Martin Lindstrom, *Buyology: How Everything We Believe About Why We Buy is Wrong*, Random House Business Books, 2009
16 Plato, *Phaedrus* from John M. Cooper and D.S. Hutchinson (eds.), *Plato: Complete Works*, Hackett, 1997
17 Marcus Aurelius, *Meditations*, Penguin, 1964
18 Quoted in Robert Bly, *The Sibling Society*, Hamish Hamilton, 1996

19 Quoted in Karen Armstrong, *Buddha*, Weidenfeld & Nicolson, 2000

20 Sigmund Freud, *Collected Papers*, Hogarth Press, 1970

21 Juan Mascaro (trans.), *The Dhammapada*, Penguin, 1973

22 Quoted in Karl Jaspers, *Socrates, Buddha, Confucius, Jesus: the paradigmatic individuals*, Harvest, 1966

23 Quoted in Armstrong, (2000) op. cit.

24 Quoted in Jaspers, op. cit.

25 ibid.

26 The statistics are in John Micklethwait & Adrian Wooldridge, *God Is Back: How the Global Rise of Faith is Changing the World*, Allen Lane, 2009

27 Spinoza, *Ethics*, Hafner Publishing, 1966

28 ibid.

29 ibid.

30 ibid.

31 Spinoza, *Ethics*, Everyman, 1993

32 Quoted in Antonio R. Damasio, *Looking for Spinoza*, Vintage, 2004

33 Quoted in Henri F. Ellenberger, *The Discovery of the Unconscious*, Penguin, 1970

34 Arthur Schopenhauer, *The World as Will and Idea*, Dent, 2004

35 Arthur Schopenhauer, *Essays and Aphorisms*, Penguin, 1970

36 Nietzsche, (1885) op. cit.

37 ibid.

38 ibid.

39 ibid.

40 ibid.

41 ibid.

42 Joseph LeDoux, *The Emotional Brain*, Simon & Schuster, 1996

43 Kenneth M. Heilman, *Matter of Mind: A Neurologist's View of Brain-Behavior Relationships*, Oxford University Press, 2002

44 J. Cohen *et al.*, 'Separate Neural Systems Value Immediate and Delayed Monetary Rewards', *Science*, 306, 2004

45 Quoted in Erich Fromm, *Marx's Concept of Man*, Ungar, 1961

46 Fiona Macdonald, 'A Truly Captive Audience', *Metro*, 4 February

2009. The quote is from Felix Paus, founder of Videogames Adventure Services. Another company offering similar services is Spy Games. The websites are www.semagoediv.com and www.spy-games.com

47 Survey quoted in *The New York Times*, 28 October 2007

48 Julian Baggini, *Complaint: From Minor Moans to Principled Protest*, Profile, 2008

49 For instance, www.unboxing.com

50 Alain de Botton, *The Art of Travel*, Random House, 2004

51 David Foster Wallace, *A Supposedly Fun Thing I'll Never Do Again*, Abacus, 1998

52 This tendency was first identified by Erich Fromm, who defined it as the 'marketing orientation', the obligation to market oneself as another commodity: 'since success depends largely on how one sells one's personality, one experiences oneself as a commodity or rather simultaneously as the seller and the commodity to be sold. A person is not concerned with his life and happiness, but with becoming saleable.' In Erich Fromm, *Man For Himself*, Routledge, 1949

53 The three who have found these innovative ways to fame and fortune are William Burroughs, Damien Hirst and Ozzy Osbourne

54 Seneca, *Moral Essays*, Loeb Classical Library, 1989

55 Aurelius, op. cit.

56 Seneca, *Moral Essays*, Loeb Classical Library, 1989

57 ibid.

58 ibid.

59 Aurelius, op. cit.

60 ibid.

61 Epictetus, *The Discourses*, Loeb Classical Library, 1989

62 Aurelius, op. cit.

63 Matthew 10:34

64 Matthew 7:28

65 Matthew 12:11

66 Matthew 22:21

67 Fromm, (1942) op. cit.

68 Jean-Paul Sartre, *Being and Nothingness*, Routledge, 2003

69   Søren Kierkegaard, *The Sickness Unto Death*, Princeton University Press, 1951

70   Jean-Paul Sartre, *Being and Nothingness*, Philosophical Library, 1956

71   Sartre, (2003) op. cit.

72   Albert Camus, *The Myth of Sisyphus*, Penguin Classics, 2000

73   ibid.

74   Samuel Beckett, *Happy Days*, Faber, 1963

75   Jonathan Haidt, *The Happiness Hypothesis*, Heinemann, 2006

76   Nicholas Epley & David Dunning, 'Feeling holier than thou', *Journal of Personal and Social Psychology*, 79, 2000

77   For instance, Richard Layard, *Happiness: Lessons From a New Science*, Penguin, 2005

78   Walter Mischel *et al.*, 'Predicting adolescent cognitive and self-regulatory competencies from preschool delay of gratification: Identifying diagnostic conditions', *Developmental Psychology*, 26, 1990

79   Richard Easterlin, 'Explaining Happiness', *Proceedings of the National Academy of Sciences*, 100, 2003

80   Schopenhauer, (2004) op. cit.

81   Leon Festinger, *A Theory of Cognitive Dissonance*, Stanford University Press, 1957

82   Quoted in Carol Tavris and Elliot Aronson, *Mistakes Were Made (but Not by Me): Why We Justify Foolish Beliefs, Bad Decisions and Hurtful Acts*, Pinter & Martin, 2008

83   This statistic is hard to believe but it is quoted in two scrupulously researched books – Carol Tavris and Elliot Aronson, *Mistakes Were Made (but Not by Me): Why We Justify Foolish Beliefs, Bad Decisions and Hurtful Acts*, Pinter & Martin, 2008; and Francis Wheen, *How Mumbo-Jumbo Conquered the World*, HarperPerennial, 2004

84   Susan A. Clancy, *Abducted: How People Come To Believe They Were Abducted By Aliens*, Harvard University Press, 2005

85   Louis Menand, 'The Devil's Disciples', *New Yorker*, 28 July 2003

86   Leo Tolstoy, *War and Peace*, Penguin, 1957

87   For instance, Daniel Nettle, *Happiness: The Science Behind Your Smile*, Oxford University Press, 2005

88 Arthur Schopenhauer, *Parerga and Paralipomena: Short Philosophical Essays*, Oxford University Press, 1974

89 Nettle, op. cit.

90 D.T. Lykken & A. Tellegen, 'Happiness is a stochastic phenomenon', *Psychological Science*, 7, 1996

91 J.B. Handelsman, *New Yorker*, 16 September 1996

92 Steven Rose, *Lifelines: Life Beyond The Gene*, Vintage, 2005

93 David Blanchflower & Andrew Oswald, 'Is well-being U-shaped over the life cycle?', *Social Science & Medicine*, Vol. 66, Issue 8, April 2008

94 Richard Layard, *Happiness: Lessons From a New Science*, Penguin, 2005

95 V. Medvec, S. Madey, T. Gilovich, 'When less is more: Counterfactual thinking and satisfaction among Olympic medallists', *Journal of Personality and Social Psychology*, 69, 1995

96 Schopenhauer, (1974) op. cit.

97 William Shakespeare, *Henry VIII*, Act 4, Scene 2

98 Aaron Beck, *Cognitive Therapy and the Emotional Disorders*, International Universities Press, 1976

99 Albert Ellis and Windy Dryden, *The Practice of Rational Emotive Behavioural Therapy*, Springer, 2007

100 ibid.

101 Oliver James, *The Selfish Capitalist: Origins of Affluenza*, Vermilion, 2008

102 Jonah Lehrer, *The Decisive Moment: How the Brain Makes Up Its Mind*, Canongate Books, 2009

103 Nettle, op. cit.

104 Schopenhauer, (1974) op. cit.

105 Damasio, (2004) op. cit.

106 Robert Nozick, *Anarchy, State, and Utopia*, Basic Books, 1974

107 *The Times*, 21 August 2007

108 Sigmund Freud, *Civilization and Its Discontents*, Penguin Books, 2002

109 John Armstrong, *Conditions of Love: The Philosophy of Intimacy*, Penguin, 2002

110 Jaspers, op. cit.

111   Christopher Peterson & Martin Seligman, *Character Strengths and Virtues: A Handbook and Classification*, Oxford University Press, 2004

112   There are several examples in Haidt, op. cit.

113   Rainer Maria Rilke, *Briefe an einen jungen Dichter*, Insel Verlag, 1929

114   Rainer Maria Rilke, *Letters on Life*, Modern Library, 2006

115   Joseph Campbell, *The Hero with a Thousand Faces*, Fontana, 1993

116   ibid.

117   ibid.

118   Matthew 10:34

119   Quoted in Jaspers, op. cit.

120   Franz Kafka, *The Zürau Aphorisms*, Schocken Books, 2006

121   Franz Kafka, *The Complete Short Stories*, Vintage, 2005

122   Farid Ud-Din Attar, *The Conference of the Birds*, Penguin, 1984

123   To match the twelfth-century Islamic parable of the Simorgh there is this first-century Jewish aphorism from Rabbi Tarphon, also sounding remarkably like Kafka: 'You are not required to complete the work, but neither are you free to desist from it.'

The existentialist Karl Jaspers: 'The goal of life cannot be formulated as a state which is attainable and, once attained, perfect. Our states of being are only manifestations of existential striving or failure. It lies in our very nature to be on the way.'

Nietzsche, the father of existentialism, was more succinct: 'There is no Being, only Becoming.'

Sartre's version was turgidly abstract: 'Existence precedes essence.'

The Buddhist version was zestfully concrete: 'Asked, "What is Zen?" the master said, "Walk on."'

And Proust expressed it in fiction: 'We do not receive wisdom, we must discover it for ourselves, after a journey through the wilderness which no one else can make for us, which no one can spare us, for our wisdom is the point of view from which we come at last to regard the world.'

124   Constantine Peter Cavafy, *Poiemata*, Ikaros, 1963

125 'Hi-tech is turning us all into time-wasters', *Observer*, 20 July 2008

126 Jerald Block, 'Issues for DSM-V: Internet Addiction', *The American Journal of Psychiatry*, March 2008

127 'Driver wins £20,000 damages for stress of parking tickets', *Observer*, 8 February 2009

128 Jean-Paul Sartre, *Being and Nothingness*, Routledge, 2003

129 'Don't worry, Woody: anxiety is in the genes, study finds', *Independent*, 11 August 2008

130 'It's not you, dear, it's me: the genetic reason why some men are just born to cheat', *The Times*, 2 September 2008

131 John Gray, *Straw Dogs: Thoughts on Humans and Other Animals*, Granta, 2002

132 Antonio Damasio, *Descartes' Error: Emotion, reason, and the human brain*, Putnam, 1994

133 LeDoux, op. cit.

134 Damasio, (2004) op. cit.

135 ibid.

136 Matt Ridley, *Nature Via Nurture: Genes, Experience and What Makes Us Human*, HarperPerennial, 2004

137 Hilary Rose & Steven Rose (ed.), *Alas Poor Darwin: Arguments against Evolutionary Psychology*, Vintage, 2001

138 Steven Rose, *Lifelines: Life Beyond the Gene*, Vintage, 2005

139 For a full account see Norman Doidge, *The Brain That Changes Itself*, Penguin, 2007

140 D.A. Christakis *et al.*, 'Early television exposure and subsequent attentional problems in children', *Pediatrics*, 113, 2004

141 William Shakespeare, *Hamlet*, Act 3, Scene 4

142 Editorial, *British Medical Journal*, 2 June 2001

143 Quoted in the *Guardian*, 13 December 2001

144 'Asleep at the Wheel', BBC One documentary, 26 October 2004

145 Muzafer Sherif, *Group Conflict and Co-operation: Their Social Psychology*, Routledge & Kegan Paul, 1966

146 Don DeLillo, *White Noise*, Viking, 1984

147 E. J. Langer & J. Rodin, 'The effects of choice and enhanced personal responsibility for the aged: A field experiment in an

institutional setting', *Journal of Personality and Social Psychology*, 34, 1976

148 S.E.R. Asch, 'Studies of Independence and Conformity: A Minority of one Against a Unanimous Majority', *Scientific American*, November 1955

149 G.S. Berns, J. Chappelow, C.F. Zin, G. Pagnoni, M.E. Martin-Skurski, and J. Richards, 'Neurobiological Correlates of Social Conformity and Independence During Mental Rotation', *Biological Psychiatry*, 5, August 2005

150 T. Blass, *Obedience to Authority: Current Perspectives on the Milgram Paradigm*, Lawrence Erlbaum Associates, 1999

151 Philip Zimbardo, *The Lucifer Effect*, Rider, 2007

152 Flaubert, op. cit.

153 Gloria Mark *et al.*. '"Constant, Constant, Multi-tasking Craziness": Managing Multiple Working Spheres', *Proceedings of CHI*, 2004

154 J.Rubinstein *et al.*, 'Executive Control of Cognitive Processes in Task Switching', *Journal of Experimental Psychology: Human Perception and Performance*, August 2001

155 Rene Marois *et al.*, 'Isolation of a Central Bottleneck of Information Processing with Time-resolved FMRI', *Neuron*, December 2006

156 Jonathan Sharples and Martin Westwell, 'The impact of interruptions from communications technologies upon the ability of an individual to concentrate upon a task', *Institute for the Future of the Mind*, 2007

157 A. Newberg *et al.*, 'The measurement of regional cerebral blood flow during the complex cognitive task of meditation: a preliminary SPECT study', *Psychiatry Research: Neuroimaging*, 106, 2001; and O. Flanagan, 'The Colour of Happiness', *New Scientist*, 178, 2003

158 Meister Eckhart, *Die Deutschen und Lateinischen Werke*, Verlag, 1936

159 Spinoza, *Ethics*, Oxford University Press, 2000

160 Albert Ellis, *The Myth of Self-Esteem*, Prometheus Books, 2005

161 R. F. Baumeister *et al.*, 'Exploding the Self-Esteem Myth', *Scientific American*, 292, January 2005

162 Oliver James, *Affluenza*, Vermilion, 2007

163 Carol S. Dweck et al, 'Praise for Intelligence Can Undermine Children's Motivation and Performance', *Journal of Personality and Social Psychology*, 75, 1998

164 William Shakespeare, *As You Like It*, Act 5, Scene 1

165 D. Kahneman *et al.*, *Well-Being: The Foundations of Hedonic Psychology*, Russell Sage, 1999

166 Bly, op. cit.

167 'Out of the Ether, Creating the Persona of Celebrity', *The New York Times* in the *Observer*, 4 November 2007

168 Rilke, (1929) op. cit.

169 T. S. Eliot, 'Ash Wednesday' in *Collected Poems*, Faber, 1974

170 Quoted in Hannah Arendt, *The Life of the Mind*, Harvest, 1981

171 Charles Wright, *Negative Blue: Selected Later Poems*, Farrar, Straus and Giroux, 2000

172 Jules Laforgue, *Selected Writings of Jules Laforgue*, Greenwood, 1972

173 Reported in 'A Little Less Conversation', *Guardian*, 11 October 2008

174 Juan Ramón Jiménez, *The Complete Perfectionist*, Doubleday, 1997

175 'Hard to eat oranges are losing a-peel', *Metro*, 3 June 2008

176 'To Think or Not to Think, Ponder the Pensive French', *The New York Times* in the *Observer*, 29 September 2007

177 Pierre Bayard, *How to talk About Books You Haven't Read*, Granta, 2008

178 Mascaro, op. cit.

179 Ecclesiastes 7:6

180 Wheen, op. cit.

181 Gray, op. cit.

182 ibid.

183 ibid.

184 Arendt, (2001) op. cit.

185 Primo Levi, *The Drowned and the Saved*, Joseph, 1988

186 Barry Schwartz, *The Paradox of Choice: Why More is Less*, HarperCollins, 2004

187 Ben R. Newell, 'Think, Blink or Sleep on it? The impact of modes of thought on complex decision making', *Quarterly Journal of Experimental Psychology*, forthcoming paper

188 Chuang Tzu, *The Inner Chapters*, Counterpoint, 1998

189 Arendt, (2001) op. cit.

190 ibid.

191 Aristotle, *The Nicomachean Ethics*, Dent, 1949

192 Anthony Storr, *Solitude*, Flamingo, 1989

193 Jonah Lehrer, 'The Eureka Hunt – why do good ideas come to us when they do?', *New Yorker*, 28 July 2008

194 Spinoza, *Ethics*, Heron, 1980

195 Arendt, (2001) op. cit.

196 Kierkegaard, (1951) op. cit.

197 Quoted in Andrew Smith, *Moondust: In Search of the Men Who Fell to Earth*, Bloomsbury, 2005

198 R. Kubey *et al.*, 'Television addiction is no mere metaphor', *Scientific American*, February 2003

199 Richard E. Nisbett, *The Geography of Thought: How Asians and Westerners Think Differently . . . and Why,* Free Press, 2003

200 Walter Benjamin, Hannah Arendt and Harry Zohn, *Illuminations*, Vintage, 1999

201 ibid.

202 Marcel Proust, *Remembrance of Things Past*, Chatto & Windus, 1981

203 James Joyce, *Ulysses*, The Bodley Head, 1960

204 William Shakespeare, *Henry IV: Part II*, Act 5, Scene 5

205 Quoted in Caleb Crain, 'Twilight of the Books', *New Yorker*, 24 December 2007

206 Marcel Proust, *Against Sainte-Beuve and Other Essays*, Penguin, 1988

207 Jonah Lehrer, *Proust was a Neuroscientist*, Houghton Mifflin, 2007

208 Maryanne Wolf, *Proust and the Squid: The Story and Science of the Reading Brain*, Icon, 2008

209 Carl Landhuis *et al.*, 'Does Childhood Viewing lead to Attention

Problems in Adolescence? Results from a Longitudinal Study', *Pediatrics*, 120, 3 September 2007

210 Heather A. Lindstrom *et al.*, 'The relationships between television viewing in midlife and the development of Alzheimer's Disease in a case-control study', *Brain and Cognition*, 58, 2 July 2005

211 Flaubert, op. cit.

212 For details see Barbara Ehrenreich, *Dancing In The Streets: A History of Collective Joy*, Granta, 2007

213 Quoted by Peter Avery in the Introduction to *The Ruba'iyat of Omar Khayyam*, Penguin, 1981

214 Jelaluddin Rumi, *The Essential Rumi*, HarperCollins, 1995

215 Spinoza, (1966) op. cit.

216 Susan Greenfield, *ID: The Quest for Meaning in the 21st Century*, Hodder & Stoughton, 2008

217 Jill Bolte Taylor, *My Stroke of Insight*, Hodder & Stoughton, 2008

218 ibid.

219 For instance, A. Newberg *et al.*, 'The measurement of regional cerebral blood flow during the complex cognitive task of meditation: a preliminary SPECT study', *Psychiatry Research: Neuroimaging*, 106, 2001; and O. Flanagan, 'The Colour of Happiness', *New Scientist*, 178, 2003

220 Mihaly Csikszentmihalyi, *Flow: The Classic Work on How to Achieve Happiness*, Rider, 2002

221 Daisetz Taitaro Suzuki & Erich Fromm, *Zen Buddhism and Psychoanalysis*, Souvenir Press, 1974

222 Nietzsche, (1885) op. cit.

223 ibid.

224 Friedrich Nietzsche, *Daybreak: Thoughts on the Prejudices of Morality*, Cambridge University Press, 1992

225 Nietzsche, (1885) op. cit.

226 Friedrich Nietzsche, *Beyond Good and Evil*, Modern Library, 1968

227 Quoted in Suzuki & Fromm, op. cit.

228 Friedrich Nietzsche, *Ecce Homo*, Modern Library, 2000

229 William Shakespeare, *A Midsummer Night's Dream*, Act 3, Scene 2

230 ibid.

231 Erich Fromm, *The Fear of Freedom*, Routledge & Kegan Paul, 1960

232 'As Office Attitudes Shift, Love Blossoms in Cubicles', *The New York Times* in the *Observer*, 25 November 2007

233 Nicholson Baker, *The Mezzanine*, Granta, 1989

234 ibid.

235 Joshua Ferris, *Then We Came to the End*, Viking, 2007

236 ibid.

237 Adrian Gostick and Scott Christopher, *The Levity Effect: Why It Pays to Lighten Up*, John Wiley, 2008

238 Stephen C. Lundin *et al.*, *Fish! A Remarkable Way to Boost Morale and Improve Results*, Hodder & Stoughton, 2001

239 'On Anger' in Seneca, *Dialogues and Letters*, Penguin, 1997

240 Frederick Herzberg, *The Motivation to Work*, John Wiley, 1959

241 Edward L. Deci & Richard M. Ryan, *Intrinsic Motivation and Self-Determination in Human Behaviour*, Plenum Press, 1985

242 E. Deci *et al.*, 'A meta-analytic review of experiments examining the effects of extrinsic rewards on intrinsic motivation', *Psychological Bulletin*, 125, 1999

243 Matthew 6:25

244 Aleksandr Solzhenitsyn, *One Day In The Life Of Ivan Denisovich*, The Bodley Head, 1971

245 Wim Meeus and Quinten A.W. Raaijmakers, 'Obedience in Modern Society: The Utrecht Studies', *Journal of Social Issues*, 51, 1995

246 Fromm, (1960) op. cit.

247 Hannah Arendt, *On Revolution*, Faber & Faber, 1964

248 Jeffry Simpson *et al.*, 'The Association between Romantic Love and Marriage', *Personality and Social Psychology Bulletin*, 12, 1986

249 Erich Fromm, *The Art of Loving*, George Allen & Unwin, 1957

250 Stendhal, *De L'Amour*, Garnier Frères, 1959

251 ibid.

252 Helen Fisher, *Why We Love: The Nature and Chemistry of Romantic Love*, Holt, 2004

253 D. Marazziti *et al.*, 'Alteration of the platelet serotonin transporter in romantic love', *Psychological Medicine*, 29, 1999

254 Giuseppe Tomasi di Lampedusa, *The Leopard*, Collins Harvill, 1960

255 In Leo Tolstoy, *The Kreutzer Sonata and Other Stories*, Penguin, 2008

256 Avner Offer, *The Challenge of Affluence: Self-control and Well-being in the United States and Britain Since 1950*, Oxford University Press, 2006

257 Rilke, (2006) op. cit.

258 Fromm, (1957) op. cit.

259 Quoted in James Gleick, *Chaos: Making a New Science*, Penguin, 1989

260 John Milton, *Paradise Lost*, Wordsworth, 1994

261 Rush W. Dozier, *Why We Hate: Understanding, Curbing and Eliminating Hate in Ourselves and Our World,* Contemporary Books, 2002

262 Alex Comfort, *The Joy of Sex*, Quartet Books, 1972

263 Alex Comfort & Susan Quilliam, *The New Joy of Sex*, Mitchell Beazley, 2008

264 B. Whipple *et al., The G Spot and Other Discoveries about Human Sexuality*, Holt, Rinehart & Winston, 1982

265 Macdonald, op. cit.

266 David Levy, *Love and Sex with Robots: The Evolution of Human–Robot Relationships*, Duckworth, 2008

267 D. Read *et al.,* 'Diversification Bias: Explaining the Discrepancy in Variety Seeking Between Combined and Separated Choices', *Journal of Experimental Psychology*, 1, 1995

268 Rainer Maria Rilke, *Duino Elegies*, Carcanet Press, 1989

269 Blanchflower & Oswald, op. cit.

270 'The Body May Age, But Romance Stays Fresh', *The New York Times* in the *Observer*, 25 November 2007

271 Douwe Draaisma, *Why Life Speeds Up As You Get Older: How Memory Shapes Our Past*, Cambridge University Press, 2004

272 'A Rise in Midlife Suicides Confounds Researchers', *The New York Times* in the *Observer*, 2 March 2008

273 L. Carstensen & J.A. Michels, 'At the Intersection of Emotion and Cognition', *Psychological Science*, 14, 2005

274 Howard S. Friedman, 'Psychosocial and Behavioural Predictors of Longevity', *American Psychologist*, February 1995

275 George E. Vaillant, *Aging Well: Surprising Guideposts to a Happier Life from the Landmark Harvard Study of Adult Development*, Little, Brown & Co., 2002

276 H. Van Praag *et al.*, 'Functional neurogenesis in the adult hippocampus', *Nature*, 415, 2002

277 William Shakespeare, *The Two Noble Kinsmen*, Act 5, Scene 4

278 Rilke, (2006) op. cit.

279 E. M. Cioran, *The Trouble With Being Born*, Quartet Books, 1993

280 Sigmund Freud, *The Complete Psychological Works*, Hogarth Press, 1970

281 Homer, *The Odyssey*, William Heinemann, 1962

282 Quoted in Jaspers, op. cit.

283 Aurelius, op. cit.

284 Quoted in John Updike, *Due Considerations*, Hamish Hamilton, 2007

285 Quoted in John Richardson, *Late Picasso*, Tate Gallery, 1988

286 ibid.

287 ibid.

288 ibid.

289 Quoted in Whitney Balliett, *Collected Works: A Journal of Jazz*, St. Martin's Press, 2000

290 William Shakespeare, *The Winter's Tale*, Act 5, Scene 1

291 Leo Tolstoy, *The Death of Ivan Ilyich and Other Stories*, Wordsworth, 2004

292 William Yeats, *Collected Poems*, Macmillan, 1939

293 ibid.

294 Quoted in J. LaFarge, *A Talk About Hokusai*, W.C. Martin, 1896

295 Tu Fu and David Hinton, *The Selected Poems of Tu Fu*, Anvil Press, 1990

296 Sarah Hills, 'It's time for snap, crackle and Spock', *Metro*, February 2008

297 Alex Godfrey, 'Enterprise Reprised', *Guardian*, 2 May 2009

298 Jacob Weisberg, *The Deluxe Election-Edition Bushisms*, Simon & Schuster, 2004

299 Quoted in Wheen, op. cit.
300 Quoted in Smith, op. cit.
301 ibid.
302 ibid.
303 ibid.

Index

Journal of the Acoustical Society of America, 108
Joy of Sex, The, 196
Joyce, James, 72, 138–40, 148, 150

Kafka, Franz, 22, 57, 72, 73, 219, 223
Kant, Immanuel, 8
Kierkegaard, Søren, 45, 65, 133
koans, 155

Laforgue, Jules, 107
Lampedusa, Giuseppe Tomasi di, 189
language, 153, 170–1, 175, 214
 left brain and, 126
 libraries and, 108
 love and, 185
 misuse of, 221
 sign, 152
 thinking and, 122
 Wolf on, 142
 words banned from, 86
Lao Tzu, 69
LeDoux, Joseph, 28, 81–2
Levi, Primo, 122
levity, 170
Libet, Benjamin, 80, 82
London Review Bookshop, 110
love, 7, 53, 73, 99
 absurdity of, 182–200
 emotion and, 121
 fault and, 185
 freedom and, 46
 Fromm on, 185, 193

language and, 185
mature, 193
neuroscience and, 188–9
reality TV and, 104
romantic, 187–9
self-, 187
striving for, 208
Tolstoy on, 13
unconditional, 39
luxury cruises, 37–8
Lykken, David, 57–8

Magic Christian, The, 156
Mahon, Derek, 4
Mangan, Terence, 225
Manicheism, 7, 80, 122, 147
Mara, 22
Marx, Karl, 9, 31–2, 64
meditation, 23, 84, 97, 150–1
memory, 139, 140, 190
 anger and, 60–1
 distortion, 54
 loss, 201
 purposive thought and, 123, 126
 U-shape graph of, 207
Menand, Louis, 55
metaphysics, 24, 202
midlife crisis, 205–7
Milgram, Stanley, 91–2
Mill, John Stuart, 6
Milton, John, 194
mindfulness, 23, 68, 92, 136, 137, 193, 208
Mischel, Walter, 51
misogyny, 66

The Age of Absurdity